# The *Smart* Executive's Guide
# to Major American Cities

## by *William G. Flanagan*

*WILLIAM MORROW AND COMPANY, INC.*

*NEW YORK    1975*

Printed in the United States of America.

1  2  3  4  5  79  78  77  76  75

**Library of Congress Cataloging in Publication Data**

Flanagan, William G
  The smart executive's guide to major American cities.

    1. Hotels, taverns, etc.—United States—Directories. 2. Restaurants, lunch rooms, etc.—United States—Directories. I. Title.
TX907.F52      647′.9473      75-15710
ISBN 0-688-02944-2

Design: H. Roberts

# The *Smart* Executive's Guide
# to Major American Cities

# FOREWORD

This book is sympathetically dedicated to the weary business traveler. He (or, increasingly, she) is indeed peripatetic: businessmen who travel make an average of 14 business trips a year, covering over 12,000 miles. More than a third of business travelers log over 20,000 miles a year.

But as important as he is to the travel industry, the businessman rarely if ever gets a discount on an airline or at a restaurant or hotel—the way the tourist does. In fact, he often pays substantially more for his travel needs because they are on a "demand" basis—he has to fly on certain dates and stay at a destination on given days, and so he pays more. In effect, the business traveler subsidizes other travelers.

Further, like Rodney Dangerfield, the business traveler "can't get no respect." He is considered a mark by bellboys, prostitutes, maître d's, bartenders, newsstand dealers, taxi drivers, pickpockets, muggers, panhandlers, and cops.

A kingpin on his home turf, the business traveler is often battered into ignominy when he takes to the road. See him on a business trip to New York—which, like Paris, can be every bit as rude as it is exciting. Watch our hero struggling with his bags into the Asia-sized lobby of the New York Hilton, after having overtipped a garrulous cabbie who took him the long, wrong way in from LaGuardia or Kennedy. After a painful wait at the registration desk a surly clerk finally finds his reservation form. A bellboy now wrestles the bags out of his hands and leads the way to a cheerless $50-a-day room (after a long wait for the elevator) and sneers at the $2 tip.

Lacking the energy to investigate the whereabouts of a decent bar or restaurant—or perhaps worried for his safety—our traveler settles for a martini or two at the hotel bar. It is full of bored business travelers like himself—plus some high-priced ladies of the evening.

Dinner in the hotel consists of an overpriced steak and lettuce-only salad. The red wine is served chilled.

Television caps the evening, and our traveler sleeps fitfully amid periodic hoots from boozed-up conventioners. Obviously, this is no way to prepare for an important day of business on the morrow—physically or psychologically.

But none of this need be—especially in a large city where there are plenty of options for lodging, dining, and entertainment. The savvy traveler, for example, takes the Carey bus in from the airport, then grabs a cab in town. This saves him $10 or more. He stays at the St. Regis instead of the Hilton, and for the same rate has a quaint, quiet room, and no threat of convention revelers. The bellboy even remembers his name.

Without putting a foot outside the hotel, he can enjoy a convivial bar, eat at an elegant restaurant, and watch a good show. And nary a hooker will be in sight. For a post-prandial walk, he can stroll along Fifth Avenue, and convince himself that New York is a great place to visit and do business in—and he is prepared for same the next day.

No matter where your origin, visiting any large city with which you are unfamiliar can be frustrating. But with some planning, and some solid advice on which to base those plans, your stay in any city can be a lot more productive and a lot more enjoyable. It can also be a lot cheaper.

This book is no mere smorgasbord of possibilities. We have made the judgments on hotels, restaurants, etc., and don't mince words. No one has a vested interest in this book—it is not being supported in any way by oil companies, rent-a-car companies, airlines, or restaurant or hotel chains. We call 'em as we see 'em. There will doubtless be quibblers who will take issue with us here and there—so be it. De gustibus, and all that.

We welcome your comments if you are so moved or if you are disgruntled by any of our evaluations.

We have included in this volume information on 22 North-American cities. They are frequent destinations of business travelers—American and foreign. The ten largest cities in the U.S. by population density are, of course, included. Beyond that, the list is somewhat arbitrary. We have included some relatively small cities that nonetheless attract lots of convention business (Honolulu and Miami), and we have included some cities that business travelers try to visit with their families (Seattle and Montreal).

We hope we will be able to expand our list in future editions.

WILLIAM G. FLANAGAN

# ACKNOWLEDGMENTS

All guidebooks must, of course, rely on contributors. No one—not even the globe-trotting Mr. Fielding—can take in everything, everywhere, himself. While I have personally visited all of these cities at least once, the basic judgments were made by those who know and live in those cities. They did all the basic research in their areas, as I did in New York. It's worth mentioning that our contributors paid their own way when visiting restaurants. Our judgments are as objective as possible, but of course based on our own opinions and on conditions as they existed at the time of our last visits.

## *Contributors*

ATLANTA—Tony Heffernan, bureau chief for *Business Week,* 100 Colony Square, 18th Floor, 1175 Peachtree Street, Atlanta, Georgia 30309.

BOSTON—Gordon and Margaret McKibben. Gordon is bureau chief for *Business Week,* McGraw-Hill Building, Copley Square, Boston, Massachusetts 02116.

CHICAGO—Jim Bliwas, *Business Week* correspondent, 645 North Michigan Avenue, Chicago, Illinois 60601.

CLEVELAND—Michael Kelly, reporter, *Cleveland Plain Dealer,* 1801 Superior Avenue, Cleveland, Ohio 44114.

DALLAS—Dudley Lynch, *Business Week* correspondent, 1722 Goodwin, Garland, Texas 75041.

DENVER—Sandra Atchison, bureau chief of *Business Week,* Tower Building, 1700 Broadway, Denver, Colorado 80202.

DETROIT—Steve Wildstrom, *Business Week* correspondent, 1400 Fischer Building, Detroit, Michigan 48202.

HONOLULU—Ray Manecki, *Honolulu Star Bulletin,* Honolulu, Hawaii 96802.

HOUSTON—Mark Morrison, *Business Week* correspondent, 2270 Humble Building, Houston, Texas 77002.

LOS ANGELES—Tom Bush, *Business Week* correspondent, 3200 Wilshire Boulevard, South Tower, Los Angeles, California 90010.

MIAMI—Ethel Blum, travel writer, One Lincoln Road, Miami Beach, Florida 33139.

MONTREAL—Reggi Dubin, *Business Week* correspondent, Suite 1507, Carlton Towers, 2 Carlton Street, Toronto, Ontario, Canada.

NEW ORLEANS—Paul Atkinson, reporter, *Times-Picayune,* 3800 Howard Avenue, New Orleans, Louisiana 70125.

NEW YORK—William Flanagan, Personal Business Editor, *Business Week,* 1221 Avenue of the Americas, New York, New York 10020.

PHILADELPHIA—Sheila Cunningham, *Business Week* correspondent, 3 Parkway, 19th Floor, Philadelphia, Pennsylvania 19100.

PITTSBURGH—Charles Hauck, formerly bureau chief, *Business Week,* 4 Gateway Center, Pittsburgh, Pennsylvania 15222.

ST. LOUIS—Ted Schafers, *St. Louis Globe Democrat,* 12th and Delmar Boulevard, St. Louis, Missouri 63101.

SAN FRANCISCO—Judy Curtis, *Business Week* correspondent, 425 Battery Street, San Francisco, California 94111.

SEATTLE—Dave Brewster, editor, *Argus* magazine, White-Henry-Stuart Building, 1318 4th Avenue, Seattle, Washington 98101.

TORONTO—Reggi Dubin, *Business Week* correspondent, Suite 1507, Carlton Towers, 2 Carlton Street, Toronto, Ontario, Canada.

WASHINGTON, D.C.—Dan and Else Moscowitz. Dan covers, among other beats, the Supreme Court for *Business Week* and other McGraw-Hill publications. National Press Building, 529 14th Street, N.W., Washington, D.C. 20004.

Note: Our Baltimore contributor preferred to remain anonymous.

# CONTENTS

# The Smart Executive's Guide to Major American Cities

# ATLANTA

When Atlanta's late mayor, William Hartsfeld, was asked how his city avoided the racial conflict that plagued so much of the Deep South, he replied that it was "a city too busy to hate."

In a city that loves to characterize itself in slightly non-Southern terms, the phrase is still widely quoted—and punned upon. Andrew Young, a black Atlanta Congressman, recently quipped that what Hartsfeld really meant was: "A city too busy making money to have time to hate."

Indeed, what was a medium-sized Southern city just a generation ago has blossomed into the region's business capital and now boasts a population of more than 1.5 million. There is as much hustle downtown during the business hours as you will encounter Up North, but after hours there is still plenty of evidence of that old Southern charm.

Despite the city's emergence as a business and convention capital, most Atlantans are gracious and polite, which, in turn, brings in more and more business and conventions. But the typical businessman's stay is short—rarely more than a few days.

If you'll be moving around the city much, rent a car. Transportation is generally not good, although a rapid transit system is under construction. Cabs are cheap enough, but often scarcer than January magnolias.

Besides the lack of good public transportation, some of the other undesirable side effects of rapid growth can be seen in Atlanta, too. The air can be very Northern on some days, and though the Chatta-hoochee River might not yet be a fire hazard, it's getting there.

Still, you'll probably enjoy your stay in this city—most business visitors do.

## Hotels

Unfortunately, Atlanta is still pitifully shy of an adequate number of good hotels, although help is on the way as two new hotels are a-building. Meantime, the **Hyatt Regency, Marriott, Stouffer's Atlanta Inn** and **Atlanta Internationale** are best. Reserve one of these hostelries well in advance, or you will have to settle for the **Admiral Benbow, Atlanta American, Rodeway Inn Lenox,** or **Sheraton-Biltmore.** Failing those, it's the **Holiday Inn Downtown,** the **Riviera Hyatt House,** the **Royal Coach Inn,** or the **TraveLodge at Executive Park.**

## Restaurants

Before Horn and Hardart gave up on the Automats in New York City, it tried to get more New Yorkers into its cheaply priced but plain-Jane cafeterias by advertising "You can't eat atmosphere." In New York the campaign had mild success; in Atlanta it would have been hooted down worse than a heckler at a Falcons' home game. Atmosphere is very much a part of the local dining scene, so much so that in some cases food definitely takes a back seat.

The current favorite in town is the **Midnight Sun,** which as the name implies has a Scandinavian motif. Located right downtown at Peachtree Center South and designed by John Portman, it is both a lunchtime favorite of businessmen and an evening dining spot for Atlantans of every stripe (if not color). The cuisine served ranges from honest-to-Stockholm to tableside flambés.

If you stay in or near the Hyatt Regency, don't miss **Hugo's,** another interesting restaurant with fine Continental cuisine. In Underground Atlanta the **Rue de Paris** is more authentically French, but more in atmosphere than in food. Still a good bet.

The **Chateau Fleur de Lis** has its critics among gourmets, but its elegant setting and excellent service can amply compensate unless you are a purist of haute cuisine—in which case you'll be out of luck in Atlanta anyway.

Other popular restaurants include **Herren's** (seafood), and the **Diplomat** (steak).

## Potpourri

Atlanta is a mecca for young singles and would-be singles, which means that visiting businessmen and conventioners can (*a*) have a

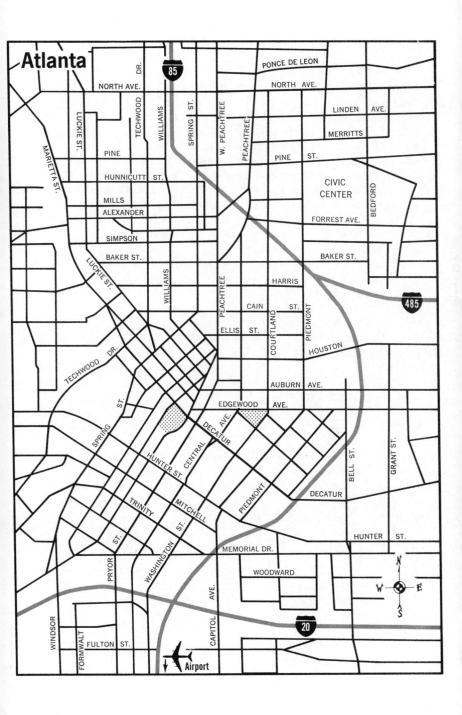

ball, (b) get into a lot of trouble, (c) be bored stiff, or (d) all of the above.

If you like bouncing around swingles bars, check a. There are plenty of watering holes for mingling New York-style—you get a drink and simply walk through mazes of people until you find yourself in proximity to someone suitable. Barbaric, but effective. The accents you hear come from all over the U.S. Maybe that is why these kinds of places are more popular than discotheques—Atlanta hasn't homogenized its own dancing style yet.

Best known are **Clarence Foster's,** the **Tree on Peachtree, Second Sun,** the **Clock O Fives** in the Hyatt Regency, and the **Brothers Two** in Colony Square. But remember that swingles don't patronize any one spot for too long. Marriage, husbands, wives, old bar tabs, and other maladies keep these types peripatetic—ask a local contact to make sure of what's happening.

If you are looking for the more professional talents, check b above. There are ladies of the evening in certain areas, and pickup joints. Watch out: Atlanta's Southern hospitality doesn't necessarily apply to pros, and you run the same risks here as elsewhere.

If your tastes run more to the cultural side, sorry, check letter c. With the exceptions of the **Atlanta Symphony Orchestra,** under the direction of Robert Shaw, and a few road shows, there is little to recommend. There aren't even many good nightclubs for top-flight entertainers. Only the **Club Atlantis** features stars regularly. It's good—but expensive.

If you want a little of everything, check d and head for Underground Atlanta. This tremendously varied three-block stretch of clubs, restaurants, and novelty shops, formerly the heart of old Atlanta, has got it all—good and bad. You can hear good entertainment in **Dante's, Down the Hatch,** or **Scarlett O'Hara's,** grab everything from a snack to a gourmet meal in any of a dozen restaurants, have Irish coffee, and buy a Lester Maddox T-shirt—personally autographed by same. Let it hang out.

If your family is along, make sure to rent a car. **Stone Mountain Park,** the world's largest mass of exposed granite, should be part of your visit. On it are etched the visages of Jefferson Davis, Stonewall Jackson, and Robert E. Lee, lest we forget.

**Six Flags Over Georgia** is a fine amusement theme park. Thirty-five miles to the south of town is **Lion Country Safari.** The **Atlanta Zoo** and nearby **Cyclorama,** featuring an enormous three-dimensional rendering of the battle of Atlanta—again, lest we forget—are also worth taking in.

For shopping, there are **Neiman-Marcus, Saks Fifth Avenue,** and **Lord & Taylor** outlets. **Rich's** is the best local department store.

## *Nitty Gritty*

## HOTELS

### *Superior*

**ATLANTA INTERNATIONALE** (450 Capitol St. across from Atlanta Stadium). Among the newest. Has nicely appointed rooms, good service. Located on the fringe of a high-crime area, however. There have been security problems. Management has provided the most extensive security system in the city.

**HYATT REGENCY ATLANTA** (In the heart of Peachtree Center). The best. A breathtaking lobby.

**MARRIOTT** (Courtland & Cain sts.). Convenient, busy convention hotel. Excellent service, a 24-hour restaurant. After 11:00 P.M., watch out for hookers.

**STOUFFER'S ATLANTA INN** (590 W. Peachtree St.). Sophisticated. Rooms are spacious and elegant. Some have what management calls swimming pools; guests call them over-sized baths.

### *Good*

**ADMIRAL BENBOW** (1470 Spring St.). A good bet if you don't have to stay downtown. Comfortable, but not elegant. Moderate rates.

**ATLANTA AMERICAN** (160 Spring St.). Downtown. Rooms are comfortable but many overlook the air-conditioning unit, which is noisy in summertime. Restaurants poor. Rates moderate.

**RODEWAY INN LENOX** (3387) Lenox Rd.). North of downtown, next to the city's two best shopping centers. No frills but well run, with moderate rates.

**SHERATON-BILTMORE** (817 W. Peachtree St.). Old Atlanta landmark that has been nicely refurbished. Popular for conventions. Just north of downtown.

### *Acceptable*

**HOLIDAY INN DOWNTOWN** (175 Piedmont St.). No oasis, but located downtown, across from the back of the Hyatt Regency.

**RIVIERA HYATT HOUSE** (1630 Peachtree St.). Away from downtown but near Interstate exits and popular with businessmen because of tennis courts. Good cocktail lounge.

**ROYAL COACH MOTOR INN** (Interstate 75 & Howell Mill Rd.). Attractive English castle. Car a must.

**TRAVELODGE AT EXECUTIVE PARK** (Interstate 85 at N. Druid Hills Rd.). A cut above the average. Attractive, comfortable accommodations, well run. Located just within the city limits, far from downtown. Waterbed suites available.

## RESTAURANTS

**THE ABBEY** (\*\*) (669 W. Peachtree St.). A converted Unitarian church with a rarified atmosphere and the service bar on the altar. Waiter and wine stewards don monks' robes. Divine food and service. One of the best wine lists in town. But, annoyingly, many Heavenly reservations are called, but few are chosen at dinner hours. Dinner for two: approximately $35.

**BRENNAN'S** (\*) (103 W. Paces Ferry Rd.). Same menu as the New Orleans landmark, but far, far away. Service below-par. The gumbo is fine and the shrimp creole dinner is recommended. Small wine list. Open for breakfast, lunch, and dinner seven days. Dinner for two: $30.

**CHATEAU FLEUR DE LIS** (\*\*\*) (Interstate 85 & Cheshire Bridge Rd.). Haute cuisine, at its finest, for Atlanta. Best wine list in the city. Elegantly appointed. Service is formal and precise. Dinner for two: $45.

**COACH AND SIX** (\*\*) (1776 Peachtree St.). Little atmosphere, but popular with businessmen for lunch. Steak au poivre is a good bet. Even with reservations you'll probably have to wait. Dinner for two: $30.

**DIPLOMAT** (\*\*) (Spring & Harris sts.). Opulent. Broad menu selection. Steaks and prime ribs best. Located in the heart of downtown. Dinner for two: $30.

**HARBOUR HOUSE** (\*) (Marriott Motor Hotel). Nice atmosphere. Recommended only for its lobsters, which are flown in daily. Dinner for two: $35.

**HERREN'S** (\*\*\*) (84 Luckie St.). For the seafood fan. Live lobster, many house specialties. Long a favorite among Atlantans. Dinner for two: $28.

**HUGO'S** (\*\*\*) (Hyatt Regency Atlanta). Elegant. Excellent Continental cuisine. Reservations a must. Dinner for two: $45.

**ICHIBAN** (\*) (151 Ellis St.). Japanese-style food for the American palate. Teppan-style steaks and chicken prepared at your table. Dinner for two: $23.

**JOE DALE'S CAJUN HOUSE** (\*\*) (3209 Maple Dr.). Excellent creole cooking at reasonable prices. Try the shrimp and the oysterman dinners. Reservations not accepted on weekends. Dinner for two: $26.

**McKINNON'S LOUISIANNE** (**) (2100 Cheshire Bridge Rd.). An intimate place that serves good creole food. Trout marguery is popular. Deferential service. Reservations only. Dinner for two: $27.

**MIDNIGHT SUN** (***) (235 Peachtree St.). One of the most attractive restaurants ever, designed by John Portman. First-rate Continental menu. Service is formal, sometimes curt. Dinner for two: $50.

**THE OUTER MARKER** (*) (In the Scott Hudgins Bldg., across from the airport). Best restaurant in the airport area. Good prime ribs and steak Diane. Service is good. Dinner for two: $26.

**RUE DE PARIS** (***) (Underground Atlanta). Very French restaurant. The sliced mushroom salad is a delight. Best service in town. Extensive wine list. Has a sister, Rue de Paris, in the Northeast section of the city on fashionable East Paces Ferry Road. It, too, is tops. Dinner for two at either: $43.

**SIDNEY'S JUST SOUTH** (*)(4225 Roswell Rd.). This offbeat place is a favorite among Atlantans. Reservations a must. Only five selections on the menu. The Phoenix Emperor Chicken is the house specialty. Order well in advance. No cocktails. American wines only. Dinner for two: $20.

*Restaurants Not Recommended*

**CROSS ROADS** (1556 Peachtree St.). Once a favorite, has deteriorated through the years. Dinner for two: $20.

**TRADER ENGS** (300 W. Peachtree St.). A Polynesian restaurant with unauthentic food. Dinner for two: $22.

## Recommended Reading

THIS IS ATLANTA by John Crown. (Atlanta Board of Realtors, Healy Building, Atlanta, Ga. 30303, $15). Very well-illustrated volume on sights and happenings around the city.

WELCOME by Tracy Warren. (Marco Publications, 215 Piedmont Ave., N.E., Suite 402, Atlanta, Ga. 30312, $3.95). Good general guide to hotels, etc., updated annually. Partial to its advertisers, which include most of the better spots.

# BALTIMORE

Baltimore has been traditionally, and unjustly, maligned as a place to avoid. Before the Harbor Tunnel thruway was constructed, the city was viewed as just a traffic jam on the way to New York. Then after the tunnel was built, Baltimore won new respect—for building a shortcut under the city.

For those who visit Baltimore on business or choose to stop for pleasure, however, the rewards may be surprising. While it is an industrial city, Baltimore is steeped in history, is a center for the arts, and is a comfortable place to live with a leisurely, outdoorsy life-style. And it's a city that has its own language, too. Locals refer to the city as "Ballamer." And the cop on the beat is a *PO*-leece-man to everyone in town.

Also unique to Baltimore are the white-stooped houses downtown that have seen various waves of immigrants come to the city, thrive, and move on. Some may make it to the more fashionable neighborhoods like Homeland, Guilford, and Roland Park, the turf of the modern-day gentry. Today, the woman scrubbing the marble stoop might be Black, or German, or Italian—but the steps shine nonetheless.

Baltimore is an old city, and in addition to the historic sights, there are numerous vestiges from the past that are slow to yield to the architect and builder. The bustling downtown area still has its ancient spires and horse-drawn vegetable wagons alongside the rebuilt business district of Charles Center. And the old piers and wharves in the waterfront area only accentuate the modernity of the McCormick Building.

Baltimore is also a sports center. Besides housing the big-league Colts and Orioles, it is the lacrosse capital of the world and an important horse racing center. The Preakness, middle jewel in the

Triple Crown, is held every May at Pimlico, and the Washington, D.C., International grass-course event is staged every fall at nearby Laurel Race Course. Don't miss them if you are in town then.

Fishing and boating on Chesapeake Bay are also popular pastimes for many Baltimoreans.

## Hotels

In a word, the hotel picture is lousy. First-rate hotels simply do not exist.

The best, without question, is the **Baltimore Hilton,** downtown in the Charles Center. It is just a few steps from the area's major indoor arena, the Civic Center, and from the Morris Mechanic Theatre. Some of the city's best restaurants are nearby. In the same area, the **Holiday Inn Downtown** is a good alternative as is the **Lord Baltimore.** As for lodging away from the downtown area, motels are the best bet, and they are plentiful. There are nine **Holiday Inns** alone scattered about, besides the one downtown. Several cater to dog lovers and have kennels available.

## Restaurants

Baltimore is rich in outstanding eateries and ranks with the best-known restaurant cities. Its specialty is Chesapeake Bay seafood delicacies: crabs, clams, oysters, all sorts of fish, diamond-backed terrapin, you name it. One local specialty, crab cakes, are simply not duplicated anywhere—and die-hard fans from all over the East have been known to drive hundreds of miles to satisfy their craving.

Don't be put off by "name" restaurants. World-famous **Haussner's** and the equally noted **Chesapeake** are as popular with locals as visitors. Haussner's, an art gallery as well as a restaurant with an almost endless menu, is located in the white-marble-step district. The Chesapeake has unbeatable seafood and beef, served in ample helpings. **Jimmy Wu's New China Inn** is the place for Cantonese selections.

A special treat to see, or place to snack or buy delicious food of all sorts to take home, is the long-standing **Lexington Market,** which dates back to 1792. More than 100 stalls operated by individual merchants feature food from all over the world.

## *Potpourri*

There are few worthwhile evening diversions. Though some well-known entertainers often perform at the **Civic Center,** most bypass the city for Washington. The **Mechanic Theatre** is the best bet for Broadway-bound plays while a number of small theater groups, such as **Center Stage,** offer decent productions. In addition, the **Baltimore Symphony** is quite good.

You've doubtless heard about The Block—a row of tawdry strip joints on East Baltimore Street, where Blaze Starr et al. do their thing. The on-stage shows are actually quite tame compared to what is on the boards in other cities, but watch out at the bar where the fine art of the rip-off has been highly polished. A brief conversation with a bar girl usually finds you paying dearly for her weak drink. Any longer liaison is strictly at your own risk—and expense. It's there, though, if you are interested.

A city short on good late-hour entertainment, Baltimore is more of a place to soak up history. Dozens of sites are available, most open only during the day.

High on the list of historic sights is **Fort McHenry,** overlooking the harbor, where the U.S. national anthem was written while the city was under bombardment from the British. Another must is the **Mount Vernon Place** area, where the first Washington Monument stands. The **Peabody Conservatory** and **Walters Art Gallery** are nearby.

Other noteworthy sites include the U.S. frigate **Constellation** at Pratt Street; **Mount Clare Mansion,** the city's oldest colonial home; the **townhouse of Charles Carroll** of Carrollton, signer of the Declaration of Independence; the **Peale Museum,** oldest museum building in the U.S.; and **Edgar Allan Poe's grave.**

A religious center, the city is the site of the first Roman Catholic Cathedral built in the U.S., the **Basilica of the Assumption,** located downtown at Cathedral and Mulberry streets.

The new **Roman Catholic Cathedral,** on fashionable North Charles Street, might be the last lavish Catholic cathedral to be built. It is one of the most elegant modern structures in the country. En route there, one passes the Federal-period Homewood campus of **Johns Hopkins University**—the famous hospital center in East Baltimore.

If your children are along, other sites include the **Baltimore Zoo,** the **Number Six Engine House,** the **Baltimore Streetcar Museum,** and the **Baltimore & Ohio Transportation Museum,** which features the

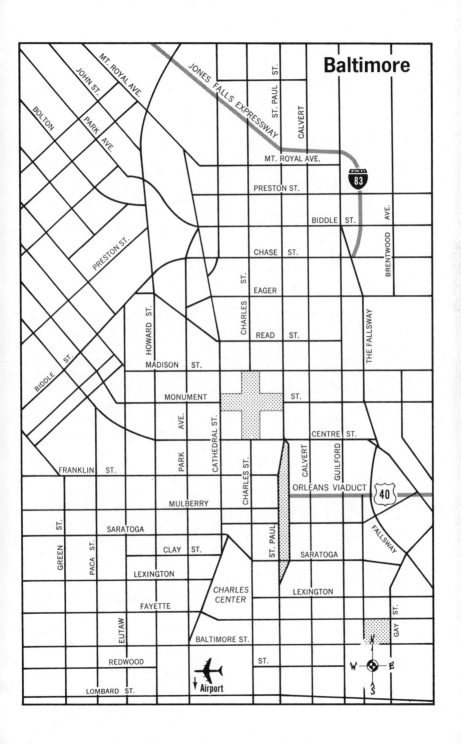

world's largest collection of locomotives, railroad equipment, and models.

## Nitty Gritty

### HOTELS

*Good*

**BALTIMORE HILTON** (101 W. Fayette). Best hotel in Baltimore, such as it is. 350 rooms. Bright, well-appointed rooms. Second tower with convention center has been completed. Convenient location across street from Civic Center and Morris Mechanic Theatre. Rooftop pool.

**CROSS KEYS INN** (Route 29, Columbia). Located on lakefront in the new city of Columbia, eight miles southwest of Baltimore. Pleasant country atmosphere, yet convenient to both Baltimore and Washington.

**CROSS KEYS INN** (5100 Falls Rd. near Northern Pkwy.). Small hotel in quiet village setting. Convenient to Pimlico and Towson and only minutes from downtown by I-83.

**HILLTOP MOTOR INN** (1660 Whitehead Ct.). West Baltimore location off Beltway (I-695), exit 17. Near the Social Security Administration National Headquarters.

**HOLIDAY INN DOWNTOWN** (Howard & Lombard). Somewhat tacky decor but the location is the chief feature, across the street from the Civic Center and within walking distance of office buildings and best stores. Revolving rooftop restaurant.

**HOLIDAY INN GLEN BURNIE** (6600 Ritchie Highway). Eight miles south of city on Route 2, Beltway (I-695), exit 3.

**HOLIDAY INN NORTH** (Loch Raven Blvd. at Joppa Rd.). Accessible to Memorial Stadium, Towson, John F. Kennedy Turnpike, and north. Kennel available.

**HOLIDAY INN WEST** (6401 Baltimore National Pike). Located eight miles west of city on Route 40, one-half mile west of Beltway (I-695), exit 15. Kennel available.

**HUNT VALLEY INN** (Shawan Rd. on I-83). Quiet, country atmosphere, yet just 15 to 20 minutes from city via interstate. Golf course, tennis courts.

**LORD BALTIMORE** (Baltimore and Hanover). Recently renovated, long-established downtown convention hotel. 600 rooms. Garage free.

**QUALITY INN TOWSON** (1015 York Rd., Towson). Good suburban motel convenient to northern suburbs.

**QUALITY INN WEST** (5801 Baltimore National Pike, Catonsville). Seven miles west of city on Route 40 at Beltway (I-695), exit 15.

**WARREN HOUSE MOTOR HOTEL** (407 Reisterstown Rd., Pikesville). 1½ miles south of Beltway (I-695), exit 20. Accessible to Pimlico, western Maryland.

*Acceptable*

**FRIENDSHIP INTERNATIONAL** (Baltimore-Washington International Airport, formerly Friendship Airport). Good, functional airport hotel.

**SHERATON INN-BALTIMORE** (400 N. Broadway). East Baltimore location opposite Johns Hopkins Hospital.

**TOWN HOUSE MOTOR HOTEL** (5810 Reisterstown Rd.). Three miles south of Beltway (I-695), exit 20.

# RESTAURANTS

**BERNIE LEE'S PENN HOTEL** (*) (15 W. Pennsylvania, Towson). The best place to eat in the Towson suburban area. Large portions. Excellent crab dishes. Dinner for two: approximately $16.

**BRENTWOOD INN** (**) (Fifth & Brentwood, one block northeast of Dundalk & Holabird aves.). An out-of-the-way south Baltimore delight. Steak and seafood are the specialties along with some good French dishes. Very good wine cellar. Dinner for two: $20.

**CHARCOAL HEARTH** (*) (1 W. Baltimore). Located in the Morris Mechanic Theatre building. Seafood and steaks are features. Well-appointed dining rooms complete with leather captain's chairs and walnut paneling. Dinner for two: $18.

**CHESAPEAKE** (***) (1701 N. Charles). Award-winning and nationally famous seafood and beef house. Early American decor. Lives up to its reputation. Outstanding crab and other Chesapeake Bay dishes. Pen and Quill Lounge has a piano bar. Dinner for two: $23.

**CINNAMON TREE** (*) (Shawan Rd. on I-83). Intimate atmosphere. Located in Hunt Valley Inn. Veal Rosemary and filet St. Joseph are two house specialties. Pleasant entertainment featured in adjoining Paddock Bar. Dinner for two: $20.

**DANNY'S** (**) (1201 N. Charles). Possibly the biggest award-winner in the city—but has been overshadowed. Steak and lobster hard to beat. Chesapeake Bay seafood outstanding. Dinner for two: $25.

**EAGER HOUSE** (***) (15 W. Eager). Continental, American

menu. Charcoal grill and lobster tank featured. Pleasant nautical decor. Dinner for two: $18.

**GORDON'S OF ORLEANS STREET** (**) (243 N. Patterson Park Ave., at Orleans). Stellar East Baltimore crab house. Wide seafood selection. Judged the best crab cakes in recent National Crab Cooking Olympics. Dinner for two: $16.

**HARVEY HOUSE** (**) (920 N. Charles). Unpretentious, but good. Friendly place with large menu. Continental, American. Seafood and prime ribs are the specialties. Dinner for two: $18.

**HAUSSNER'S** (***) (3236 Eastern Ave.). A must. A unique stop located in the white-marble-step, East-side German area. German specialties. Old-World atmosphere. An art gallery as well as a restaurant, with paintings adorning almost every inch of wall space. Best at lunch. Note: no reservations or credit cards. Dinner for two: $16.

**HORN & HORN** (*) (304 E. Baltimore). The original of a cafeteria/restaurant chain located on Baltimore's famous Block. Recommended for lunch only. Customers range from businessmen to Block entertainers. Lunch for two: $8.

**JIMMY WU'S NEW CHINA INN** (***) (2430 N. Charles). Advertises the "best Chinese food this side of China"—well, this side of Baltimore, anyway. A local institution. Excellent Cantonese. Informal atmosphere. Exotic drinks by Won Long Pour. Eight minutes from downtown. Dinner for two: $18.

**JOHNNY UNITAS' GOLDEN ARM** (*) (6354 York). A shopping center restaurant owned by the former Colt star and Bobby Boyd, frequented by jocks. Standard seafood and steak fare. Dinner for two: $18.

**KARSON'S INN** (**) (5100 Holabird Ave.). A pleasant stop by the harbor with rustic decor. Can't miss with seafood dishes. Dinner for two: $18.

**MAISON MARCONI** (**) (106 W. Saratoga). Small, elegant downtown restaurant. French, Italian menu. Closed Sundays, Mondays. Specialties: lobster Cardinal, chicken Tetrazzini. Dinner for two: $25.

**MARIA'S "300"** (***) (300 Albemarle). Outstanding Italian cuisine. Features lobster Fra Diavolo, shrimp oregano, veal Maria, crab Sorrento, and homemade pasta. As in all Little Italy restaurants, prices are very moderate. Dinner for two: $15.

**MILLER BROTHERS** (*) (101 W. Fayette). Located in the Baltimore Hilton. This new version of a famous eatery fails to match its elegant predecessor. Dinner for two: $25.

**ORCHARD INN** (*) (1528 E. Joppa Rd.). Fine all-around fare with music. Near Towson and northern suburbs. Dinner for two: $18.

**OYSTER BAY** (*) (4 N. Liberty). Mass-production eatery across the street from the Civic Center. Vast menu. Try the crab soup and stuffed rockfish. Dinner for two: $17.

**PEABODY BOOKSHOP AND BEER STUBE** (*) (913 N. Charles). Folk music and varied beverages add to the dining atmosphere in room to the rear of authentic old bookstore. Extremely moderate. Dinner for two: $10.50.

**PIMLICO HOTEL** (*) (5301 Park Heights Ave.). Adjoining Pimlico Race Track. Standard Maryland fare excellently prepared. An odds-on favorite after a day at the races. Cavalier Lounge usually has good entertainment. Dinner for two: $18.

**THE PRIME RIB** (**) (Calvert & Chase). Self-proclaimed as the "21 Club" of Baltimore, this New York-style restaurant is about a "17"—but it does have the best prime ribs in the city, and some great steaks. Dinner for two: $25.

**SABATINO'S** (***) (901 Fawn). Little Italy's best. Like stepping into the dining room of a Southern Italian home. Completely unpretentious, a sheer delight. Dinner for two: $15.

**THOMPSON'S SEA GIRT HOUSE** (**) (5919 York). An informal seafood house in north Baltimore—worth the short trip from downtown. Established in 1885, this remains a family-operated establishment best known for its Crab Imperial. Dinner for two: $15.

**VELLEGGIA'S** (**) (204 S. High). Probably the largest restaurant in Little Italy. Specializes in Southern Italian dishes, uniformly good. Dinner for two: $15.

## Recommended Reading

MARYLAND ACCOMMODATIONS GUIDE   Published annually. Free, from the Maryland Hotel and Motor Inn Association, P.O. Box 180, Severna Park, Md. 21146.

HISTORICAL GUIDE TO BALTIMORE   Free from the Peale Museum, 225 Holiday St., Baltimore, Md. 21202.

BALTIMORE TODAY: ITS PLEASURES, TREASURES & PAST by A. Aubrey Bodine. (Bodine, $1.95).

# BOSTON

Dame Boston, the nation's oldest big city and its most important business center until New York overtook it in the 1840s, is a fascinating, compact blend of the very old and the very new. Bostonians like to brag about the city's liveability, its manageable size compared with New York or Chicago, and its easy access to Cape Cod, the coast of Maine, and the mountains of northern New England.

It's a city of contrasts, the faded elegance of Back Bay and Beacon Hill coexisting in a remarkable fit with the "let it all hang out" style of the city's huge student population.

Boston's age shows everywhere. Well-preserved revolutionary shrines such as Faneuil (rhymes with flannel) Hall and the Old State House, started in 1713, are standouts. Even the current statehouse, a gold-domed Bullfinch structure at the peak of Beacon Hill, was started in the late eighteenth century. There, in the Senate chamber, the sacred cod still hangs, a reminder of commercial priorities in the era before electronics and mutual funds.

Mixed with the old are some fine examples of modern architecture, such as the great City Hall set back in a large brick plaza that once was Scollay Square, the city's tenderloin district. The "pregnant" First National Bank tower with its bulge in the middle is easily spotted, as is the 60-story, all-glass John Hancock tower. By and large, Boston escaped the mindless urban renewal that has plagued many cities because it got started so late, in the 1960s, that it learned from the mistakes of others. Its rebuilding has been accomplished with a respect for saving the best of the past.

This city of 2.5 million persons is frequently and correctly compared with San Francisco in terms of setting and personality. To a striking degree its character is set by an undisciplined army of 200,000 students and hangers-on from Harvard, MIT, Boston University,

Boston College, Northeastern, Tufts, Brandeis, and other schools sprinkled liberally throughout the metropolitan area. Young people spill over the city's sidewalks and parks without reverence for ethnic or occupational turf, mixing with Irish, Italians, blacks, Yankees, and others who come together from nine to five, but retreat to such ethnic neighborhoods as Irish South Boston and the Italian North End at night. Boston's famous orators talked a lot about the American melting pot. But Boston never really melted—witness its school desegregation problems.

This panorama is easily seen by visitors because Boston is so compact. A taxi will get you most places for a couple of bucks, and a couple of dollars more will get you anywhere and back in Boston, Brookline, and neighboring Cambridge, across the Charles River. The Charles, incidentally, despite centuries of pollution, may well be America's loveliest urban waterway, especially in the spring when sailboats vie with racing shells in its broad lower stretches.

If the weather is good—only an even bet in a coastal city that suffers some truly wretched weather—visitors can and should walk in this city scaled for walking. Unfortunately, night walking on the darker streets and Boston Common is no safer here than in most major cities.

At any rate, do not drive; repeat, do not drive. Boston is loaded with ill-tempered drivers of all ages who have been taught that law and order belong in streets elsewhere, but not in Boston. For the adventuresome, there's an ancient, creaking underground trolley system that gets around, but it's hard to figure out.

## Hotels

Any hotel you choose in Boston or Cambridge will be only two or three miles from close-in Logan airport. Except for rush-hour traffic, especially in the late afternoon, when traffic clogs the tunnel under the harbor, it's a quickie 15-minute cab ride to and from hotels. Don't fuss with airport limousines. Cabs are quick and the run is only a few dollars.

The **Boston-Sheraton** hotel at Prudential Center in the Back Bay is the city's largest hotel, host to most conventions. Book the Tower suites if you want luxury with a view. Note: Make reservations early. Boston has a scarcity of good rooms.

Close to the Boston-Sheraton is the new **Colonnade Hotel,** geared to executives' tastes. It is off the main drag just enough so that a last-minute room reservation might be handled.

For those with a yen for the quiet elegance of the old Boston, the **Ritz-Carlton** across from the Public Garden and the **Copley-Plaza** near the Public Library are truly gracious. The Ritz, purchased by local people when it was about to fall into non-Boston hands, retains its expensive, tasteful air, the kind of place where even the coffee shop serves fresh croissants and herring for breakfast. It's beloved by senior academics, visiting diplomats, international businessmen, and established Broadway stars. The Copley Plaza is a regular habit with businessmen who prefer its quiet, its oversized rooms, and its excellent restaurants and facilities.

In the old downtown heart near the financial district and Government Center, the **Parker House** stands as the sole quality hotel. This venerable hostelry is trying to make a comeback after a long period when its reputation sagged like Parker House rolls without the yeast. It was completely refurbished in 1973.

Only in Boston, perhaps, will you find a **Howard Johnson** motor lodge touted as one of the half-dozen best places to spend the night. The high-rise Hojo's on Stuart Street is in a tacky part of town, though close to the city's few legitimate theaters and handy to the Massachusetts Turnpike. It boasts large, pleasant rooms and even some suites that compare in price and size—if not period furniture—with the Ritz.

There is little else in Boston. Stay away from the **Statler Hilton,** a very busy convention hotel, unless you want to take a chance on landing in a room not much larger than a closet at the better hotels. Cambridge is so easily reached from Boston that businessmen with appointments in the cerebral suburb can easily stay in Boston. In Cambridge itself, though awkwardly located, the **Sonesta Motor Inn** offers sound quarters.

Note for the businessmen who must head for the Rte. 128 industrial and research belt that rings the city: such Rte. 128 towns as Needham, Westwood, Wellesley, Waltham, Lexington, Burlington, and Woburn are reachable only by car, which can be rented either at the airport or at downtown hotels. A large, well-run hotel on Rte. 128, at the Mass Turnpike interchange in Newton, is the **Marriott.**

### Restaurants

Dining in Boston, even for the man who automatically asks for steak, ought to include a sampling of New England's excellent seafood. You'll probably think at once of **Anthony's Pier 4** and **Jimmy's**

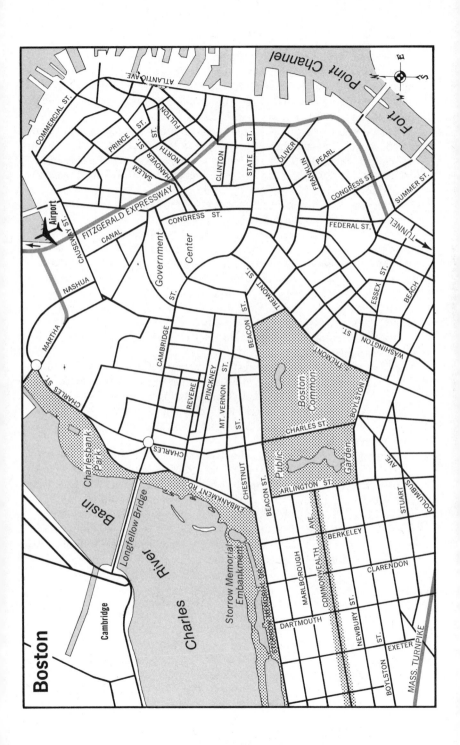

**Harborside,** two very large, popular restaurants a couple of miles from downtown in South Boston, and that's all right. They are worth the trip and even the inevitable wait because the food is excellent and the drinking is good aboard the *Peter Stuyvesant,* a saloon ship that holds waiting patrons at Anthony's.

Back in town, seafood is featured at most restaurants. Spell it scrod or schrod—and never mind the joke about the visitor who asked the taxidriver the best place in town to get scrod—this moderately priced delicacy is on every respectable menu. It's a young cod or haddock.

Some restaurant choices are obvious, but don't let that stop you. **Locke-Ober** and its Back Bay branch, **Joseph's,** serve excellent Continental fare in a cosmopolitan setting of black-tied waiters and starched tablecloths. The Sea and Surf's **Admiralty Room** is a fine restaurant overlooking the new City Hall. **Maison Robert,** located in the old city hall, has won a wide following.

On the largely shipless waterfront, which looks much the same as it did during the Clipper Ship era, with several granite piers and warehouses as reminders, restaurants are sparking what could be a successful rebirth of the area. **Dom's** and **Stella** are both worthwhile experiences, with Dom's a special winner.

A few of the city's best restaurants are hidden in byways and not much given to shouting. **Café Budapest,** considered by some critics to be the city's best, is reached via the lobby of an undistinguished hotel in a nondescript block near Copley Plaza. **Lechner's** is a new spot in an old brick house in a drab part of the financial district. Both are worth the search.

And, of course, there's a whole class of ethnic and off-beat restaurants in the city and in Cambridge. Such places as the **No Name** on Boston's Fish Pier, the **Legal Seafood** in Cambridge, the **Red Fez** in a tough area of Boston, **India Sweet House** and **Acropolis** in Cambridge, and many more fit this bill. Find out about others from friends or, if you want to see Harvard Square on your own, from books such as the perceptive *Cheap Eats* (see Recommended Reading) researched by hungry Harvard students.


## *Potpourri*

Boston night life is on the quiet side. Of course, several clubs attract the sort of "who's that" star that rates high with Boston's student hordes. Many are concentrated in the Kenmore Square area, but they don't appeal to business visitors. Stay away from Combat Zone strip joints and lounges in the downtown red-light district.

Two good jazz clubs share the same basement address, 733 Boylston Street, across from the Prudential Center. **Paul's Mall** and the **Jazz Workshop** bring big-name musicians to their rather small settings.

The **Sugar Shack** at 110 Boylston brings in top Black entertainers and is the city's leading soul club.

Sports stars are a big deal in this sports-crazy city, and a few have made a go of their own restaurant-lounges. Gino Capelleti, a long-time place kicker with the Patriots, runs **The Point After** at 271 Dartmouth Street, just off Copley Square, while playboy hockey-star Derek Sanderson has a piece of the action in the well-regarded lounge, **Daisy Buchanan's,** on Newbury at Gloucester, and at **Zelda's,** 1194 Commonwealth Avenue. The Boston-Sheraton has dinner and dancing every night except Sunday and Monday at the **Café Riviera,** and there's dancing at the **Top of the Hub,** at the summit of the 58-story Prudential Center, where the view is spectacular day and night.

At the Copley Plaza Hotel, the massive stand-up oak bar in the cornball Edwardian setting of **Copley's** has quickly become one of the most popular bars in town, with a heavy trade from insurance and advertising types. For traditionalists, the same hotel still offers the **Merry-Go-Round** bar, with entertainers perched in one corner.

There are plenty of singles clubs, though they tend to shift in popularity as fickle patrons drift from one to another. You might try **Brandy's,** 1110 Commonwealth Avenue; **Brandy's II,** 1222 Commonwealth; **T.J.'s,** 528 Commonwealth; or **Lucifer's,** 523 Commonwealth, if you're of that mind. In the same building as Lucifer's is **K-K-K-Katy,** offering beer, peanuts, Dixieland, and sometimes rock.

Boston gets a good number of pre-Broadway shows at the city's legitimate theaters; *No, No, Nanette* was polished here, for example. And there is plenty of good repertory theater in Cambridge and Boston. Check the papers, particularly the *Globe,* which covers the entertainment best with a thorough and critical sweep.

The city is rich in cultural attractions. The **Boston Symphony** is one of the world's finest, and director Seiji Ozawa adds excitement. Symphony Hall frequently sells out but check anyway, or write to Symphony Hall, 255 Huntington Avenue, Boston 02115.

In May and June you can catch the schmaltzy **Boston Pops** with Arthur Fiedler—tables and chairs replace seats on the first floor, and champagne and wine are sold in liberal quantities as corks pop and trumpets blow. Most Pops concerts are sellouts, so inquire ahead or lean on business contacts.

Bostonians are devoted to big-time sports, with more radio chatter and sportspage gossip given over to jocks than one might expect of the Athens of America. **Hockey,** Boston Bruins-style, is undisputed king, and tickets simply cannot be bought, nor usually borrowed. But you can usually pick up tickets at the last minute to watch the Celtics blow opponents off the court. Both the Bruins and the Celts play at the ancient, grimy Boston Garden, built in the days when big-time fights were the rage, and worth a visit before it comes down —or falls down.

The Boston Red Sox also offer a chance to watch **baseball** in a park that was up to date in the 1930s, when it was built. Fenway Park, right in town, only holds about 27,000 persons, but it gives a pleasant taste of the past to anyone used to the sterile suburban baseball parks that many cities now boast.

The New England Patriots **football** team sometimes has seats, depending on the Pats' performance—but if you go, reserve all day Sunday, because it's an 80-mile round trip to the boondocks of Foxborough.

Except for Boston College football, trying for the big time again, college sports in the Boston area is small scale. But it is not without its traditions and excitement. Attend a Harvard-Yale football game and see. Check out the Charles River for as many as a dozen men's and women's eight-oared racing shells practicing for the spring-summer season.

Boston makes it easy for history lovers to indulge in the city's rich heritage. Just follow the red brick path imbedded in sidewalks for the famous **Freedom Trail** that starts at Boston Common and winds for 1.5 miles through 15 important sites. It ends at Old North Church, where the lantern that started Paul Revere's ride to Lexington and Concord is hung. Freedom Trail maps are available from the information booth on the Tremont Street side of the Common— watch for strange hours at some of the shrines. And when you come to the busy corner that marks the site of the Boston Massacre, watch out for the five-way traffic or you may fall victim to another massacre.

From the Old North Church it is a short taxi ride to the Charlestown berth of the U.S.S. **Constitution**—Old Ironsides—a must if there are kids along. You may as well move on to the **Bunker Hill monument** on nearby Breed's Hill, with an excellent view of Boston —if you feel up to climbing 294 steps.

A less strenuous way to view the city is aboard a **harbor tour** boat —particularly the cocktail cruise that runs Monday through Friday at 5:30 during summer months (Massachusetts Bay Line, 542-8000; or Bay State Spray Cruises, 742-5707). Or if fresh water is your thing, and there are children along, head for the famous Swan Boats that are pedaled around the pond in the Public Garden—a surprisingly good skyline view of the city is yours from this beautiful inner city park.

Museums fit the Boston stereotype and they abound. Foremost is the **Museum of Fine Arts** at 479 Huntington Avenue, where collections of Old Kingdom works and Asiatic arts are considered among the best in the world. The great French Impressionist collection includes 34 Monets. The works of Paul Revere are an important part of an American silverware collection.

Harvard University has a wealth of museums, including the **Fogg Art Museum** (Quincy Street), next door to the striking **Carpenter Center for the Visual Arts,** the only U.S. building by Le Corbusier. The **Peabody Museum of Archaeology and Ethnology** is rated as one of the supreme collections of its kind in the world. And while there, stroll through Harvard Yard, then take in the signs and sounds of frenetic Harvard Square, one of America's more vibrant commercial districts with some interesting gift-buying possibilities. In Boston, incidentally, boutiques, galleries, and "little restaurants" abound on Newbury Street in the Back Bay, near Copley Square.

If children are along, a treat is the **Children's Museum,** several miles from downtown, where everything is touch and try. Depending on your time and wants, Gray Line tours to Lexington and Concord to visit revolutionary war shrines and literary homes are popular at all seasons.

## Nitty Gritty

## HOTELS

### Superior
**RITZ-CARLTON** (15 Arlington St.). The incomparable Ritz, so Proper Bostonian that everyone seems to be a Cabot or a Forbes (which isn't too surprising since it is now owned by Cabot, Cabot & Forbes), offers superb and restrained service. Many rooms overlook the Public Garden.

### Good
**COPLEY PLAZA** (Copley Sq.). This hotel, formerly the Sheraton Plaza, remains very popular with businessmen who want to avoid the bustle of convention hotels yet be close to the thick of things. Rooms, which have been totally refurbished, are frequently oversized and make up for older plumbing with fine furnishings.

**PARKER HOUSE** (60 School St.). The hotel that made the rolls famous is back in the Boston hotel scene to stay and deserves to be there. Management has poured $3.5 million into refurbishing every room in this aging hotel where Charles Dickens once lived. It's a favorite with political figures.

**SHERATON-BOSTON** (Prudential Center). Biggest hotel in New England. It suffers the crowding and mix-up problems of any high-traffic hotel, though Tower Rooms at the upper levels get away from the bustle.

*Acceptable*

**COLONNADE** (120 Huntington Ave., at Prudential Center). The city's newest and one of its plushest hotels. Excellent location and garage facilities if you're driving.

**HOWARD JOHNSON'S 57** (57 Stuart St.). Large rooms, a hotel in fact as well as in name, in a complex that includes an excellent independent restaurant and two movie theaters. Parking garage.

**MARRIOTT** (Route 128 and Massachusetts Turnpike, Newton). Large, busy motor lodge, popular with electronics executives. Several dining rooms and bars, easy access to both Boston and western suburbs.

**SONESTA MOTOR INN** (5 Cambridge Pkwy., Cambridge). The Sonesta is a high-rise motor lodge located near a bridge to Boston, just below the MIT campus. Terrific view across the river to Boston skyline.

# RESTAURANTS

**ANTHONY'S PIER 4** (***) (Northern Ave.). Possibly the largest restaurant in the U.S. and worth a visit despite the aggravation of a no-reservations policy and a certain wait. Excellent seafood of every size and shape. A hangout of the famous and would-be famous. Dinner for two: $30.

**BORASCHI'S** (*) (793 Boylston St.). An Italian restaurant in a plush Back Bay setting. Dinner for two: $25.

**THE BULL AT THE SOMERSET** (**) (Somerset Hotel, Commonwealth Ave.). Beef lovers call it The Bull, in what's left of the famous old Somerset Hotel (no longer in business). Serves the biggest steak in town. Dinner for two: $20.

**CAFÉ BUDAPEST** (***) (90 Exeter St.). Opulent, superb Hungarian food and wines, with knowledgeable waiters to guide selections. Try the cold cherry soup. Fills up fast for dinner. Adjacent lounge with gypsy fiddler. Dinner for two: $30.

**CASA ROMERO** (**) (Gloucester St.). Hidden off an alley in the Back Bay, this handsome Mexican restaurant is an elegant spot with high-backed chairs, bright inlays, and Mexican fare that runs hot, hotter, and hottest, as opposed to the blander Mexican-American foods so many restaurants serve. Popular with the Gillette crowd and others from nearby Prudential Center. Dinner for two: $30.

**COPLEY'S** (**) (Copley Plaza Hotel, Copley Sq.). The setting steals the show in this new room at the Copley Plaza, where everything from mooseheads to the original White Rock Girl painting adorn the walls and the waiters are decked out in turn-of-the-century dress. A fairly limited menu but sumptuous portions of good food. Dinner for two: $30.

**DOM'S of Newbury St.** (***) Some rate it the city's best. North Italian and French cooking are featured in this fairly new, renovated warehouse on the waterfront. No tipping—and this allows Dom's to use serious youngsters as waiters in an apprenticeship system borrowed from certain European traditions. Dinner for two: $26.

**DUNFEY'S LAST HURRAH** (**) (60 School St.). In the ground floor of the Parker House hotel, this looks like the place where every Irish pol in Boston should eat, including Mayor James M. Curley. Huge blown-up photos of bare-fisted boxers, Gibson Girls, and James Michael himself. Meats and fish priced by weight, serve-yourself salads, special chowders and stews, and plenty of beer flowing from the bar. Dixieland at night. Dinner for two: $25.

**DURGIN PARK** (*) (30 North Market St.). Everyone's heard of Durgin Park, where diners sit eight or ten to a table and the waitresses run you down if you don't duck. Not for relaxed dining, but good for an experience. College types like it. Much of the food is ordinary, but the huge prime ribs of beef are exceptional. Dinner for two: $18.

**FELICIA'S** (**) (145-A Richmond St.). Another fine North End Italian restaurant. A specialty is the chicken-mushroom-artichoke dish called Chicken Verdicchio. Dinner for two: $22.

**57 RESTAURANT** (**) (57 Stuart St.). One of the better large restaurants downtown, with an extensive menu and a good wine list. Dinner for two: $25.

**HALF-SHELL** (*) (743 Boylston St.). Seafood prepared in plain and fancy manners in a dark room so filled with nets and glass balls it's hard to girl-watch sometimes. Try the scallops en maison, brewed in a broth with shallots. Dinner for two: $25.

**JIMMY'S HARBORSIDE** (***) (242 Northern Ave.). Another large, famous, excellent seafood restaurant patronized by the great and near-great as well as by legions of business visitors. Jimmy's sometimes takes reservations. Dinner for two: $24.

**JOE TECCE'S** (**) (53 Washington St.). Tell the cabdriver the

exact address and look for the two red lanterns over the door—
there's no sign at this offbeat Italian family restaurant. Lots of noise,
schmaltz, overdone decorations, homemade wine served in jumbo
Coke bottles, and loads of good Italian food. Dnner for two: $12.

**JOSEPH'S** (\*\*) (279 Dartmouth St.). Joseph's, under Locke-
Ober's management, is located in an old Back Bay structure near
Copley Square and offers an identical menu in a more relaxed but
less interesting setting with a higher proportion of little old Boston
ladies. Dinner for two: $40.

**JOYCE CHEN** (\*\*) (500 Memorial Dr., Cambridge). If you want
Chinese food, this large restaurant on the banks of the Charles
River is plusher than the Boston Chinatown places, and specializes in
Northern Chinese cooking. Joyce herself has visited Peking, and
came back with some new recipes. Dinner for two: $18.

**LECHNER'S** (\*\*\*) (21 Broad St.). Lechner's is an impressive
restaurant with an air of Continental elegance. Authentic German
cooking plus such Boston favorites as the ubiquitous scrod. Handsome rooms, attentive service. Dinner for two: $40.

**LOCKE-OBER** (\*\*\*) (3 Winter Pl.). Perhaps the most famous
restaurant in Boston. The downstairs bar is masculine-ornate. The
upstairs dining rooms are plain, but the food is not. Lobster Savan-
nah, Sweetbreads Eugène are among the specialties, as are the Baked
Oysters Dartmouth. Dinner for two: approximately $40, with higher-
priced options.

**MAISON ROBERT** (\*\*\*) (45 School St.). An expanding restaurant located in the old city hall. Try the steak au poivre. One of
the rooms is called Ben's Café—for old Francophile Ben Franklin,
born in Boston. A statue of Ben directly outside the window is surrounded by tables in the summer months. Dinner for two: $30.

**NINETIES** (\*) (90 Broadway). Located in a tough part of town,
this popular restaurant packs in a lot of customers. The Beef Wellington is recommended. Dinner for two: $22.

**RITZ CARLTON** (\*\*\*) (15 Arlington St.). A great kitchen pre-
pares fine meals in a setting that is totally proper Boston. If you are
in no rush, and you should not be, ask for the superb Soufflé Grand
Marnier for dessert, which takes 45 minutes to prepare. Dinner for
two: about $40. (Light suppers served in the French Room for the
after-theater crowd.)

**SEA 'N SURF** (\*\*) (Sears Crescent Building, Government Center). The Admiralty Room upstairs offers relaxed dining in a bright,
cheerful room with a great view of the striking new City Hall. Good
seafood. Dinner for two: $30.

**STELLA** (\*\*) (74 East India Row). This old North End favorite
moved to glassy new waterfront quarters across from the Aquarium,

but the maître d' swears the quality of the food remains the same, which is to say, good. Veal Marsala is a specialty. Dinner for two: $24.

**UNION OYSTER HOUSE** (*) (41 Union St.). The building is 300 years old and once served as the home of exiled King of France Louis Philippe. It's been a restaurant for almost 150 years. Meals can be great, but inconsistent. Downstairs oyster bar is one of the city's wonders. Dinner for two: $20.

**ZACHARY'S** (**) (Colonnade Hotel, 120 Huntington Ave.). A plush expensive new dining spot. Dinner for two: $30.

## *Recommended Reading*

COMPREHENSIVE GUIDE TO BOSTON by Jerome and Cynthia Rubin (Emporium Publications, Box 539, Newton, Mass. 02158. 1972, $3.50). This comprehensive guide includes hotels, restaurants (but few ratings), a subway map, walking tours, and detailed information right down to where you will find a drinking fountain for animals.

IN AND OUT OF BOSTON WITH CHILDREN by Bernice Chesler. (Barre Westover, 419 Park Ave. S., New York, N.Y. 10016. Revised 1972, $3.95). Despite its name, this book is also great for people without children, particularly on day trips out of Boston. It includes a monthly calendar of special events, i.e., festivals in Boston's North End Italian section, fall fairs in New Hampshire. The only restaurant listings are geared to children.

BOSTON DINING OUT by Cynthia and Jerome Rubin. (Emporium Publications, Box 539, Newton, Mass. 02158, $2.50). A directory of Boston restaurants with commentary on specialties, atmosphere, hours, prices—but without ratings. This book includes menus from some of Boston's best-known restaurants and some favorite restaurant recipes.

CHEAP EATS by Kathrine C. Haspel and Paul A. Silver. (Harvard Student Agencies, Inc. 1972, $1.95.) Don't be put off by the title of this one. Although it does an excellent job of focusing on Boston's inexpensive restaurants—of which there are many in a variety of nationalities—it also lists, under the heading "Not Cheap At All," the city's better restaurants.

GREATER BOSTON SPECTATORS GUIDE by Jerome and Cynthia Rubin. (Emporium Publications, Box 539, Newton, Mass. 02158, $1.50). Seating charts as well as listings of addresses, phone numbers, and managers of Boston theaters, music halls, and sports stadiums.

# CHICAGO

For generations Chicago has labored under the stigma of being the Second City, a poor country bumpkin compared to the Big Apple in the east, New York. Well, now the city sports the world's tallest building, the Sears Tower, and it can point with mixed feelings of pride and embarrassment to Mayor Daley's cleaner streets, lower crime rate, and less orneriness than New York.

But make no mistake about it. Chicago is still the Second City. Under its brawny muscle lurks the heart of a pure prairie town. Not that any apologies are needed. The citizens are friendlier, the atmosphere for doing business more spontaneous (your word is your bond here), and there are fewer class distinctions.

Chicago grew up as a railroad town serving the huge stockyards that once perfumed the West Side. Manufacturers soon spotted the transportation advantages—rail and lake—and industry came in. From those early days, laborers and company presidents were often side by side, and even today the $100,000-a-year-corporation president and the $15,000-a-year steel worker may share a seat on the commuter railroad on the way home at night.

Its central location helps to make Chicago a big convention city, and rare is the metropolis that can absorb huge groups with so few dislocations. (The 1968 Democratic National Convention excepted, of course.)

Most of the city's business is still conducted in or near the famed Loop—a circle of elevated mass-transit tracks. In the Loop, LaSalle Street is the financial center. A few minutes' cab ride away are some of the newer high-risers, along Michigan Avenue (the Hancock Center, Standard Oil Building, Illinois Center) or on Wacker Drive (Sears Tower, Riverside Plaza). A few firms have abandoned the city entirely for the suburbs—particularly Kraftco and International

Minerals—but the city's splendid commuter rail service to the out-lying areas, where executives are usually ensconced, has made many corporate officers reluctant to abandon the inner city—unlike the case in New York.

The chic shops—like the big companies—have likewise stayed downtown. Saks and I. Magnin are fixtures on North Michigan Avenue, and State Street simply wouldn't be the same without Marshall Field's, perhaps the last exciting large department store in the country.

Getting around Chicago is a breeze. Streets are wide and traffic is not too bad (except at rush hours), and parking is plentiful, if ex-pensive. If you don't want to rent a car, however, you'll find taxis plentiful and fairly cheap.

## Hotels

As befits a crossroads city, Chicago has plenty of first-class hotels. The **Palmer House Towers** (not to be confused with the drab stan-dard Palmer House rooms) in the Loop provides the best center-city luxury space. Otherwise, you might check into the plush **Continental Plaza,** which has a new wing, or the **Drake,** both on North Michigan. The **Ritz-Carlton,** a few blocks up Michigan Avenue from the Con-tinental Plaza, is a 1975 entry. The **Westbury,** another near-North first-class hotel is at Huron and St. Clair.

Also plush and expensive, but somewhat away from the center of things, are the **Ambassadors** (East and West). Long a favorite with traveling movie stars, celebrities, and the jet-set, the **Ambassador East** is home of the Pump Room, where Booth 1 often finds such notables as Frank Sinatra holding court for vice-presidents and former vice-presidents. A surprisingly efficient and pleasant hotel, also near-North, is the **Astor Tower,** where only suites are offered—at single and double rates.

If your expense account is a bit more pinched, the **Sheraton-Chi-cago** offers remodeled rooms and an indoor pool. The **Executive House,** after a brief decline, is regaining favor as it attempts to live up to its reputation of old. If you are attending a convention at McCormick Place, the **McCormick Inn** is convenient, although the staff cares only about your credit card. The **Conrad Hilton** is also a favorite, although it seems to have more twin-sized beds than any other hotel in the world. If you are six feet or over, or just prefer a double bed, be sure to specify one when making a reservation. The **Sheraton-Blackstone** and **Pick-Congress** also offer decent rooms.

There are also **Holiday Inns** ringing the Loop, including one on the Lake with a spectacular view.

Hotels that have lost their gleam but remain popular with businessmen include the **LaSalle** and the **Bismarck.**


## *Restaurants*


For a town that holds a reputation for being all beef and potatoes, there are a lot of places for exotic, unusual foods. You can sample cuisine ranging from Armenian to Szechuan, besides getting a juicy New York-cut steak.

Some of the better known expensive eating spots include the **Pump Room, Maxim's de Paris, Biggs,** the **Cape Cod Room** (in the Drake Hotel) and the **Empire Room** (at the Palmer House), and **The Bakery.**

The food at these establishments does not always equal the reputation, but if you are out to impress, they will do just fine. Chicagoans themselves tend to avoid such places, and enjoy "discovering" out-of-the-way joints, which soon, of course, become tourist haunts themselves. This is what has recently happened to the once unknown Bakery, now becoming a popular tourist haunt.

If your appetite alone is your guide—not the decor, reputation, or price—the best advice is to select which type of cuisine you want to eat, then opt for the best. Here are some suggestions: French: **Jovan, Le Bastille, Consort, Le Mignon, Chez Paul, Champs-Elysées, L'Epuisette.** Chinese: **Abacus, Mongolian House.** Mexican: **Acapulco, Su Casa.** Italian: **Armando's, Italian Village, Riccardo's.** Seafood: **The Sea Gull.**

For the best view in town, try the **Ninety-Fifth,** on the you-guessed-it floor of the Hancock Center. Food is expensive and ordinary, so choose a good, clear evening.


## *Potpourri*


Chicago jumps until 4:00 A.M. Top-name entertainment frequents the **Empire Room, Mr. Kelly's** (North Rush Street), **The Blue Max** (in the Hyatt Regency O'Hare), **Mill Run** (Golf Road and Milwaukee Avenue in suburban Niles), and the **Playboy Club** (919 North Michigan—but you must be a member). Also there are a number of smallish night spots that occasionally book surprisingly

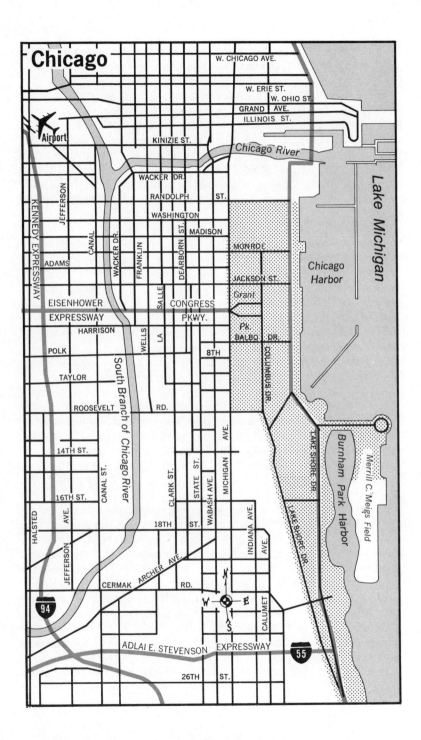

good talent in the 1000 North Rush Street block. For blues and folk-rock, a trip to the **Quiet Knight** (953 Belmont) is a must. **Ratso's** (2464 North Lincoln) is also a blues and jazz haven.

There are a number of singles bars in Chicago, as well, most of them clustered around the intersection of Division and Rush streets. Also you might try the lobby bar in the **Playboy Hotel** (next door to the club) during the cocktail hour, or the **Buttery** in the Ambassador West after ten. One problem: the drinking age in Illinois is nineteen, so the Rush-Division Street bars are often jammed with teeny-boppers, while the Buttery and the Playboy bar are often frequented by the type who expects a very smooth line and a Porsche in the parking lot.

If you don't score at the singles bars, by all means avoid the hookers who hang around the strip joints on Rush Street. They are notoriously dangerous. Their sisters, who are B-girls inside, will only rush you for as many quick, expensive drinks as they can hustle. If you are seriously looking for a lady of the night, $10 and a discreet word to the Bell Captain in your hotel will often produce a much safer liaison. Plan to spend a minimum of $50.

Note: Chicago is a big city with all of the big-city problems of crime. Do not go on foot inside the Loop at night. If you don't know your way around, the price of a cab to and from your destination can save you needless trouble in an unsavory neighborhood.

For **sports** buffs, Chicago is the home of the pro-football Bears, the baseball Cubs and White Sox, the basketball Bulls, and hockey Cougars and Blackhawks. In addition, north in Evanston, the North-western University Wildcats hold forth. Tickets for everything but Blackhawk hockey are readily available, but if the Bears are having a passable season, ask a contact to arrange for ducats in advance.

If you have some spare time or have brought your family along for the ride, there is plenty to do in Chicago. Besides the usual parade of museums and exhibits (marching orders include the **Art Institute, Museum of Science and Industry, Adler Planetarium, Field Museum of Natural History**), there are literally hundreds of small art galleries in which to while away (or waste, depending upon the exhibit) your time. There are also two zoos, **Lincoln Park** and **Brookfield,** and one aquarium—**John G. Shedd,** 1200 South Lake Shore.

There are also daily sight-seeing **tours** of varying length and fares to haul a family around while you are tied up in meetings. A cheap, fun diversion for children is the Loop shuttle. Board on the inner track and ride as long as you please—but remember where you got on because the L stations are all decorated in a style best described as Early Chicago Decrepit and look alike.

## *Nitty Gritty*

## HOTELS

### *Superior*

**AMBASSADOR EAST and WEST** (1300 N. State Pkwy., at Goethe St.). Out of the way, but an elegant pair of dowagers that watch over show-biz celebs and jet-setters as they pass through town. The Buttery is a singles bar where men must wear jackets, and the Pump Room is THE Pump Room.

**ASTOR TOWER** (1300 N. Astor St.). Slightly out of the way, but Old-World flavor and charm more than compensate. Its spaciousness makes it popular with executives who need extra room.

**CONTINENTAL PLAZA** (909 N. Michigan Ave.). On the Gold Coast, it offers a seasonal swimming pool and year-round health club along with an array of shops and restaurants. Popular with movie stars and executives alike.

**DRAKE** (N. Michigan Ave., at Lake Shore Dr.). The original Gold Coast luxury hotel. Very efficient, with large, spacious rooms kept up to date but not "plastic modern."

**HYATT REGENCY O'HARE** (two miles from O'Hare Airport). A favorite with traveling executives who need to fly into town for a meeting and leave again in the morning. Features the famous soaring architectural style of Hyatt. A good nightclub offsets its out-of-the-way location.

**PALMER HOUSE TOWERS** (State & Monroe sts.). Not to be confused with the dreary Palmer House standard rooms, the Towers offer executives an "honor bar" where they mix their own drinks and write their own tab. Nobody's watching . . . watching . . . watching. Gracious rooms and suites.

**WESTBURY** (160 E. Huron St.). New. Hallways narrow, but rooms are tastefully furnished and large. They successfully walk the thin line between modern and showy, with efficient service.

### *Good*

**ARLINGTON PARK TOWERS** (Arlington Heights). Adjacent to the race track, it is trying for convention business. Pleasant rooms which fill up with second-honeymooners on Thursday and Friday. Nightclub is so-so, and there is a pool.

**CONRAD HILTON** (720 S. Michigan Ave.). There is a bureaucratic structure to check in and check out, so don't try to rush it, and be patient. Also, if you need or like a double bed, specify when reserving a room and again when you check in. Big drawback: there are a lot of large conventions headquartered here and often you must stand in line for an elevator.

**EXECUTIVE HOUSE** (71 E. Wacker Dr.). A dramatic hotel trying hard to live up to its reputation as a good executive hotel; it occasionally slips, and when the staff is having a bad day, the service is poor. Other times, moderately pleasant with up-to-date rooms and a good dining room.

**HOLIDAY INN AT THE LAKE** (Lake Shore Dr. at Ohio St.). An unusual Holiday Inn with little of the chain's usual tacky appearance. A bit off the track, but a good place to camp if the family is along. The lake is across the street and there is a fun rooftop restaurant.

**MARRIOTT MOTOR HOTEL** (8535 West Higgins Rd.). Near O'Hare, another meeting specialist with oversized rooms and beds, and a shuttle to the airport. Convenient, but service is a bit abrupt.

**MC CORMICK INN** (At McCormick Place). Convenient if you are attending a show or convention, but the service is bleak and the food marginal. It is also away from the city, and you'll spend quite a bit in cab or train fares going back and forth. Stay no longer than necessary.

**PICK-CONGRESS** (520 S. Michigan Ave.). Remodeled in the past decade, this old hotel is a businessman's favorite for its quick, efficient service. Large banquets are noisy, and waiters still clear dishes during the program; but the rooms are large and the beds surprisingly comfortable.

**O'HARE INTERNATIONAL TOWER** (O'Hare Airport). Connected by tunnels to the baggage claim, it's a great layover hotel and convenient for meetings, etc. A bit brassy. And despite the ads, you can hear the planes.

**SHERATON-CHICAGO** (505 N. Michigan Ave.). Recently remodeled rooms offset a decidedly commercial feel to the hotel, and there is a pool and health club on the 16th floor for guests. Convenient to North Michigan Avenue shops and businesses.

*Acceptable*

**ALLERTON** (701 N. Michigan Ave.). A fading relic, it offers passable rooms and service, but nothing to write home about. Not expensive.

**BISMARCK** (171 W. Randolph St.). One of the early commercial hotels, it has bypassed major remodeling. Relatively inexpensive for tight expense accounts.

**LA SALLE** (LaSalle St. at Madison St.). Remember those over-stuffed chairs found in hotel lobbies? Here they are in one of the city's grand old hotels with a political history longer than Mayor Daley's. Once THE center for political high jinks, this is now a bustling middle-level commercial hotel.

**PALMER HOUSE** (State & Monroe sts.). The rooms are small and dreary and the maze of corridors would confuse a Daedalus. Check out with lots of time to spare because it takes forever, regardless of when you pay your bill (except perhaps at midnight). Registering isn't much faster. But it does offer an indoor pool and some good restaurants.

**PLAYBOY TOWERS** (163 E. Walton Pl., near N. Michigan Ave.). It is the old Knickerbocker trying to cash in on the Playboy name now that Hefner owns it. But all it has is a name and a jumping lobby bar—the bunnies are all next door at the club.

**SHERATON-BLACKSTONE** (S. Michigan & E. Balbo aves.). This is where the smoke-filled room in politics originated, and its lower-level club is still a luncheon favorite of politicos. But this is a sad hotel that needs renovation.

# RESTAURANTS

**ABACUS** (**) (2619 N. Clark St.). An imaginative menu representing four regions: Cantonese, Mandarin, Shanghai, and Szechuan, with items such as pork with bitter lemon, beef with pickles. No liquor, but 80 entrées. Dinner for two: approximately $12.

**ACAPULCO** (**) (908 Belmont). Outstanding Mexican food with sparkling entertainment. Dinner for two: $25.

**ADOLPHS** (**) (1045 N. Rush St.). Huge portions of Italian food and items such as bluepoint oysters included with complete dinners. Dinner for two: $20.

**ARMANDO'S** (**) (100 E. Superior St.). Mama mia, Armando and his wife add ambiance to good food and an intimate upstairs dining room specializing in veal parmigiana and beef Capri. Dinner for two: $25.

**THE BAGEL** (*) (4806 N. Kedzie). Away from downtown but authentic Yiddisha-moma cooking that's fun to enjoy. Luncheon under $10.

**THE BAKERY** (***) (2218 N. Lincoln Ave.). Excellent food and efficient service means the place is always full. Start with paté, work your way through a superb dinner—try duck with cherry sauce, stuffed lamb, or quail in season—and end with one of five surprising desserts. Dinner for two: $45.

**BENIHANA OF TOKYO** (*) (166 E. Superior St.). Part of the chain; reasonably good food is tempered by the rush act you get during dinner. Definitely an in-eat-and-out place. Dinner for two: $30.

**THE BERGHOFF** (*) (17 W. Adams St.). Ja, dis es da platzen mit Schnitzel cordon bleu, fresh seafood and fine steaks. Be prepared to be rushed by the all-male staff. Dinner for two: $20.

**BIGGS** (**) (1150 N. Dearborn St.). Set in a restored mansion; dining is in a series of smallish rooms that add intimacy to the meal. Try the roast lamb. Dinner for two: $30.

**CAMELLIA HOUSE** (**) (Drake Hotel). A famous eating place in Chicago noted for beef Stroganoff. Seafood is good but better you step downstairs to the Cape Cod Room. Dinner for two: $40.

**CAPE COD ROOM** (**) (Drake Hotel). One of the best seafood restaurants in the city, it has a surprisingly large selection of fresh seafood dishes. Their chowder is world-famous, as is their small charge for bread and butter. Dinner for two: $40.

**CASA BONNIFEATHER** (**) (2449 N. Lincoln Ave.). A kicky little hole-in-the-wall that features cheese dishes superbly prepared by the young staff. Bring your own wine and try the quiche. Dinner for two: $14.

**CHAMPS-ELYSÉES** (***) (260 E. Chestnut St.). Haute cuisine served excellently in a handsome balconied room. Dinner for two: $40.

**CHEZ PAUL** (*) (660 N. Rush St.). Overrated and noisy; the food is slightly better than average. The turbot is among the best, however, as are the quenelles of pike. Good wine list. Dinner for two: $35.

**CHICAGO CLAIM COMPANY** (**) (2314 N. Clark St.). Very much an in-spot. The menu is printed on gold-mining pans. Try the kabob, or steak-lobster teriyaki. How they manage to keep their salad bar so fresh is a delightful mystery. Dinner for two: $17.

**COMO INN** (**) (546 N. Milwaukee Ave.). One of the better-known Italian restaurants popular for large gatherings of paisanos. Great cacciatore and pheasant. Dinner for two: $25.

**CONSORT** (***) (Continental Plaza Hotel). One of the best in the city, it has a broad menu which includes five salads, 23 entrées— try the tournedos—a wide selection of vegetables and desserts, and a fantastic wine list. There's a $3 cover charge after 8:00 P.M. Dinner for two: $60.

**DIANA** (*) (310 S. Halsted St.). A warm, friendly, outgoing Greek restaurant located behind a warm, friendly, outgoing grocery store. Huge portions characterize this popular spot, and they are noted for squid and octopus or braised lamb. Wine served by the bottle, but you only pay for what you drink. Don't ask where the rest goes. Dinner for two: $18.

**DON THE BEACHCOMBER** (\*\*) (101 E. Walton St.). Part of the chain, but better than some of the others around the system. Surprisingly moderate prices from an extensive Cantonese menu. Dinner for two: $25.

**ELI'S, THE PLACE FOR STEAK** (\*\*) (215 E. Chicago Ave.). Lots of stars hang out here when in town and the steaks are good. Dinner for two: $18.

**EMPIRE ROOM** (\*\*) (Palmer House). Splashy nightclub featuring big-name entertainers. Decent conglomerate cuisine. Dinner for two: $35, plus cover.

**FLORENTINE ROOM** (\*) (In Italian Village restaurant, 71 W. Monroe St.). In an Italian garden setting; the food is often spotty and service obtrusive. But when everything goes right, it's one of the better places in the Loop. Dinner for two: $35.

**FOUR TORCHES** (\*\*) (1960 Lincoln Pk. W.). Another in-spot for celebrity watching. Their reputation for great steaks is backed up by an amazing list of appetizers. There is also a good selection of seafood. Dinner for two: $50.

**FUJI** (\*) (76 W. Lake St.). The only true Japanese eatery in the Loop. Diners may elect to eat in a native teahouse. They are strong on fish specialties, all done well. Dinner for two: $16.

**GHISELA'S** (\*\*) (612 N. Wells St.). An unusual Romanian restaurant where you'd do well to sample the brisket with vegetables in a superb tomato wine sauce. Great service with personal attention from the management. Dinner for two: $16.

**ITALIAN VILLAGE** (\*) (71 W. Monroe St.). See Florentine Room.

**JOVAN** (\*\*\*) (16 E. Huron St.). A prix-fixe dinner of $12.50 includes tempting Continental appetizers, soup, salad (preferably served after the entrée and dessert). An Old-World jewel where the owner personally selects vegetables each morning. Dinner for two: $40.

**LA CREPERIE** (\*) (2845 N. Clark St.). All-crêpe menu in a storefront restaurant; try the spinach crêpe. No liquor. Dinner for two: $10.

**LE BASTILLE** (\*\*\*) (21 W. Superior St.). A rustic old dining hall with outstanding service and good food. Dinners include seafood, stuffed trout, coq au Chambertin, frog's legs. Extensive, well-prepared wine list. Dinner for two: $50.

**LE MIGNON** (\*\*\*) (712 N. Rush St.). A young upstart to its neighbor, Chez Paul, Le Mignon runs circles around it. Superb food in a delightful series of small, intimate dining rooms. And what is this?—an outstanding domestic wine list to go along with the French wines. Dinner for two: $30.

**L'EPUISETTE** (***) (21 W. Goethe St.). Seafood is the specialty, French the style. Small but chic—and expensive. Dinner for two: $50.

**MAXIM'S DE PARIS** (***) (1300 N. Astor St.). Direct from Paris, the staff here runs perhaps the best single dining room in town. The broad menu offers an incredible sampling of delightful food, such as Dover sole prepared in vermouth, steaks cooked in a delicate wine sauce and marrow. You have an option of selecting a complete dinner, which each month is native to a different French province. But all good things must be paid for, and hopefully the boss pays for this one. Dinner for two: $75.

**MONGOLIAN HOUSE** (**) (3410 N. Clark St.). Ever tried skewered shark? This Mandarin restaurant has all sorts of delicacies served in a homey atmosphere by a friendly staff. Dinner for two: $14.

**NINETY-FIFTH** (*) (John Hancock Center). Another tab for the boss. The food is adequate, but much of the price goes for the view—which on a clear night is spectacular. Generally overpriced and over-rated; there is nothing spectacular on the menu. Dinner for two: $60.

**THE PRESIDENTS** (*) (First National Plaza). This restaurant has a carefully drawn menu that specializes in domestic dishes such as beef tenderloin cooked in bourbon. But why must they serve so many dishes flambé? Dinner for two: $40.

**PUMP ROOM** (***) (Ambassador East Hotel). The one and only. Flaming sword dishes predominate. Chicken sauté Ambassador is a favorite—and check out who is sitting in Booth 1: Isn't that what's his name? Dinner for two: $75.

**RICCARDO'S** (**) (437 N. Rush St.). The newsmen of the town gather to eat and water here in the shadow of the Wrigley Building. The tetrazzine is overrated but you'll do well by the scallopine. Dinner for two: $25.

**SAGE'S EAST** (**) (181 E. Lake Shore Dr.). A terribly English sort of place, where beef dishes dominate the menu. Seafood is done nicely too. Dinner for two: $25.

**SCHWABEN STUBE** (**) (3500 N. Lincoln). Tasty is the way the native German dishes are described, and that's on target for the Sauerbraten und Schnitzel. The duck is surprising. Dinner for two: $20.

**THE SEA GULL** (***) (400 E. Randolph). Of course a seafood restaurant, and one of the best in the city. There are some meat dishes, but stick to the turbot. Dinner for two: $30.

**SU CASA** (**) (49 E. Ontario St.). Everything in the place reportedly from Mexico except the water. They take ordinary dishes, such as butterfly steak, and dress them up with guacamole sauce and turn the Mexican food hater into a devotee. Dinner for two: $20.

**TRACK ONE** (*) (LaSalle St. Station). Unusual place—a dining

CHICAGO 51

car meal served in a real dining car. Nothing to write home about, except it's hard to find dining cars anymore. Lots of fun. Dinner for two: $15.

**TRADER VIC'S** (\*\*) (Palmer House). Trader Vic Bergerone spreads out another South Seas delight that is better than the original in San Francisco. But it's always crowded and noisy and best to avoid on weekends, when headwaiters greet you with palms outstretched. Dinner for two: $35.

**WRIGLEY BUILDING RESTAURANT** (\*) (410 N. Michigan Ave.). Good lunches, but mostly fun to spot Philip K. Wrigley, the man who gave you the Doublemint twins. He eats here daily with cronies from his gum empire. Don't mention the Cubs. Dinner for two: $15.

## Recommended Reading

CHICAGO: AN EXTRAORDINARY GUIDE by Jory Graham. (Rand McNally, $2.95).

INSTANT CHICAGO: HOW TO COPE by Jory Graham. (Rand McNally, $2.95).

CHICAGO GUIDE MAGAZINE (Monthly. $1). Best current restaurant guide around.

CHICAGOAN MAGAZINE (Monthly. $1). Cutesy, overwritten listings of things to do and see, but helpful nonetheless.

# CLEVELAND

Not too many years ago, George E. Condon, local columnist for *The Plain Dealer,* wrote a book about his favorite city, *Cleveland: The Best Kept Secret.*

Ohio's largest city has long been considered a joke—much like Philadelphia was to the late W. C. Fields. But Cleveland is not a joke to American industry.

The city plays host to 31 of *Fortune*'s 500 top industrial companies, including major producers of steel, machine tools, and vital parts for Detroit's insolent chariots. And, if you include Akron, 35 miles south, the area takes on added significance, because of the presence there of four of the five major American tiremakers.

Cleveland is also an international city of sorts. Ships enter the Port of Cleveland from all corners of the world. It is the largest iron-ore receiving port in the world, since so many steel mills are fed through this port. Many of the major iron-ore companies still call Cleveland home, even though their major ore deposits are in Minnesota, Wisconsin, Michigan, Canada, Brazil, or Australia.

Indeed, your first glimpse of Cleveland—if you fly in—will be the Cuyahoga River valley ablaze with glowing fires from three major steel mills. But the steel mills, and other industrial plants along the Cuyahoga, have done their share of polluting. Indeed, the Cuyahoga was once so full of wastes that it literally was on fire.

Cleveland is split by the Cuyahoga into the East and West sides, and the distinction between the sections is more than geographic.

Cleveland's downtown section still remains the city's business and economic hub, although some business and industry have fled to the suburbs. The center of downtown is Public Square, which was laid out by General Cleaveland's initial surveying party as a transplanted bit of New England. It never really took root.

Cleveland's Union Terminal, which no longer has any passenger train service, is southwest of Public Square. The rapid transit from the airport uses this terminal, as does the Shaker Heights rapid transit system. Connected with the Union Terminal are the 52-story Terminal Tower, several major office buildings, the Sheraton-Cleveland Hotel, and the Higbee Co., one of the city's major department stores. A second department store, the May Co., and the federal courthouse, are just across from the Terminal.

Euclid Avenue, still Cleveland's main business and shopping street, begins at the southeast end of the square. Several hotels, Halle's department store (a division of Chicago's famed Marshall Field & Co.), Cleveland State University, and the Playhouse Square area all are just a few minutes up Euclid from Public Square.

Also within easy walking distance is the Convention Center, which includes a 10,000-seat public auditorium, a 3,000-seat music hall, and a large underground exhibition area.

If you fly in, you'll find Cleveland Hopkins International Airport handy. It is only 12 miles southwest of downtown, and if you have only light luggage you might use the rapid transit line that makes it downtown in only 20 minutes. A taxi or airport limousine takes 35 to 55 minutes, depending on traffic.

The city also has another airport, Burke, just 5 minutes by cab from downtown on the Lake Erie shore. The only commercial air service available at Burke is to and from Detroit, but it's the logical choice if you are coming in on the company plane.

## Hotels

The city has a good number of decent hotels. Nothing spectacular, but you should have no trouble finding a decent room. Downtown, your best choices are the **Hollenden House, Keg & Quarter Motor Inn, Holiday Inn,** and **Sheraton-Cleveland**—as long as the convention crowd isn't too noisy.

A number of new hotels are: the **Bond Court Hotel** right across the street from the Convention Center, the **Holiday Inn Lakeside,** and the **Clinic Inn,** near Case Western Reserve.

On the West Side, try the **Marriott Motor Inn,** the **Sheraton-Hopkins Hotel,** or the **Hospitality Motor Inn.** On the East Side, make it **Stouffer's Somerset Inn** in Shaker Heights, or the **Hospitality Motor Inn** in Willoughby Hills.

## Restaurants

The Stouffer's chain of restaurants was born here in Cleveland, but if that name makes you wrinkle your nose, don't despair. Three Stouffer's restaurants here are at least one notch above the typical chain establishments elsewhere, and there are many other worthwhile restaurants as well.

The best Stouffer's entries include the **Top of the Town,** which offers, along with a good steak, a very good skyline view from one of the city's tallest buildings. Another room with a view—on the shores of Lake Erie—is **Pier W,** which specializes in lobster and steak. **Shaker Square,** one of the original Stouffer's, lacks a view, but has a cozy, pub-style atmosphere that enhances the good, if basic, menu.

If you're looking for French cuisine, two spots are good—if not très parisien. **Père Jacques** does Gallic justice to Dover sole and steak au poivre. The unlikely named **Wagon Wheel** is owned by the chef, and he must love frog's legs—a delicious specialty.

Meat and potato fanciers have a good choice of spots to dine. Best and most expensive is the **English Oak Room** in the Terminal Tower, very handy if you are staying at a downtown hotel. Besides beef, **Jim's Steak House** serves good trout, as befits a restaurant that overlooks the water. (Rest assured: the seafood doesn't come from Lake Erie.)

The **Blue Fox** has Italian dishes along with seafood and steak, and has many local fans. But true pasta lovers favor **Guarino's** and the **Golden Bowl** in the city's Little Italy section.

## Potpourri

A swinging city Cleveland ain't. It does have its crime problems—as do most major cities—but you no longer need an armed guard to venture out after dark. The East Side can still be a little tough, however, and isn't recommended as a place to take a constitutional, or go pub crawling with your conventioneer's name tag plastered to your lapel.

For some congenial quaffing and light entertainment, there are two **Pat Joyce's** taverns, **Fagan's, Pickle Bill's,** and **Diamond Jim's,** all on the banks of the Cuyahoga River. The **Theatrical Grill** on

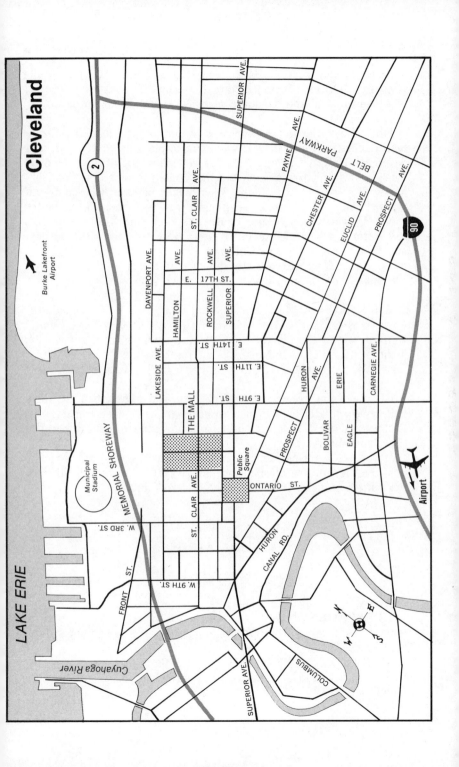

Vincent Avenue near the Hollenden House is popular with out-of-towners. **The Last Moving Picture Company,** on Playhouse Square, is a haunt of real and would-be swingles, especially on Fridays.

No fooling—the city does have a vibrant cultural life. The **Cleveland Orchestra,** which is widely acclaimed, plays its winter season at Severance Hall in University Circle, five miles east of downtown on Euclid Avenue. In the summer, the orchestra moves to Blossom Music Center in the Cuyahoga River Valley between Cleveland and Akron. Pop stars and rock groups take the stage when the orchestra rests. (University Circle also houses the **Cleveland Museum of Art,** the **Natural Science Museum, Western Reserve Historical Society,** and **Case Western Reserve University.**)

Within walking distance are the three theaters of the **Cleveland Playhouse,** and **Karamu House,** which stages interracial theater.

The 80,000-seat Municipal Stadium is an easy walk from downtown. It is on the Lake Erie shore just past the Cuyahoga County courthouse and Cleveland City Hall. The stadium is, of course, the home of the **baseball** Indians, and the **football** Browns. With 80,000 seats, it's usually not too difficult to get football tickets, even on short notice.

Cleveland's two other major league teams, the **basketball** Cavaliers and the World **Hockey** League Crusaders are at the Coliseum in West Richfield, about a 25-minute drive from downtown, midway between Cleveland and Akron.

If you are a **racing** fan, there are two tracks easily accessible by bus from downtown. Thistledown has the flat races, Northfield Park the trotters at night. Both are in the eastern suburbs.

## Nitty Gritty

## HOTELS

*Superior*

**HOLLENDEN HOUSE** (E. 6th St. & Superior Ave.). Best in town. Good location, comfortable rooms, excellent restaurant (Marie Schrieber's Tavern).

**MARRIOTT MOTOR INN** (W. 150th St. at Interstate 71). Modern, clean, good West Side location, midway between Cleveland Hopkins International Airport and downtown Cleveland. Good restaurants.

## Good

**CLINIC INN** (9545 Carnegie Ave.). Modern-style hi-riser, comfortable. Very handy to Case Western Reserve and adjacent to famed Cleveland Clinic, where even Arab sheiks come in for check-ups.

**HOLIDAY INN DOWNTOWN** (E. 22d St. & Euclid Ave.). Currently the newest of the downtown area hotels and motels. Across the street from Cleveland State University and near Playhouse Square area.

**HOLIDAY INN-LAKESIDE** (1111 Lakeside Ave.). Representative of the clan. Convenient, just a five-minute walk from Convention Center, City Hall, and federal office buildings. Entertainment in barlounge.

**HOSPITALITY MOTOR INNS.** There are two. The West Side Inn is at Interstate 71 and Bagley Road, 10 minutes from the airport. East Side Inn at Interstate 90 and SOM Center Road, near heavily industrialized areas of Euclid and Mentor. No suites.

**KEG & QUARTER MOTOR INN** (E. 18th St. & Euclid Ave.). Close to Playhouse Square and Cleveland State University. Nicesized rooms, excellent dining facilities.

**SHERATON-CLEVELAND** (Public Sq.). The center of downtown. Large hotel, host to many conventions and trade groups, with 2000-seat ballroom, many restaurants and bars. Direct passage to many corporate offices and Terminal Tower, including rapid transit to Airport.

**SHERATON INN-HOPKINS** (Entrance to Hopkins Airport on Ohio 237). Newly built section, plus remodeled area. Very handy to airport and West Side business. High-rise section.

**SOMERSET INN** (Warrensville Center and Northfield rds., Shaker Heights). Close to the homes of many corporate executives, also handy to race tracks, good golf courses, and most East Side business firms. Easily reached from downtown by Shaker Heights Rapid Transit line. Operated by Cleveland-based Stouffer Corp.

## Acceptable

**CLEVELAND PLAZA** (E. 12th St. & Euclid Ave.). Has new name (formerly Statler-Hilton), new management, and is trying hard for a new image. Not easy for a 65-year-old. Good downtown location with excellent dining (Marie Schrieber's restaurant). Indoor parking available.

## Not Rated (under construction)

**BOND COURT** (E. 6th St. & St. Clair Ave.). Under same ownership and management as nearby Hollenden House. Should be in the same league. Good location across from Cleveland Convention Center.

# RESTAURANTS

**BLUE FOX** (\*\*) (W. 117th St. & Clifton Blvd., Lakewood). Just a block from the Gold Coast (a high-rise apartment section), caters to these residents. Steak, seafood, Italian dishes. Dinner for two: about $35.

**BLUE GRASS** (\*) (Northfield & Rockside rds., Bedford Heights). Average food, but a swinging spot, both for the entertainment it offers on stage, and in the type of people who come to eat and drink. Dinner for two: $30 to $35.

**BROGLIO'S** (\*\*) (5568 Brecksville Rd., Independence). A favorite luncheon spot for local salesmen, just 15 minutes by freeway from downtown Cleveland. Lunch for two: about $30.

**CAPTAIN FRANK'S** (\*) (E. 9th St. Pier, 100 feet south of Lake Erie). A good view of downtown Cleveland and the bustling lakefront. Within walking distance of Municipal Stadium, it's a favorite of baseball and football fans. Dinner for two: $30.

**COLONY** (\*\*) (2510 St. Clair Ave., just out of downtown). Conglomerate cuisine worth the short cab ride. Dinner for two: $35.

**ENGLISH OAK ROOM** (\*\*\*) (Cleveland Union Terminal). The local establishment lunches here everyday, with good reason. Quieter at dinner. Excellent wine list, personal service. Dinner for two: $45.

**FISHERMAN'S COVE** (\*\*) (E. 12th St. & Chester Ave.). Fish flown in fresh daily. Tasteful nautical decor, but sometimes noisy. Dinner for two: $35.

**GOLDEN BOWL** (\*\*) (12312 Mayfield Rd., just off University Circle in Little Italy). An old favorite of local pasta lovers. Dinner for two: $35.

**GUARINO'S** (\*\*) (12309 Mayfield Rd., also in Little Italy). The place for that home-style Italian meal. Dinner for two: $35.

**HOFBRAU HAUS** (\*\*) (1400 E. 55th St., just south of St. Clair Ave.). German cuisine and atmosphere, with good, inexpensive buffet both at lunch and dinner. Menu also available. Dinner for two: $30.

**JIM'S STEAK HOUSE** (\*\*\*) (1800 Scranton Rd.). A short drive from downtown with a view of the city across the Cuyahoga River. Iron-ore boats almost touch the windows as they round Collision Bend. Good steak and all the trimmings (served home-style). Dinner for two: $40.

**PAT JOYCE'S TAVERNS** (\*) (E. 6th St. & St. Clair Ave., and E. 12th St. and Chester Ave.). Two local favorite eating and especially drinking establishments. Limited dinner menu, but lots of sandwiches. Dinner for two: $30.

**KIEFERS** (\*\*) (2519 Detroit Ave., just across the Cuyahoga River from downtown Cleveland). Long-time favorite, family-run restaurant, with emphasis on German food and atmosphere. Dinner for two: $35.

**LAST MOVING PICTURE CO.** (\*\*) (1356 Euclid Ave.). A restaurant despite its name. Some young Clevelanders took over an old Stouffer's, added old-time movies, peanuts, and decent food. A favorite gathering place, especially on Friday nights. Dinner for two: $40.

**NIGHTTOWN** (\*\*) (12383 Cedar Rd., Cleveland Heights, just up the hill from University Circle). Favored watering hole of singles. Limited but good menu. Dinner for two: $35.

**OHIO CITY TAVERN** (\*\*) (W. 28th St. & Bridge Ave.). Some West Side residents are renovating houses in what used to be called Ohio City. This former neighborhood tavern has been remodeled in the same spirit. Includes murals from an old, local church. Dinner for two: $35.

**PERE JACQUES** (\*\*) (34015 Chagrin Blvd., Orange). Off the beaten path, but draws considerable crowds who love its French-style cuisine. Dinner for two: $55.

**RED FOX INN** (\*) (Chagrin River Rd., Gates Mills). Out in the Chagrin River Valley, where many business executives live. Another spot well off the beaten path, but worth the trip. Dinner for two: $45.

**SETTLER'S TAVERN** (\*\*) (12906 Buckeye Rd., just off Shaker Sq.). Cleveland is home to many Hungarian-Americans, and this is one of their favorites. Dinner for two: $30.

**STOUFFER'S.** Cleveland was the home of this restaurant chain, and still has some of its best restaurants. They are:

**Top of the Town** (\*\*) (38th floor of 100 Erieview Plaza), Good view of the city from one of its tallest buildings. Dinner for two: $40.

**Pier W** (\*\*) (12700 Lake Ave., Lakewood, right in the Gold Coast). Waves wash up to big picture windows in this just-below-the-ground restaurant. Dinner for two: $40.

**Shaker Square** (\*\*) (on Shaker Sq.). One of the oldest Stouffer's with good atmosphere, especially the Tack Room. Dinner for two: $40.

**THEATRICAL RESTAURANT** (\*\*) (711 Vincent Ave., just behind the Hollenden House hotel). Known for big-band entertainment and the assortment of political and business leaders who eat here. Dinner for two: $40.

**WAGON WHEEL** (\*\*\*) (13114 Woodland Ave., just off Shaker Sq.). Don't let appearances fool you. Looks like a simple neighborhood tavern. But there's an excellent French restaurant in the basement, and it's worth hunting for. Good wine selection. Dinner for two: $50.

## *Recommended Reading*

Not much here. Best book still is:

CLEVELAND: THE BEST KEPT SECRET by George Condon. (Doubleday, $5.95). It's dated (1967) but still an excellent guide to the city. Available in most bookstores in town.

CLEVELAND MAGAZINE   Published monthly and available at newsstands for $1, will give you current listings and reviews.

# DALLAS

Let the sun get low in the western Texas sky, and a funny thing happens in Dallas—nothing. The downtown area becomes as desolate as a pumped-out well, in less time than it takes to skin a rattlesnake. After a series of ill-attended nighttime cocktail hours along Main Street, one dumbfounded Canadian diplomat wryly observed: "There's more life in Calgary in the middle of a snowstorm."

But stay-at-home Dallas is slowly starting to change. It has been only a few years since it became legal to buy liquor by the drink, so you have to give the boys a chance. There are other challenges to the folkways of the nation's largest inland city, too. There has been an influx of *real* big-city folks from elsewhere, and Dallas has also had to take on the necessary, if reluctant, role as big financial center of the Southwest.

Moral for the visitor: There are some good times to be had, but you have to keep an eye out, and cover a lot of territory. By all means, rent a car when you arrive. Without wheels, you will be confined to your hotel or motel, and there's no one watering hole in the town that's worth any long stay.

## Hotels

The **Fairmont,** with its twin towers piercing the downtown skyline, its New York prices, and Texas-style hospitality, is the best place to stay in town. The Fairmont is actually the city's only one-stop shopping center for eating, entertainment, and lodging. It houses the best restaurant in town—the Pyramid Room—and the leading night spot, the Venetian Room. It's a bit young yet to have perfected its natural character, but its comfort and service are unequaled in town.

61

Elsewhere in Dallas, it is strictly also-ran. A couple of adequate downtown entries are the **Sheraton-Dallas** and the **Statler Hilton,** the latter more conveniently located. Both are busy, convention-minded abodes. On the other hand, if it is a touch of high-ceilinged, thanks-for-the-memories lodging you are looking for, book the **Adolphus,** built in 1912, or the **Baker,** just across Commerce Street. If their walls could talk, there would be heavy stories to tell. Unfortunately, it's more often the plumbing that sings.

To the north, along the city's traffic spine, the North Central Expressway, there are two possibilities. The architects deserve a bow for the stately **Hilton Inn,** at Mockingbird, already a midtown landmark. At 6060 North Central, **Ramada Inn** has just bowed in with a creditable venture in luxury motels. Far to the north, along the LBJ Freeway, make it the **Marriott Inn North.**

## *Restaurants*

The visiting gourmet should sample the Fairmont's **Pyramid Room.** But make reservations, as it seats only seventy. Beneath a million-dollar, six-ton, metal sculpture, European waiters whisk by with platters of filet of sole en croute, Maine lobster, Beluga caviar, and beef Wellington. For all this, the tab will pleasantly surprise the New Yorker or Chicagoan.

**Mario's,** a few dollars' cab ride from downtown, is hardly what it claims to be: "one of the great restaurants of the world." But it is certainly one of the best in Dallas. The menu stresses Northern Italian cuisine, seafood, and steaks.

Other spots worth trying (all require a cab ride of a few minutes): **Daddy's Money,** a stab at split-level elegance in the Old Town development; **The Railhead,** a steak house for railroad buffs; **Peking Palace,** a Mandarin-style establishment.

For the travel-weary, there are these downtown eateries of note: **Brennan's,** with its touch of French New Orleans; **Clocks of Five,** a steak place that takes its name from the antique clocks stashed about, and **Ports O'Call,** featuring South Seas dishes with a 37th floor view.

## *Potpourri*

As Coach Tom Landry of the Dallas Cowboys football team might say of the entertainment possibilities, the first string is adequate, but there's no depth at all.

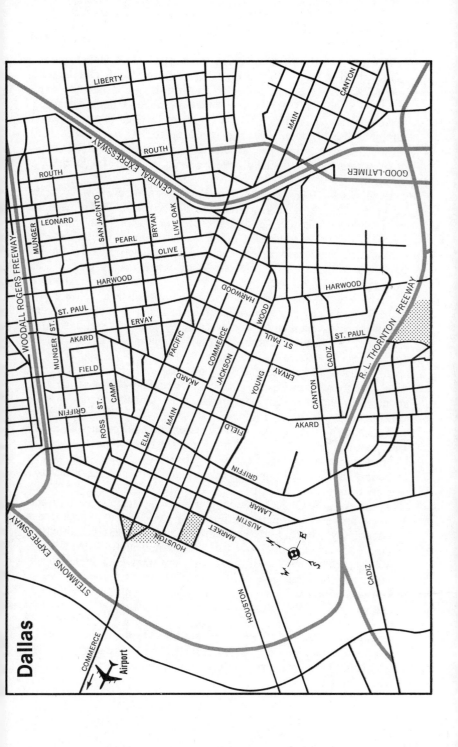

If you are traveling solo, avoid the topless night clubs and strip joints which seem to cluster on Cedar Springs Road and Lemmon and McKinney avenues, north of downtown. And, just as in any major U.S. city, it's not best to ambulate around the sidewalks of downtown alone in the late or wee hours. Muggings are relatively rare, but the Midnight Cowboy is asking for it. As for the really high-crime areas, they are to the west and south of downtown—areas where there is usually little reason for an overnight guest to be traveling.

Despite the 1971 passage of a liquor-by-the-drink law in Texas, liquor regulations in Dallas remain weird. Says the Dallas Chamber of Commerce: "Liquor, except for beer and wine, may be served by the drink only in licensed public bars. In many public bars and restaurants, unlicensed to serve mixed drinks, setups are furnished but the patron must bring his own liquor. . . . To assure a pleasant evening it would be well for the visitor to check with the hotel or motel in which he is registered. . . ." In a nutshell, if you are after a drink, don't descend on a restaurant in a dry precinct. You can, however, get a drink in a dry precinct by purchasing a temporary membership in a private club. It costs a couple of bucks and is good for seventy-two hours.

The likes of Peggy Lee, the Supremes, Richard Harris, Mel Torme, et al., stop over at only one place: the **Venetian Room** at the Fairmont. Two shows nightly, starting at 7:30. Concern about reservations depends on the entertainer.

**The King's Club,** in the Hotel Adolphus, features decent, if less than famous, entertainers, and more than decent prices.

Also worth a try: the **Big D Jamboree,** a country-and-western swingfest at Sportatorium. Saturday nights only. It's no black-tie scene. Nosirreee!

**The Levee,** 5615 East Mockingbird, for Dixieland, country-and-western, and audience-participation singing on Friday and Saturdays.

**Greek Key Club and Restaurant,** 2920 Northwest Highway, for Greek food, Greek music, and Greek belly dancing.

**Villager Club,** 3531 McKinney, the only jazz club in town with both coat-and-tie and casual clienteles.

**Harper's Corner,** Hilton Inn, 5600 North Center Expressway, a nice quiet place with a great view and a good pianist.

Legitimate theaters? Just two: **Dallas Theater Center,** which stages its productions in a Frank Lloyd Wright-designed structure, and **Theater Three.** The former tends to stage old favorites, the latter is more daring.

**The Dallas Civic Opera** usually offers three or four production runs of a few days in the late fall. Metropolitan Opera visits in the spring. And there are always musical events scheduled at Southern Methodist University. Consult visitor's guides and newspaper calendars for times and places.

In **sports,** there are the Cowboys to watch, of course, if you can get tickets. The Texas Rangers (baseball), the Dallas Black Hawks (hockey), and the Dallas Tornados (soccer) also provide divertissement.

On the college scene, Southern Methodist University often fields respectable teams in Southwest Conference football, basketball, baseball, and swimming. In the summer, there is rodeo on Friday and Saturday nights at Mesquite, just east of Dallas.

An array of museums and exhibits is available at **Fair Park,** the site each October of the Texas State Fair. These include the **Dallas Health and Science Museum and Planetarium,** the **Dallas Museum of Natural History,** the **Dallas Garden Center,** the **Dallas Aquarium,** and the **Dallas Museum of Fine Arts.** All are free. Critic's choice: the fine arts museum, with its permanent collection of twentieth century art, pre-Columbian artifacts, Congolese sculpture, and works from ancient Greece.

If you have time to visit the environs, head west to Arlington, halfway between Dallas and Fort Worth.

In Arlington, there's **Six Flags Over Texas,** a family amusement center billed as "Texas' leading tourist attraction." The park's 95 rides and historical-themed landscaping draw two million visitors yearly. Except for summers, the park is open weekends only. One $6 ticket for adults covers all; children ages 3 to 11 pay less. Plan to spend the day and sleep tight that night.

Two other amusement centers are nearby. **Lion Country Safari** is the usual zoo-in-the-round. **The Southwestern Historical Wax Museum** preserves 142 life-sized Western characters. A park to avoid: **Seven Seas,** an educational sea-like amusement center that tried to go nautical with the Six Flags approach—and missed.

A "must" stop for the family in north Dallas is the **Olla Podrida,** an endless collection of tiny shops and artisan hideaways in a monstrous barn which also houses **Granny's Dinner Playhouse.** The kids can watch craftsmen, artists, and collectors at work. At lunchtime, a stopover in order is **The Upper Crust,** a home-cooking operation run by two sisters who serve up simple makings in delightfully casual surroundings.

Other family stopovers: **John F. Kennedy Plaza** at Commerce and Market Streets, and the nearby private **Kennedy Museum**; and the

**Marsalis Park Zoo,** with its collections of 2,000 birds, reptiles, mammals, and amphibians.

Note: the **Dallas/Fort Worth Regional Airport,** 17 miles from downtown Dallas on State Highway 114, is as much an attraction as it is a means of access and egress. Touted as the world's largest, it is geared to handle the region's burgeoning air needs into the twenty-first century.

## *Nitty Gritty*

## HOTELS

*Superior*

**FAIRMONT** (Ross and Akard sts.). The finest in town. The decor is a little much, but interesting. Convenient to financial district, but away from the crush. Superb restaurants.

*Good*

**HILTON INN** (5600 N. Central Expy.). Built with a nod to Southwestern architectural styles. Convenient to Southern Methodist University, North Dallas, and the Park Cities.

**HOLIDAY INN DOWNTOWN** (1015 Elm St.). A hotel, really. Caters to the businessman and conventioner. Close to the city's governmental complex.

**HYATT HOUSE** (899 Stemmons Freeway). At the edge of the industrial district, but still a popular convention setting, close to Market Center. Recently redecorated. Quite suitable for conferences and meetings.

**MARRIOTT INN NORTH** (7750 LBJ Freeway). Part of the Park Central development in North Dallas. Convenient to Texas Instruments Co. Its Currency Club is relaxing.

**RAMADA INN** (6060 N. Central Expy.). A midtown inn, several cuts above the roadside standards. Tweedy surroundings in the bar and restaurant. Good atmosphere for meetings.

**SHERATON-DALLAS** (Southland Center). Big, bustling, modern convention hotel. Convenient to northside downtown office complexes. Interconnected with the 40-story Southland Center building.

**STATLER HILTON** (1914 Commerce St.). Right in the heart of things. Lobby often a madhouse. Inadequate front drive usually jammed with cabs and unhappy drivers.

*Adequate*

**ADOLPHUS** (1321 Commerce St.). Built in 1912 and shows it. High ceilings and slow elevators. Easy walk to and from main office centers and noted shopping stops. Moderate rates.

**BAKER** (1400 Commerce St.). Another famous old Dallas hotel. Its many remodelings haven't hid all the scars. Moderate rates.

## RESTAURANTS

**THE BEEFEATER INN** (\*\*) (2425 Cedar Springs St.). Elegant atmosphere. House specialty is a filet mignon served on wild rice. Some say the best beef in town. Dinner for two: approximately $30.

**BRENNAN'S** (\*\*) (One Main Place). New Orleans fare, sans flair. Nice place for breakfast. A favorite downtown spot for executive lunches. Dinner for two: $35.

**CLOCKS OF FIVE** (\*) (One Main Place). Plush decor featuring old clocks and objets d'art. Prime beef and French recipes top the menu. Dinner for two: $25.

**DADDY'S MONEY** (\*) (5500 Greenville Ave.). A contemporary, multilevel setting in Old Town. Menu features rack of lamb, beef, sea food. Live entertainment, plus late-night menu. Dinner for two: $25.

**MARIO'S** (\*\*\*) (135 Turtle Creek Village). Deserving of its reputation for fine northern Italian and French cuisine. Dinner for two: $45.

**MR. PEPPE** (\*\*) (5617 W. Lovers Lane). Local favorite. French and Continental cuisine. Excellent steak au poivre. Entrées each night limited to three. Dinner for two: $35.

**OLD SPAGHETTI WAREHOUSE** (\*) (1815 Market). Cleverly antiqued. Popular family spot. Menu limited to spaghetti with ten varieties of sauce, salad, sourdough bread. Long lines in prime dinner hours. Dinner for two: $20.

**OLD WARSAW** (\*\*\*) (2610 Maple Ave.). Don't worry—it's French, not Polish. Superb, unhurried service, fine cuisine. Excellent wine list. Dinner for two: $45.

**PEKING PLACE** (\*) (4119 Lomo Alto). The shrimp toast, wonton, ribs, and other appetizers are almost meals in themselves. Quiet despite Oriental Muzak. Menu features such delicacies as Szechuan-style chicken with peanuts and Moo Shu Pork with crepe-like Mandarin pancakes. Dinner for two: approximately $25.

**PORTS O'CALL** (\*\*) (Southland Center). Its topside view of North Dallas is almost as relaxing as its rum-based drinks. Quality foods on the exotic side. Good service. Quiet. Dinner for two: $30.

**PYRAMID ROOM** (***) (Ross and Akard sts.). No place for a man in a hurry. Gourmet menu, with superb wine selection. Service with a flourish. Rich foods, generous portions. Dinner for two: $60.

**THE RAILHEAD** (*) (6929 Twin Hills). A Victorian railway station. Menu features prime rib, steak, and lobster. Live entertainment and a fireplace in the lounge. Dinner for two: $30.

## *Recommended Reading*

DALLAS IN A NUTSHELL (Available through Darvies Art and Design, P. O. Box 28022, Dallas, Tex. 75228, $2.15). An excellent general guide to Dallas scenes and services, done with taste and style.

DALLAS MAGAZINE (Available free from the Dallas Chamber of Commerce, 1507 Pacific Ave., Dallas, Tex. 75201). Quarterly "Visitor's Guide to Dallas" has detailed summaries of coming events and service facilities.

KEY—THIS MONTH IN DALLAS  A digest-sized monthly "greeters' guide" that can be had for the asking at most hotels and motels. Advertisers win the plaudits.

PREVUE OF DALLAS/FORT WORTH  Another monthly visitors' guide usually available at lodging places.

WHERE  Yet a third free monthly visitors' guide available at lodging places.

TEXAS MONTHLY  Each issue contains a "selective" guide to dining and entertainment in five major Texas cities, including Dallas. Excellent rundowns on places and events calculated to appeal to the younger urban dweller. On most newsstands for $1.

# DENVER

If cities have personalities, call Denver schizophrenic. Long-time residents tend to think of it still as a cow town, while newcomers view it as a sophisticated center of business and finance. It is both. You'll find plenty of cowboy boots and ten-gallon hats, and a like number of pinstripe suits. But the atmosphere is generally casual—people are still nice to one another here; they smile at each other on the street and look you in the eye.

The hordes of large companies flocking to this Rocky Mountain mecca will doubtless change all that, however. Leading the list of new companies are insurance institutions. Manufacturers Life shifted headquarters here in 1973, as did Great-West Life Assurance. But few would agree with Great-West's president, James W. Burns, that it has become the "Hartford of the West." For Denver also has a number of oil company offices opening here, and is an important energy city too. (Oil men would rather live in Denver than in Gillette, Wyoming.) It is the focal point for companies interested in the vast, wild oil shale lands of western Colorado, the western low-sulfur coal deposits that will be strip-mined before long, and natural gas and oil. There are diverse companies such as Johns-Manville Corp., which recently relocated its world headquarters here.

A long-time native is Adolph Coors Co., which makes Coors Beer, the nation's fourth largest selling brew—and according to more than a few barflies, the nation's best drinking. Until recently it was family-owned, and typical of the Old West, it paid for everything in cash.

The other major family company is Gates Rubber Co. Along with producing rubber products, Gates owns IML Freight in Salt Lake City, controlling interest in Gates Learjet Corp., and Financial Programs, Inc. (mutual funds and insurance).

There is a lingering Western ethic of hard work in Denver. Johns-

Manville found it got an extra hour of work from its employees when they moved to Denver. Businessmen get to the office early—so try calling an executive before 8:00 A.M. He will probably answer his own phone. On the other hand, local businessmen make up for those longer hours Monday through Thursday by playing hooky on Friday to play golf or go skiing.

The city is beginning to have problems as it grows, of course. There are more and more days when you can't see the mountains. Traffic is bad; crime is increasing. Forget those leisurely strolls that used to be so pleasant in the evening. And suburban sprawl is setting in. It is becoming more fashionable to live in the city now, and land values in some areas have tripled in a half-dozen years.

The city is becoming more aware of its heritage. Larimer Square, a historic commercial restoration of Denver's first block, is the most sophisticated area in the city in which to dine, drink, and shop. An urban renewal project, however, has cleared lower downtown Denver away and is replacing it with office buildings and apartment complexes. Like most urban renewal projects, this one thrives on the idea of clear-cutting. Only a few of the architectural gems of the past have been saved; the new buildings lack style. And, also typical of a growing city, there are suburban industrial parks. Denver Technological Center, for instance, is considered one of the most beautiful industrial parks in the country, with its expanse of lawns and superb contemporary architecture. It is so inspiring, in fact, the women working at a small assembly facility there voted not to come to work in curlers.

But the financial heart of the city still is downtown Denver, and its hub is 17th Street—known to some as Scratch Lane.

## Hotels

There's really only one place to stay in town, the **Brown Palace** (old wing). Built before the turn of the century, the Brown was probably long overdue for a major refurbishing job just when what had simply been old suddenly became charming. Now what is charming is carefully preserved. Result: a jewel of an antique hotel, with an 8-story lobby that was the talk of all the West in the early days.

The **Denver Hilton** is well located near the Brown downtown, and is the best spot in town for a big convention. There are a handful of other hotels that are fine for a few days' stay, including the **Cosmopolitan, Greenwood Inn, Stouffer's Denver Inn,** and the **Writers' Manor.**

# Denver

## *Restaurants*

Not one of the city's strong points. For a former cow town, even the beef is not all that much to brag about, but you can get excellent prime ribs at a few spots, including the **Ship Tavern** at the Brown. For seafood, it's **Lafitte.** After that, it's strictly steak and salad bar, and some touristy spots (see following section).

## *Potpourri*

Night life is improving. You'll find name entertainment at the **Warehouse** and the **Grain Exchange.** (Denver has a penchant for erecting restaurants that look like something else.)

Denver is a college town and there is a lot of swingles activity—check with a cabbie or your bellboy, as the popular joints change overnight.

Around the Hilton there is also a slew of sleazy bars with strippers with names like Candy Barr and Flyp Topp, but only if you are desperate.

Denver is also a **sports** city. It is almost impossible to get Denver Bronco tickets in season, even if the team is on a losing streak. Tickets for Denver Spurs (hockey) and the Denver Rockets (basketball) are easier to come by.

Skiing is big of course, especially among newcomers. (It's amazing how many natives never take it up.) The Eisenhower Tunnel cuts out treacherous Loveland Pass and 30 to 60 minutes off the trip to Vail, Breckenridge, and Aspen. But don't be fooled. The tunnel has rush-hour traffic jams on weekends, and the West approach is like Loveland Pass without the curves.

There are plenty of sights around the city. The **Mint** is interesting, if you like to see money made the real way. There are tours of the **Molly Brown House** (impress the guide by calling her Maggie Brown, her real name, until Meredith Willson got hold of her). The **Denver Museum of Natural History** (in City Park) is one of the best in the country—stuffed animals in unusually real settings. The **Denver Art Museum,** designed by Gio Ponti, a contemporary crenellated castle, houses a varied and improving collection. Oddly enough, there is little Western art. You'll have to go to the galleries—**Fred Rosenstock's Books** and **Carson Gallery__**to find Western art.

*Nitty Gritty*

## HOTELS

*Superior*

**BROWN PALACE** (17th St. & Tremont Pl.). Some consider the rooms a bit dumpy, others love their charm, but it has been Denver's most prestigious hotel since Henry C. Brown built it on his cow pasture in 1892. Convenient to 17th Street. Ask for a room in the old section. Restaurants (Ship Tavern and Palace Arms) are among the city's best.

*Good*

**GREENWOOD INN** (5111 S. Valley Hwy.). Convenient to Denver Tech Center and Johns-Manville, but out of the way for good night life. No suites.

**STOUFFER'S DENVER INN** (3203 Quebec). Adjacent to the airport. Good bar.

**WRITERS' MANOR** (1730 S. Colorado Blvd.) Good family place, easy access to highways.

*Acceptable*

**COSMOPOLITAN** (18th Ave. & Broadway). Has improved in the past few years. Has a Trader Vic's.

**DENVER HILTON** (16th St. and Court Pl.). Cramped but conveniently located downtown. A favorite convention hotel, though meeting rooms can be "you can't get there from here" places—they often require riding back elevators or a brisk walk.

## RESTAURANTS

**BENIHANA OF TOKYO** (\*\*) (1050 17th St.). There's one here, too. You know, Japanese food prepared at your table with great pizzazz. Tables seat eight, so unless your party is large you sit with strangers. Dinner for two (with saki): $24.

**COLORADO MINE CO.** (\*) (4490 E. Virginia Ave.). Contrived but nice. Menu primarily beef. Bar caters to singles. Prime ribs for two: $25.

**THE FORT** (\*\*) (Morrison, Colorado, a half hour from Denver). Touristy but great Old West atmosphere. Food and drink prepared from authentic early trapper and Indian recipes. Rocky Mountain Oysters what you suspect. Drinks served in Mason jars. Dinner for two: $27 (buffalo steak is more).

**LAFFITE** (\*\*\*) (14th and Larimer sts.). Only place in Denver for seafood. Service is showy. Prepare for a wait (in the Oyster Bar) even with reservations. Dinner for two: $24.

**LEO'S PLACE** (\*\*\*) (4 E. 16th Ave.). Luncheon spot for Denver businessmen. Heavy Edwardian decor, combined with architectural relics of Denver eateries. Dinner is more leisurely. Dinner for two: $25.

**PALACE ARMS** (\*\*) (Brown Palace Hotel). A bit stuffy and starchy, but food is good and service professional. Ideal place to dine with a client. Dinner for two: $25.

**PTI** (\*\*) (3425 S. Oleander Ct.). Favorite of Denver advertising men. Ultramodern with chrome and Helvetica type. Specializes in skewered things. Dinner for two: $24.

**QUORUM** (\*\*) (233 E. Colfax Ave.). A favorite of the gourmets. Service with lots of panache. Across from the state capitol, it can be crowded at lunch when the legislature is in session. Dinner for two: $30.

**SHIP TAVERN** (\*\*\*) (Brown Palace Hotel). Something businessmen barque about. But despite the nautical decor, best "seafood" is trout. Prime ribs excellent. Jammed at lunch, no reservations, so come early. Dinner for two: $28.

**STROMBERG'S** (\*\*) (1317 14th St.). Haute cuisine, a favorite with the expense-account crowd. The bar is small; you're expected to eat, not drink. The restaurant is poorly marked. Look for Maudie's Flea Market, off Larimer Square. Stromberg's is downstairs. Dinner for two: $30.

**TANTE LOUISE** (\*\*) (4900 E. Colfax Ave.). Country relative of the Quorum (operated by the same family). Try specialties like Canadian Hare. Dinner for two: $28.

**TRADER VIC'S** (\*\*) (Cosmopolitan Hotel). One of the better in the chain, though service can be indifferent. Dinner for two: $25.

## Recommended Reading

YESTERDAY'S DENVER by Sandra Atchison. (Freeman Publishing, $9.95). 1975. The old cow town of frontier days in glowing prose and living sepia.

CENTENNIAL by James Michener. (Random House, $12.50). The old master spent some time in Colorado, and has the place beautifully pegged in this yarn.

# DETROIT

A few years ago, a raw graduate of the Columbia Journalism School landed a highly prized job with a national publication and was assigned to Detroit. But when he gave his wife what he thought was good news, she broke into tears. "Detroit? Oh my God!" she moaned. Well, Detroit may not be all that bad, but a swinging city it certainly ain't.

The nation's fifth largest city is the oldest city in the Upper Midwest, having been founded in 1701 as a French fur trading outpost. Unfortunately, few traces of that early history remain, and the French heritage survives only in street names such as Cadieux and Livernois (pronounced Cad-joo and Liver-noy).

By the late nineteenth century, Detroit was well on its way toward becoming a major industrial center, turning out wagons, machinery, and stoves. The invention of the automobile, the early concentration of its manufacture in Michigan, and the acumen of Henry Ford sealed the city's destiny. For the first half of the century, immigrants, first from Central and Southern Europe, then from the hills of Appalachia and finally Blacks from the Deep South, poured into Detroit making it what it is today: a polyglot, beer-and-potatoes factory town. In the popular song of a few years back, "Detroit City," the singer lamented: "By day I make the cars and by night I hit the bars/Oh, how I want to go home." That somehow symbolizes this city, where even many second-generation Detroiters consider somewhere else to be "home."

Since the 1950s, Detroit has been undergoing a Los Angeles-style decentralization, with massive business centers in the western and northern suburbs threatening to render downtown obsolete. The central business district, though, remains the center for banking and finance and is not quite ready to be written off. About a billion dollars worth of redevelopment is underway, including the $500 million, John Portman-designed Renaissance Center, which will feature offices, apartments, shops, restaurants, and the vast 70-story Detroit Plaza Hotel. Phase One of the center, including the hotel, probably won't open until late 1976.

## *Hotels*

The **Detroit Plaza,** to be run by Western International, will undoubtedly be downtown's best hotel. But until then, the visitor staying downtown has to contend with the chronic shortage of good hotels. Best choice is the **Hotel Pontchartrain.** While it would not be considered a great hotel in most other cities—though new it always seems slightly tired—the Pontch is the best downtown has to offer. Its La Méditerranée dining room is a big cut above most American hotel eateries and its La Salamandre Bar, with jazz in the evenings, is one of the town's best. The Top of the Pontch offers entertainment and a sweeping view of the Detroit River and southern Ontario.

Elsewhere downtown, the choices are slim. The **Sheraton Cadillac** and the **Detroit Hilton** are typical of older downtown Hiltons and Sheratons. Also centrally located is **Howard Johnson's Downtown**— clean, modern, and very HoJo-ish. Watch out for the **Holiday Inn Downtown.** There's nothing wrong with the place itself except that it is not actually downtown—it is separated from the central business area by a freeway and is in a somewhat dubious neighborhood.

Unless you are coming to Detroit for one of the growing number of conventions at Cobo Hall, or unless your business is to be concentrated in the downtown area, there is really no reason to stay there. Detroit is a sprawling city with severe traffic congestion during rush hours and by staying close to the site of your business, you can save much valuable time. The businessman staying at a suburban hotel will need a car, but he would anyway if he stayed downtown and had business in the suburbs.

Fortunately, recent years have seen a major boom in construction of outlying hotels. And some of these are full-service hostelries, not just ports in a storm. Best are the **Somerset Inn** in Troy and the **Michigan Inn** and **Shiawassee Inn** in Southfield.

If your business is with General Motors, Burroughs, or some other company headquartered in the New Center area, a few miles north of downtown, the **St. Regis** is a good choice. Built several years ago as an attempt at a grande luxe hotel, it never quite came off, but is a

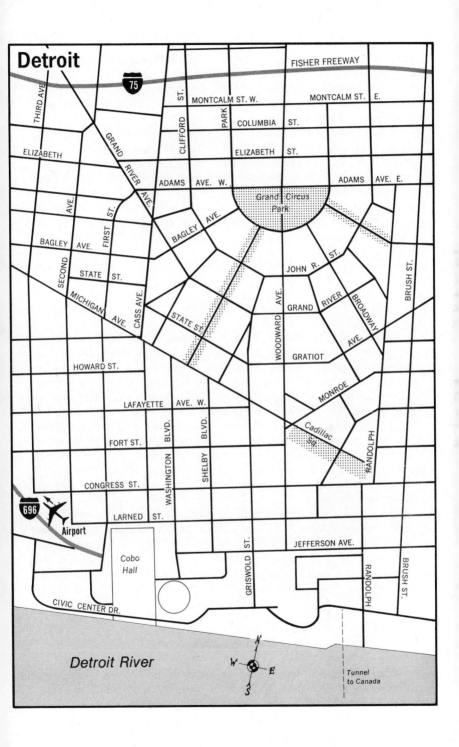

good hostelry. Another new center choice is **Howard Johnson's New Center,** a carbon copy of the one downtown.

In Dearborn, very close to Ford headquarters, is the **Dearborn Inn,** an uncommonly comfortable place. Soon to open in this area is a big new **Hyatt House.**

In Southfield, where dozens of businesses have moved their offices, the best existing hotel is **Stouffer's Northland Inn,** a good suburban motor inn. Both the **Shiawassee Inn,** built by the owners of the Pontchartrain, and Western International's **Michigan Inn** offer better than average accommodations. In Troy, very close to the offices of S. S. Kresge and the Budd Company and in the middle of an office boom, is the **Somerset Inn,** a very attractive new hotel, with Fifth Avenue-style shopping in the adjoining Somerset Mall. The **Troy Hilton** and a **Holiday Inn** are also nearby.

## Restaurants

While hotels are diffusing into the suburbs, the best restaurants are still concentrated in the central city. The **London Chop House** has long been regarded as the city's best, and while the food from the Continental menu generally lives up to that reputation, the service often does not. The tab is high by Detroit standards, easily $40 to $50 for two for dinner. The **Pontchartrain Wine Cellars,** the closest thing in town to a French bistro, serves excellent food at much more moderate prices. **Joe Muer's** serves the best seafood in town, some say in the Midwest. Though there is a good selection of traditional seafood, such as the inevitable Dover sole and Maine lobster, try some Great Lakes local specialties, such as broiled pickerel, sautéed perch, or lake trout.

For a first-class steak in a fairly modest setting, try **Carl's Chop House.** Good Italian food is available at **Mario's and Lelli's Inn. Little Harry's** is an intimate place with a Continental menu and **Schweizer's** is a charming restaurant with a Continental flavor. As befits Detroit's varied ethnic heritage, there is also a good variety of ethnic eating places (see restaurant list).

## Potpourri

What to do after dinner can be a big problem in town. Downtown Detroit dies at 6:00 P.M. Night life is virtually nonexistent and visiting businessmen should note that local executives are early risers who are often at their desks no later than 8:30 A.M. Earlier appointments are not unusual, especially at the auto companies.

Most of the city after dark has become a fearful place; the city's homicide rate is the nation's highest and assaults are uncomfortably frequent. Walking after dark is ill-advised except on the best-lit streets downtown, and this not surprisingly tends to discourage life after dark. Unless your taste runs to skin flicks, Kung Fu thrillers, or third-rate *Superfly* imitations, don't count on a downtown movie.

For a late-night drink, the **Top of the Flame** at the Michigan Consolidated Gas Co. building has fine ambiance and a great view. **Dirty Helen's** in the Leland House draws a singles crowd, and try the **Red Garter** if you like banjos and peanuts. All the hotels have decent, if unexciting, bars.

If you must humor a dippy customer or fellow worker, the best concentration of skin flicks, porno stores, "living art" studios, and massage parlors is along Woodward Avenue in Highland Park, several miles north of downtown. The places are fairly respectable as such establishments go. The **Tender Trap** in the area offers topless (and occasionally but unofficially bottomless) entertainment. But don't let your buddy go overboard. Prostitution in Detroit is a rough game and one best avoided by the visitor. Johns frequently get more than they bargain for—a rolling or worse.

Detroit's only professional legitimate theater is the striking **Fisher Theater** in the Fisher Building (New Center area). Programs are a mixture of pre-Broadway tryouts and successful road shows. Tickets are generally moderately priced and, except for the biggest hits, are usually available at the box office quite close to show time.

The **Music Hall Center for the Performing Arts,** housed in a slightly seedy but serviceable theater downtown, presents a varied program of popular and serious musical entertainment. The **Detroit Symphony Orchestra's** quality has improved faster than its reputation outside the city, and its regular Thursday and Saturday night concerts are first rate.

Detroit has a full bill of professional **sports** and only the football Lions pose any particular ticket problems—all the good seats are sold to season pass holders. All teams except the Lions play downtown or within a short cab ride. The Lions now play in Pontiac, 25 miles away.

Detroit does not have a great number of daytime diversions. Something everyone should try to see once, with or without family, however is **Ford Motor Company's River Rouge complex,** the only place in the world capable of turning raw materials like ore and sand into a complete automobile. Free two-hour tours, which cover the steel mill, stamping plant, engine plant, and final assembly leave hourly from the Ford World Headquarters Building 9:00 A.M. to 2:00 P.M. weekdays except holidays.

Nearby, and a must if children are along, is **Greenfield Village** and the **Henry Ford Museum.** The Village is a collection of old buildings, mostly nineteenth century American, moved to Dearborn and lovingly restored under the direction of Henry Ford. Exhibits also feature nineteenth-century manufacturing processes and crafts. The adjoining museum is a marvelous attic with extensive collections of almost anything you can think of: Hepplewhite and Duncan Phyfe furniture, Chinese export pottery, McCormick reapers, aircraft, steam locomotives, and a variety of early lightbulbs. Not surprisingly, the Ford Museum's collection of automobiles is among the world's finest.

On the heavier side, the **Detroit Institute of Arts** has a splendid collection and recent acquisitions have shored up a traditional weakness in modern art. Aggressive management has consistently attracted to the museum limited engagement traveling shows, and in some cases, shows unique to North America.

## *Nitty Gritty*

## HOTELS—DOWNTOWN AND NEW CENTER AREA

*Superior*
**PONTCHARTRAIN** (Washington Blvd. & West Jefferson Ave.). Downtown's best, located across the street from Cobo Hall. First choice of visiting businessmen. Good restaurants. Heated pool.

*Good*
**DETROIT HILTON** (Washington Blvd. at Grand Circus Park). Older but with many rooms recently renovated. Extensive meeting facilities. Trader Vic's restaurant.

**SHERATON-CADILLAC** (Washington Blvd. at Michigan Ave.). Old but many rooms newly decorated. Good location and extensive meeting facilities.

**ST. REGIS** (Grand Blvd. at Cass Ave.). Across the street from the General Motors Building, but curiously off the beaten track. Very nicely done public rooms and large guest rooms.

*Acceptable*

**HOLIDAY INN DOWNTOWN** (1331 Trumbull). Motor inn, poor location on western fringe of downtown, near Tiger Stadium. Heated pool.

**HOWARD JOHNSON'S DOWNTOWN** (Washington Blvd. & Michigan Ave.). Plastic ambiance, but decent rooms. Food service only by the Orange Roof people.

**HOWARD JOHNSON'S NEW CENTER** (Grand Blvd. & Third Ave.). An uptown carbon copy of the previous listing.

## SUBURBAN HOTELS

*Superior*

**DEARBORN INN** (20301 Oakwood Blvd., Dearborn). Gracious inn in Early American tradition with period furnishing and spacious grounds, tennis courts, heated pool. Very convenient to Ford Motor Co. offices. Good restaurant.

*Good*

**HOLIDAY INN—TROY** (Rochester Rd. near Maple Rd., Troy). Typical, good suburban Holiday Inn. Heated pool.

**MICHIGAN INN** (16400 J. L. Hudson Dr., Southfield). Comfortable, reasonable, an oasis in the area.

**SHIAWASSEE INN** (17017 W. Nine Mile Rd., Southfield). New and most welcome. Full complement of facilities.

**SOMERSET INN** (2601 W. Big Beaver Rd., Troy). More than just a motel. Heated, year-round pool. Conventional facilities.

**STOUFFER'S NORTHLAND INN** (Northland Dr. at Greenfield Rd., Southfield, across from Northland Shopping Center). Something of a cross between a suburban motor inn and a true hotel. Good meeting facilities. Heated pool.

**TROY HILTON INN** (Stephenson Highway near I-75, Troy). Good suburban motor inn. Better-than-average meeting facilities, especially cozy bar. Indoor pool, sauna.

## RESTAURANTS

**CARL'S CHOP HOUSE** (**) (Grand River Ave. at John Lodge Freeway). Excellent steaks from limited menu; also live lobster. Plain and efficient surroundings. Good for a late-night sandwich, but avoid the place after major sports events. Dinner for two approximately $25.

**CHUNG'S** (*) (3177 Cass Ave. at Peterboro St.). The best Cantonese food in Detroit. Rather plain room with efficient and occasionally brusque service, but reasonable prices. No alcohol. Dinner for two is only about $11.

**GRECIAN GARDENS** (*) (Monroe Ave. at Beaubien St.). Traditional Greek specialties. Try the thin broiled lamp chops, Greek-style—ask if you don't see them on the menu. Beer and wine, liquor license pending. Dinner runs about $15 for two.

**JIM'S GARAGE** (**) (Larned St. at Washington Blvd.). Interesting dishes from a limited Continental menu. Very good scampi. Decorated with memorabilia of early automobiles. Dinner about $30.

**JOE MUER'S** (***) (2000 Gratiot Ave.). Best seafood in town or for miles around. Traditional seafood plus Great Lakes specialties. Oyster bar. No reservations accepted; be prepared for a wait. Dinner for two: $30.

**LA MÉDITERRANÉE** (**) (Hotel Pontchartrain). French and Continental specialties. Elegant setting. Dinner for two: $35.

**LELLI'S INN** (**) (7618 Woodward Ave., near Grand Blvd.). Italian food with a Northern flavor. Excellent veal dishes. Dinner for two: $25.

**LITTLE HARRY'S** (**) (2681 E. Jefferson Ave.). Intimate Continental dining. Fine service. Dinner for two approximately $30.

**LONDON CHOP HOUSE** (**) (155 West Congress St., near Griswold St.). Detroit's top see-and-be-seen, expense-account restaurant. Continental menu. Service sometimes not up to prices. Dinner for two: $45.

**MARIO'S** (**) (4222 Second Ave.). Elegant Italian food. Good veal Oscar. Dinner for two approximately $30.

**NEW-HELLAS CAFÉ** (*) (583 Monroe Ave.). Simple hearty Greek cuisine. Best Greek salads in town. Beer, wine only. Dinner for two: $12.

**PONTCHARTRAIN WINE CELLARS** (**) (234 West Larned St. near Shelby Blvd.). Charming French bistro. Birthplace of Cold Duck, a drink which here bears little resemblance to the atrocities bottled in its name. Excellent veal Cordon Bleu, not bad bouillabaise considering Midwest limitation. Dinner for two: $28.

**SCHWEIZER'S** (**) (260 Schweizer Pl., off E. Jefferson). One of Detroit's oldest restaurants and a local institution. German-American menu, good sauerbraten. Dinner for two: $25.

**TOPINKA'S** (*) (2960 West Grand Blvd.). Large servings of hearty food. Attracts big theater crowd for Fisher Theater across the street. Tends to get noisy. Dinner for two: $30.

**YAMATO** (**) (in Lelan House, at Cass and Bagley Aves.). Authentic Japanese cuisine. Get up your courage and try sashimi—succulent raw tuna in soy sauce—a lot better than it sounds to Western ears. Kimono-clad waitresses add to charm. Dinner for two: $25.

## *Recommended Reading*

There are very few good books about Detroit, not even guidebooks. It's that kind of town.

DETROIT GUIDE by Martin Fischoff. (Speedball Publications. $3.00.) Recently revised, it's a good general guidebook with some useful tips on survival in town if your stay will be longer than a few days.

Note: If you are a history buff, consult the 35-year-old Federal Writer's Project GUIDE TO MICHIGAN, available in many libraries.

# HONOLULU

Critics are calling Honolulu "another Miami Beach." And there are similarities. Oldtimers hardly recognize famed Waikiki anymore. Three decades ago there were just the Royal Hawaiian, Moana, and Halekulani hotels on the beach at Waikiki; now the two-and-a-half-mile stretch is choked with more than 100 hotels, many of them highrisers, containing some 23,000 units.

But Waikiki still attracts throngs. Of the 2.76 million visitors to the 50th State in 1974, close to half stayed at Waikiki for at least one night. Of that total, 2.17 million were from the west, mainly from the U.S. mainland and Canada, and 597,000 were from the east, principally from Japan.

Waikiki is still where the action is. And it is where the conventions are. During 1974, it hosted two of the biggest, the American Bankers Association and the American Bar Association. The American Medical Association chose it as the site for its 1975 gathering.

But for all of Waikiki's density and bustle, the state's main island of Oahu isn't wall-to-wall people. Honoluluans bristle at suggestions that vacationers should bypass Waikiki and Oahu for the "neighbor islands"—Maui, Hawaii (the "big island"), and Kauai. A drive around Oahu treats the visitor to some of the Hawaiian Islands' loveliest scenery.

More and more businessmen are sure to find themselves in Honolulu. Bookings of conventions for 1975 show an estimated head count of 225,000, up from 1974's 188,000. As a vacation destination, Hawaii has gained from dollar devaluations, inflation rates abroad, and soaring air fares to Europe. Fares between the mainland and Hawaii, while rising, remain among the cheapest in the world on a per-mile basis.

If crowds aren't your style, the local tourist trade's least busy months, in order, are December (before Christmas), September (after Labor Day), May, and November. The highest occupancy rates at Waikiki hotels occur in February, March, and August. In February, 1973, winter-weary mainlanders so jammed Waikiki that the hotels had to appeal to local citizens to take the overflow into their homes. Today, the hotels, fearful of more regulation, watch bookings closely, with required deposits the rule.

## *Hotels*

The **Kahala Hilton,** Hilton International's sole domestic operation, remains tops in prestige. It's four miles removed from Waikiki, overlooking the Waialae Country Club, site of the Hawaiian Open. In Waikiki the 1,706-unit **Sheraton-Waikiki** is centrally located and popular. It's the world's largest beachfront resort hotel. In its shadow is the still-proud **Royal Hawaiian** (also a Sheraton hotel), for those to whom tradition appeals. Safe bets are **Hilton Hawaiian Village's Rainbow Tower** and the **Ilikai,** the latter owned by UAL, Inc.'s Western International Hotel chain. A cottage-type, beachfront favorite is the **Halekulani.** The **Hawaiian Regent** is also a standout.

There are very few hotels downtown, despite a clutch of new office buildings, including headquarters towers for three of Hawaii's "Big Five" corporations. Handiest for businessmen is the **Ala Moana Hotel** (Americana), two miles east of downtown. It is near the Ala Moana Center, the islands' largest shopping complex.

## *Restaurants*

The top Western-style restaurants are the Kahala Hilton's **Maile Room**—which has a well varied menu in a tropical setting—and the Hawaiian Regent's **Third Floor**—a must if you like French cuisine. The Maile Room's three tender filets (veal, beef, and pork) are especially good. At the Third Floor the New Zealand venison and rack of lamb Provençale are especially fine.

The best steak house is **Canlis' Charcoal Broiler.** The best seafood can be found at **Nick's Fish Market.** For Italian food, there's the **Trattoria** and **Matteo's.**

As one would expect from its large Oriental population, Honolulu has some of the best Chinese and Japanese restaurants in the U.S. Peking duck serving 4 to 6 persons (order a day in advance) is

especially good at the two Cantonese places—**China House** in the
Ala Moana Shopping Center, and **Ming Palace.** Also fine are Ming
Palace's beef on crisp long rice, and China House's lemon chicken.

A short ride from the Kahala Hilton, look for the **Winter Garden.**
The winter melon soup is fine, as are crisp duck Szechuan, sweet-sour
shrimp or pork, and the novel Chinaman's Hat, which you eat on
soft, thin pastry.

For Japanese—and Japanesy—food, try **Mon Cher Ton Ton** in
the Ala Moana Hotel, **Benihana of Tokyo** at the Hilton Hawaiian
Village, or the nearby **Kobe Steak House.** All do the teppan yaki
(teh-pahn-YAH-key) style of cooking tidbits of steak, shrimp, and
vegetables in front of you. Kobe Steak House is the most attractive.

If you ask Honolulu-based Japanese businessmen where to go for
good Japanese food, they will add to the list **Manno's** in the Royal
Aloha Hotel, and the **Miyako** in the Kaimana Beach Hotel.


## *Potpourri*


Waikiki doesn't pretend to compare with Las Vegas for night life.
If you have time for just one or two shows, enjoy the lovely gals in
the low-slung skirts doing torrid Tahitian dances. They're in the
Tahiti show at **Ala Moana Hotel's** colorful Hawaiian Hut, and in
Tavana's Polynesian Spectacular at the **Moana Hotel.**

Also good are the Danny Kaleikiki show at the **Kahala Hilton,**
and the Al Harrington show at the **Hilton Hawaiian Village,** which
also has "Paradise Found," a well-staged Pacific revue laced with
history and culture.

Your wife will love Don Ho's cute show at the **Polynesian Palace**
if she's a country girl, but try to find an excuse to be elsewhere that
night, especially if you don't like crowds. Or persuade her to go
instead to hear soprano Emma Veary's grand, classy show at the
**Halekulani Hotel.**

Caution: If you go bouncing around the town at night, you'll find
that the much-advertised Aloha spirit can go just so far. In Waikiki,
as in any resort town, there are plenty of people eager to separate
you from your traveler's checks.

Stay off the streets after midnight, especially in the sight-seeing
areas—they can get dangerous. A favorite trick of streetwalkers is
to swarm all over a tipsy male, rubbing and pawing—and lifting his
wallet. And, of course, steer clear of the hostess bars, which abound
in Waikiki. They are the same as everywhere else, except the girls
are Japanese or Korean. Much phony champagne, no action.

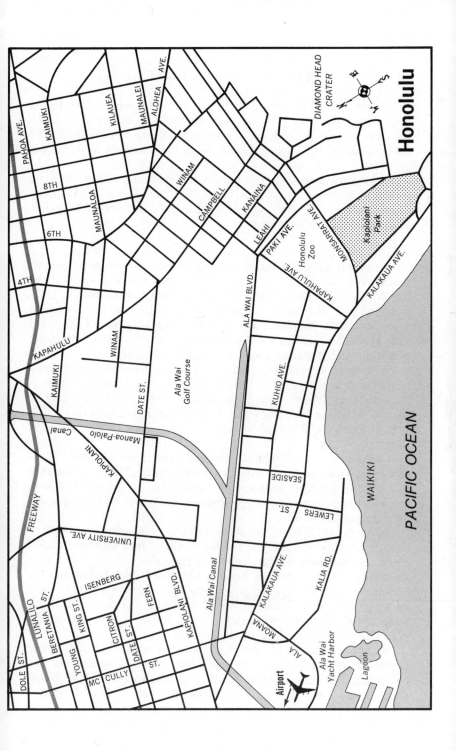

# Honolulu

Stay close to your hotel if you are looking for company—Honolulu attracts wholesome types of both sexes, remember.

For the active sportsman, there are 15 **golf** courses open to the public on Oahu. The Waialae and hilly Oahu clubs are the island's best, but private, so latch on to a member if you can. Of Oahu's 80 public **tennis** courts, some are within an easy walk of Waikiki, but are busy.

The charter **fishing** fleet is handy—a few minutes from Waikiki toward downtown, at Kewalo Basin. But the islands' sport-fishing capital in Kona on the "big island," home of the annual Hawaiian International Billfish Tournament.

How best to sight-see on Oahu—rented car, tour bus, or hired limousine—is a matter of taste. An island tour can easily be accomplished in a day. Local tour drivers usually have colorful and instructive spiels. Highlights include **Punchbowl Memorial Cemetery,** for a sweeping vista of Honolulu; **Tantalus** for a still higher-up view, from a cool forest; the **Nuuanu Pali Lookout,** overlooking Oahu's windward side; Pearl Harbor, and the **Arizona** Memorial, if only for the sense of history, and **Hanauma Bay,** a marine life sanctuary.

For a swim, stop at Hanauma (bring a face mask and snorkel) or at **Kailua Beach,** even nicer than Waikiki and less crowded. On Sundays, between March 2 and mid-August, swim in the morning at remote **Mokuleia,** then enjoy the afternoon polo match. In mid-Oahu, stop at the **Dole Pineapple** stand and enjoy peak-of-ripeness fresh fruit.

If you've time, the **Polynesian Cultural Center, Sea Life Park, Paradise Park, Valley of the Temples Memorial Park,** and **Bishop Museum** (the Islands' foremost collection of Hawaiiana) are all worthwhile—and all charge admission. The **Academy of Arts** is free—and a delightful spot for lunch.

For shopping, Waikiki has three concentrations of tourist-oriented shops: tasteful (if expensive) **King's Alley, International Market Place,** and **Rainbow Bazaar** (at Hilton Hawaiian Village). Or take a short bus ride to **Kilohana Square,** the **Ward Warehouse,** or **Ala Moana Center.** Here you know you pay what the locals pay. To load up on puka shell necklaces, many of the locals journey to the **Kam Swap Meet,** Wednesdays, Saturdays, and Sundays, at the Kam Hi-Way Drive-In Theatre, for the best prices.

Of course, you should take in a "neighbor island" or two if time permits. Each extra island costs just a few dollars more on your airline ticket. For sheer pristine beauty and a relaxed life-style, **Kauai** (the "garden island") ranks high. **Maui** (the "valley island") offers a variety of scenery from 10,025-foot Haleakala crater ("The House of the Sun") to lush, rustic Hana. The "big island" of **Hawaii** can be the most exciting if Pele, the volcano goddess, is doing her thing—as she has recently.

## *Nitty Gritty*

## HOTELS

*Superior*

**KAHALA HILTON** (5000 Kahala Ave.). Ultra-luxurious favorite of presidents and entertainment stars, with prices to match. If you can afford the rates, the taxi fares to Waikiki and downtown Honolulu won't matter.

**ROYAL HAWAIIAN** (2259 Kalakaua Ave.). Former favorite of presidents, etc., but you can't beat the beach location in the heart of Waikiki. Get one of the old rooms (luxuriously large) with an ocean view.

*Good*

**ALA MOANA** (410 Atkinson). No beach, but no Waikiki traffic jams either. Next-door neighbor to Ala Moana Shopping Center. Superior restaurants and entertainment.

**HAWAIIAN REGENT** (2552 Kalakaua Ave.). One of the newer ones, like the Sheraton-Waikiki. Central Waikiki location, but not right on the beach. Superior rooms and service; very superior restaurants.

**HILTON HAWAIIAN VILLAGE** (2005 Kalia Rd.). Beach location with fine variety of shops and restaurants. Good if you stay in a suite, the Rainbow Tower (preferable), or the Diamond Head Tower.

**ILIKAI** (Ala Moana Ave. at Hobron). Good location on Waikiki's edge, between Ala Moana Shopping Center and Hilton Hawaiian Village. Good restaurants and ocean and yacht-harbor view, but no beach. Tower Building superior because of its large rooms. If you get a suite, specify ocean or yacht-harbor view.

**SHERATON-WAIKIKI** (2255 Kalakaua Ave.). New and fine for conventions. Restaurants, shops. Good beach location, in the heart of Waikiki.

*Acceptable*

**HALEKULANI** (2199 Kalia Rd.). Small, gracious, comfortable, low-rise. Lots of folks won't go anywhere else.

**PRINCESS KAIULANI** (120 Kaiulani). Good central location, no beach. Specify tower rooms.

**SURFRIDER** (2353 Kalakaua Ave.). Good central Waikiki location on beach.

**WAIKIKIAN** (1811 Ala Moana). Low-rise advantages like the Halekulani, and good central location with fewer traffic problems. Between Hilton Hawaiian Village and Ala Moana Shopping Center; no beach. Some low-priced rooms.


# RESTAURANTS

**ARTHUR'S** (*) (Ala Moana Ave. and Hobron). Lamb Jacqueline, Dover sole, other good French food. Dinner for two: approximately $35.

**BENIHANA OF TOKYO** (**) (Hilton Hawaiian Village). Maybe it's because it is closer to Japan than any other Benihana in the chain, but this one seems more Oriental—even though it serves the same American-style food (slightly slanted). A fun place to eat and watch your magic-chef perform for your dinner. Dinner for two: $30.

**BISTRO** (*) (1647 Kapiolani). Steak Diane, sweetbreads, other fine specialties. Dinner for two: $30.

**BYRON II** (*) (Ala Moana Shopping Center). Portuguese bean soup, stuffed trout, good steaks. Dinner for two: $25.

**CANLIS' CHARCOAL BROILER** (**) (Kalakaua and Kalaimoku). Best steak house. Fresh oysters, prime ribs. Dinner for two: $40.

**CAVALIER** (*) (1600 Kapiolani). Scampi, veau Cordon Bleu, other good French food. Dinner for two: $30.

**CHEZ MICHEL** (**) (2126B Kalakaua). Mahimahi Provençale, tournedos Chasseur, other Franco-Hawaiian fare. Dinner for two: $40.

**CHINA HOUSE** (*) (Ala Moana Shopping Center). One of the best Chinese restaurants. Dinner for two: $25.

**KOBE STEAK HOUSE** (**) (1814 Ala Moana). Japanese-style steak and other dishes cooked at your table. One of the best Japanese restaurants. Dinner for two: $22.

**LE CHATEAU** (**) (131 Kaiulani, in King's Alley). Pheasant, duck, broiled lamb, other excellent French food. Dinner for two: $35.

**MAILE ROOM** (***) (Kahala Hilton Hotel). Some of the finest dining you'll ever find anywhere, in lovely tropical setting. Dinner for two: $40.

**MANNO'S** (*) (Royal Aloha Hotel, Ala Wai Blvd. and McCully St.). Authentic Japanese cuisine—and clientele. For the genuine sushi and tempura addict. Dinner for two: $25.

**MATTEO'S** (**) (Marine Surf-Waikiki Hotel, 342 Seaside Ave.). Good Italian, just like you think mama used to make. Dinner for two: $30.

**MING PALACE** (*) (1272 S. King). Ming Palace beef on crisp long rice outstanding at one of the best Chinese restaurants. Dinner for two: $25.

**MON CHER TON TON** (**) (Ala Moana Hotel). Teriyaki steak, good seafood dishes. One of the best Japanese restaurants. Dinner for two: $30.

**MIYAKO** (*) (Kaimana Beach Hotel, 2863 Kalakaua). Offers a great view of the sunset while you enjoy your sukiyaki. For true sons—and culinary cousins—of Nippon. Dinner for two: $25.

**NICK'S FISH MARKET** (***) (Waikiki Gateway Hotel, 2070 Kalakaua Ave.) Seafood is hardly rare in the island's restaurants, but rarely is it better than here. Also has Continental dishes. Dinner for two: $25.

**SUMMIT** (*) (Ala Moana Hotel). Spinach salad, roast rack of lamb, or flaming Duckling Waianae at one of the better rooftop restaurants. Dinner for two: $30.

**THIRD FLOOR** (***) (Hawaiian Regent Hotel). Venison from New Zealand or rack of lamb Provençale at Hawaii's finest French restaurant. Dinner for two: $40.

**TOP OF THE ILIKAI** (*) (Ilikai Hotel). Tournedos Perigourdine or stuffed trout at one of the better rooftop restaurants. Dinner for two: $30.

**TRATTORIA** (**) (2168 Kalia Rd.). Nothing like homemade pasta, a bottle of bardolino, and veal Marsala in a tropical environment. Dinner for two: $25.

**WHALER'S BROILER** (*) (Ala Moana Hotel). One of the best steak houses. Dinner for two: $30.

**WILLOWS** (**) (901 Hausten St.). Touristy, but what a lot of people think a Hawaiian restaurant should be like—lush foliage, tropical birds, Tahitian dancers, and fair-to-middlin' fish and poi. Worth one visit. Dinner for two: $30.

**WINTER GARDEN** (**) (Kahala Mall). Northern Chinese cuisine—livelier, spicier than most Oriental food, and you can't do better this side of the Far East. Dinner for two: $25.

## *Recommended Reading*

ALL ABOUT HAWAII edited by Charles Frankel. (Star-Bulletin Printing Co., $1.95).

ATLAS OF HAWAII by University of Hawaii Department of Geography. (University Press of Hawaii, $15).

HAWAII, A GUIDE TO ALL THE ISLANDS by *Sunset* Magazine. (Lane Magazine and Book Co., $1.95).

HOW TO PHOTOGRAPH HAWAII by Robert Wenkam. (Rand McNally & Co., $4.95).

# HOUSTON

Houston has quite a few claims to fame. There's the Astrodome, the NASA Manned Spacecraft Center, the nation's third largest seaport, and the phenomenal growth which makes it America's most rapidly growing metropolis. It is also the most thoroughly air-conditioned city in the world, and all that growth would not be possible without it. (Try walking around town in mid-August and you'll see why.)

Houston is also a major oil city—not only in terms of the number of oil companies and executives living here. Oil made Houston rich, and it brings most businessmen to town.

As befits a city where petroleum is so important, as a visitor you will rapidly become a superconsumer of it, in the form of gasoline. Houston still has no zoning regulations, and its growth has been as controlled as an uncapped oil well. If you don't drive, make your trip with someone who can, or arrange for a driver. The automobile is essential in this city, where there is no rapid transit system, very spotty bus service, and expensive, hard-to-find cabs.

The city is so spread out, in fact, that it's a good idea to check the specific locations of the places you have to call and schedule your hotel reservations accordingly. Being on the wrong side of town from your business can mean empty hours on the road.

## *Hotels*

There are three superior hotels in Houston, and fortunately, they are not all downtown. The **Hyatt Regency** stands at least one notch above all the rest. It has more than 1,000 rooms and the customary

Hyatt atrium with garden lobby and Spindletop revolving restaurant lounge on its 30th floor.

A few miles south of the Hyatt Regency is the elegant **Warwick.** It is convenient to both downtown and the Texas Medical Center. The Warwick's rooms are probably the nicest available to the traveler in Houston. It also has some above-average eating places.

In Southwest Houston, a rapidly growing business area, the standout hotel is the **Houston Oaks,** in the city's nicest shopping center, The Galleria. This would be the ideal choice for those doing business in one of the Southwest area's many corporate buildings. It would also be a logical lodging if the wife is traveling along. Neiman-Marcus and scores of other top clothing and jewelry stores are within easy walking distance.

Other good hotels downtown include the largest (607 rooms) Holiday Inn in the Continental United States. (Be sure to specify the **Holiday Inn Downtown,** not the **Holiday Inn Civic Center,** which is older and more inconvenient.) Also downtown are the **Whitehall** and the **Sheraton-Lincoln. The Hilton Inn,** near northwest Houston office parks, the **Host Airport Hotel,** connected by tunnel to Intercontinental Airport, and the **Sheraton Inn—Town & Country,** in a west Houston shopping center, are fine if your business is in those respective areas.

## Restaurants

Two restaurants are in a class by themselves: **Maxim's** (French of course) and **Tony's** (Continental). Maxim's is downtown; Tony's is down the street from The Galleria in southwest Houston. Both have excellent wine lists.

On the fringe of the downtown area, there's **Brennan's,** a cousin of the New Orleans restaurant. It's a distant cousin, but the food is still quite good. Also in the same area, you might try **Courtlandt's** for that Texas steak. Further south, near the Medical Center, there's a very good **Trader Vic's** and the **Red Lion,** good for prime ribs. Both are located in the Shamrock Hilton Hotel.

You have to take to the Interstates for local favorites. Leading the list as a steak house is **Brenner's,** an old family restaurant on Interstate 10. Nearby, the **Courtyard** is luring away some old customers with its beef dishes.

Also scattered around town are three **Look's** steak houses—better than average for a chain.

As you might expect, Houston is not exactly rich in ethnic restau-

# Houston

Buffalo Bayou

NORTH FREEWAY

Airport

I-45

COMMERCE

FRANKLIN

CONGRESS

PRESTON

SMITH

MAIN ST.

PRAIRIE

BAGBY

TEXAS

CAPITOL

TRAVIS

RUSK

CAROLINE

Sam

FANNIN

WALKER

CRAWFORD

CHENEVERT

Houston

Park

MILAM

MC KINNEY

BRAZOS

LAMAR

LA BRANCH

DALLAS

SAN JACINTO

POLK

CLAY

BELL

JACKSON

SMITH

LOUISIANA

LEELAND

AUSTIN

MAIN ST.

PEASE

JEFFERSON

CALHOUN

PIERCE

GULF FREEWAY

rants. But you might want to try the **Athens Bar & Grill** out by the Houston Ship Channel, which has pretty decent Greek fare, and better entertainment. **Las Cazuelas Taqueria** is The Spot for authentic Tex-Mex fare. And for that strictly Texas-style barbecue, try **Otto's Bar-B-Q,** a few minutes drive from downtown.


## *Potpourri*

Houston is a fairly swinging, wide-open town, considering that liquor by the drink only became legal a few years ago. Respectable swingles head for **Boccaccio 2000** in Southwest Houston, or (would you believe) **Friday's.** It's a knock-off of the New York version that somehow works.

The topless zones of the city are Market Square and Montrose, but check things out with a local before wandering in. There are a few decent, if earthy places in these areas, but there are more of the other kind. And there is more than one case on record of visiting business-men ripped off by hookers.

A better idea might be to have a nightcap in the **Galleria Roof** atop the Houston Oaks Hotel, or at the **Spindletop** at the Hyatt Regency. From those elevations, you can see the city continue outward in prac-tically every direction.

Houston offers a modest range of healthy diversions after dark. The justly famous **Alley Theater** in the Houston Civic Center usually has something worthwhile on stage. There are several notable dinner-theaters, too, especially the **Windmill.**

Locals are proud of the symphony orchestra, which performs in the **Jesse Jones Hall.**

**Sports,** of course, are a big thing—and you can usually get tickets for most events without any trouble. That is, of course, as long as the football Oilers and baseball Astros continue to finish out of the money. It's harder to get tickets to watch—of all things—hockey. Though you'll live a long time before watching a man with a Texas drawl drive home a puck in pro hockey, the Aeros are very popular, as long as the football Oilers and baseball Astros aren't winning too often.

If time allows, you might drive out to the **NASA Manned Space-craft Center.** After all, you paid for it. Call well in advance for an escorted tour.

If you are so inclined, you might want to arrange for a free boat trip down the **Houston Ship Channel,** where you can view firsthand the source of much of the city's air pollution, and much of the country's gasoline. (There's always plenty of both in Houston.)

If your kids are in town, **Astroworld** is a must. Located next to the Astrodome, this amusement park is less of a theme park than others in the country. Another stop for the small fry: the **San Jacinto battleground,** where Sam Houston's 910-man army defeated 1,200 Mexican soldiers in 1836. The battleship *Texas* is now anchored there in a channel off Galveston Bay. The **Hermann Park Zoo** is another possibility.

## *Nitty Gritty*

## HOTELS

### *Superior*

**HOUSTON OAKS** (5011 Westheimer Rd.). Relatively new hotel with 400 rooms located within city's nicest shopping center, The Galleria, and convenient to southwest Houston suburban offices. Several pleasant restaurants nearby and a good bar atop, The Galleria Roof.

**HYATT REGENCY** (1200 Louisiana St.). Grand-scale, like most Hyatts, with more than 1,000 rooms. Convenient to the downtown business district. Good restaurants and bars.

**WARWICK** (5701 Main St.). Most elegant hotel in town. Three above-average restaurants including the well-known Warwick Club on the top floor. Convenient to downtown and Texas Medical Center.

### *Good*

**HILTON INN** (2504 North Loop West). New, comfortable, near northwest Houston office parks.

**HOLIDAY INN DOWNTOWN** (801 Calhoun St.). Touted as the largest Holiday Inn in the Continental United States. It's more of the same.

**HOST AIRPORT HOTEL** (Houston Intercontinental Airport). Connected via tunnel and small train with airport. About the best one can do north of the city. Above-average revolving restaurant on top.

**SHERATON INN—TOWN & COUNTRY** (910 West Belt Dr. N.). Relatively new hotel with 240 rooms. Quiet club on top. Con-

venient to west residential area and to a top shopping center: Town
& Country Village.

**SHERATON-LINCOLN** (Milam St. at Polk St.). More than 500
rooms convenient to downtown business district.

**WHITEHALL** (Smith at Jefferson). Recently remodeled. Nice
restaurant called the Rib Room.

*Adequate*

**ASTROWORLD** (Interstate 610 at Kirby Dr.). Across the street
from the Astrodome and the Astroworld amusement park. Often in
state of confusion with vacationers and conventioners.

**MARRIOTT MOTOR HOTEL** (2100 S. Braeswood Blvd.). Convenient to both the Astrodome and the Texas Medical Center.

**RICE** (Texas Ave. at Main St.). A Houston landmark that has
seen better days. Backs up to tough commercial neighborhood.

**ROYAL COACH MOTOR HOTEL** (7000 Southwest Freeway).
A sprawling motel convenient to Sharpstown residential and commercial area.

**SHAMROCK HILTON** (Main St. at Holcombe Blvd.). Old hotel
with 800 rooms. Convention atmosphere. Convenient to Texas Medical Center and to Astrodome.

# RESTAURANTS

**ATHENS BAR & GRILL** (*) (8037 Clinton Dr.). Rustic decor.
Informally served Greek dishes made more palatable by belly dancers
and festive spirit of Greek clientele, often seamen in port. Dinner for
two: approximately $16.

**BRENNAN'S** (**) (3300 Smith St.). Not quite as good as its sister
restaurant in New Orleans, but among the top restaurants in Houston.
Service is excellent and the seafood entrées are especially well prepared. Dinner for two: $35.

**BRENNER'S** (**) (10911 Katy Freeway). A family-run restaurant
with about the best steaks that can be found in Houston. Service at
times inconsistent, but the food should not disappoint. Dinner for
two: $30.

**COURTLANDT'S** (**) (611 Stuart St.). Another New Orleans-
type restaurant that specializes in beef dishes: prime rib, Chateaubriand, beef Stroganoff. Dinner for two: $27.

**COURTYARD** (*) (Katy Freeway at Campbell Rd). Quaintly
decorated. Standout on the menu is the marinated rib eye steak. The
salad bar is the best in town. Dinner for two: $25.

**LAS CAZUELAS TAQUERIA** (*) (2221 Fulton). A working-
man's café that does not serve alcoholic beverages. Best bet is to take

your own beer and butter. The Tex-Mex food is unexcelled in the city. Try the shredded roast pork dishes. Dinner for two: a roaring $10.

**LOOK'S** (*) (212 Milam St., 9810 Main St., 6112 Westheimer Rd.). Best for steak. Meticulous service and good frills such as relish servings, cheese spreads, etc. Dinner for two: $25.

**MAXIM'S** (***) (802 Lamar St.). The best French restaurant in the city. Try the caviar dip before dinner. Regardless of what is chosen on the menu, it will most likely be perfectly prepared and served. Many Houstonians enjoy the seafood dishes, particularly those with crab. Dinner for two: $30.

**OTTO'S BAR-B-QUE** (**) (5502 Memorial Dr.). The place for that down-home, finger-lickin' meal. In Texas, it's an institution. Dinner for two: $30.

**THE RED LION** (**) (7315 Main St.). The atmosphere of a luxurious English pub. Specialty of the house is prime ribs. Bring along a hearty appetite. Dinner for two: $30.

**TOKYO GARDENS** (**) (4701 Westheimer Rd.). Most authentic Japanese food available in Houston. Outstanding service. Dinner for two: $25.

**TONY'S** (***) (1801 S. Post Oak Lane). Unfailing service and food at this southwest Houston restaurant. Continental cuisine at its best. Try the veal, a house specialty. Dinner for two: $28.

**TRADER VIC'S** (*) (Shamrock Hilton Hotel). Start off with an exotic drink like the Scorpion. After that, battle through the long menu of Polynesian specialties. Dinner for two: $22.

## Recommended Reading

ACCOMMODATIONS DIRECTORY (16 pages. Copies available free from the Greater Houston Convention and Visitors Council, 1006 Main St., Houston, Tex. 77002). A guide to most of the city's better hotels and motels containing brief descriptions of accommodations and rates.

RESTAURANT DIRECTORY (27 pages. Copies available free from the Greater Houston Convention and Visitors Council, 1006 Main St., Houston, Tex. 77002.) A directory of many of the better restaurants in the city.

TEXAS MONTHLY'S GUIDE TO HOUSTON (Texas Monthly, P.O. Box 1965, Austin, Tex. 78767, $2.95). A complete directory of places to go and things to see in Houston researched and written by Felicia Coates and Harriet Howle. Copies are available at many newsstands and bookstores. This is an excellent aid to visiting the city.

TEXAS MONTHLY   Each issue of the monthly magazine contains a guide to dining and entertainment in Houston and four other major Texas cities. Provides an excellent reference for places and events appealing to youthful urban dwellers. Available at many newsstands.

# LOS ANGELES

Los Angeles is a posh hotel in Beverly Hills where show biz types stroll around tropical gardens before slipping away to a private screening room to view the latest films. (Yes, they still do things like that—and you can too—for $150 plus the film rental charge.)

Los Angeles is smog and fog, where the bottoms of buildings disappear on the horizon. And where from mid-November through early March, Los Angeles Airport sometimes has to shut down in the early morning and late afternoon because of poor visibility (air travelers, take note).

Los Angeles is suburbia gone riot, a series of suburbs in search of a city. Most Angelenos don't know the suburbs from the city's 460-square-mile limits, and there's hardly any difference, anyway. In fact, jokesters have replanted city limits signs as far north as San Francisco and as far east as Phoenix.

But Los Angeles is also a thriving business center—for other than the entertainment industry, which, in fact, has been fading for some time. It is a financial hub, an increasingly important international trade center, as commerce in the Pacific Basin expands, an electronic and aerospace mecca, and, of course, a huge marketing area in itself—the largest city in the nation's largest state (population circa 3,000,000).

Los Angeles even has its clear days, too. On some January days, when the weather is right, you can stand in shirtsleeves at the end of a dock in Los Angeles and watch a snowstorm blow over the hilly, northern boundaries of the city. And no smog will blur your view.

It is a city then, not so much of contradictions, but one which has a personality a little more diverse than popular descriptions portray.

But if there is one cliché that is all too true, it is the freeway system. You simply must rent a car in Los Angeles, if you don't drive there.

Public transportation is simply lousy, and distances are too great to make taxis worthwhile. They are few and far between, anyhow.

You can easily put 200 or more miles a day on your rented car in the Los Angeles area, so reserve a comfortable one. Note: Some airlines will let you make auto reservations while enroute on certain flights. But to be on the safe side, reserve your car in advance through one of the major car-rental agencies. Rented cars are far from scarce, but not getting one right away—or having to settle for one you don't like driving—can make your stay that much less enjoyable.

Try to avoid the freeways during peak traffic hours of 7:30 to a little after 9:00 A.M., if you are headed from the outskirts toward downtown, that is, coming in from L.A. International. During these hours, it can take over an hour to cover 30 miles. Likewise in late afternoon, when the traffic flow reverses.

An important driving note: Rain is infrequent in Los Angeles, but when it does pour, the city is paralyzed. Oil slicks build up on streets and freeways, making them as slippery as ice.

On the whole, California drivers are skillful, which you would expect from spending so much time behind the wheel, and courteous, which you might not expect.

Much has been made about the confusion of the freeways. But if you are used to driving around any major city, you'll find them relatively easy. If, however, you are not used to belts, loops, crossovers, going right to make a left, and other vagaries of interlocking superhighways, get careful instructions first.

A word on that famous Southern California weather. It is pleasant most of the time, and downright hot some days. But many evenings in the fall, winter, and spring can get a little nippy. Medium to lightweight suits for men should fit most conditions, however, and ladies should bring a wrap for evening wear. Note: Los Angeles is a bit less formal than many other metropolitan areas.

## Hotels

If you are from New York or another Eastern seaboard city, you are likely to be pleasantly surprised by the city's hotel rates—and restaurant prices as well. Hotel accommodations vary widely, of course, but figure about $30 a day for a double room. And dinner for two, with drinks and wine, seldom exceeds $30, even at better restaurants.

If you can, stay in the Beverly Hills area, which is not too far from either downtown or L.A. Airport. It boasts some of the region's

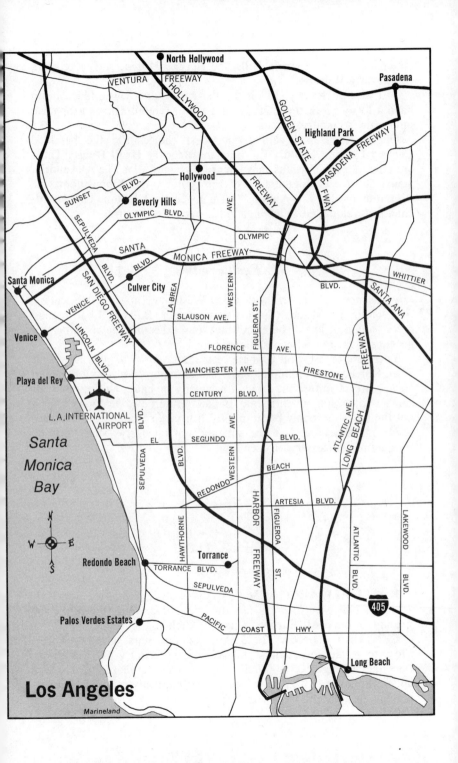

better hotels—the **Beverly Hills,** the **Beverly Hilton,** and, of course, the **Beverly Wilshire.**

Just west of Beverly Hills is the **Bel-Air,** a quiet jewel, ideal if you have a lot of work to do. It is all 1-story, reminiscent of a Spanish millionaire's country retreat.

Outside of Beverly Hills, your best choices are the heralded **Century-Plaza** in Century City and the **Regency Hyatt House.** There are other old standbys that have their followings, too: The **Alexandria,** which dates back to the turn of the century; the **Ambassador;** the **Biltmore;** and the **Los Angeles** (formerly Statler) **Hilton.** The **Americana** is developing a following, and is handy to the airport.

## *Restaurants*

Angelenos, in common with many Westerners, are big beef eaters. And, of course, Mexican food is very popular. But you'll find a good cross-section of lots of other cuisines, too, reflecting the city's heterogeneous makeup and economic mix.

There are many good Chinese restaurants, for example, as well as Thai, Korean, and Philippine spots. Restaurants featuring Continental cuisine are plentiful, but there is a paucity of haute cuisine, and for some odd reason, no first-rate Italian restaurants. Seafood, too, is not the best—probably because local fish taken from warm Southern California waters tends to be soft and not too tasty. Many seafood restaurants hence serve frozen fish.

## *Hotels*

### WEST SIDE

*Superior*

**HOTEL BEL-AIR** (701 Stone Canyon Blvd., West Los Angeles). 73 units. Not easy to find—ask directions if driving yourself. Pool, spacious rooms. All European staff in kitchen.

**CENTURY PLAZA** (2025 Ave. of the Stars, Century City). Close to restaurants, tennis and golf clubs, Century City shopping. Pool and wading pool. 800 units. Family plan; no charge for children under 18. Guests with rooms facing west frequently can watch movie-making on adjacent Twentieth Century lot.

**BEVERLY HILLS HOTEL** (9641 Sunset Blvd., Beverly Hills). 312 units. Private residence feature includes full cooking facilities. Two tennis courts, pool, cabana ($15).

**BEVERLY WILSHIRE** (9500 Wilshire Blvd., Beverly Hills). 550 units. Pool, sauna, excellent service.

**BEVERLY HILTON** (9876 Wilshire Blvd., Beverly Hills). 700 units. Two pools. Guest privileges at Rancho Park Golf Club (5 minutes away) and Riviera Golf Club (25 minutes away). Restaurant of note: L'Escoffier.

## WILSHIRE AREA

*Superior*

**AMBASSADOR HOTEL** (3400 Wilshire Blvd., L.A.). 500 units. Pool, putting green, health club. Close to Wilshire and downtown shopping.

**WILSHIRE HYATT HOUSE** (3515 Wilshire Blvd., L.A.). 400 units. Pool.

**SHERATON-WEST HOTEL** (2961 Wilshire Blvd., L.A.). 300 units. Lanai, pool, sauna, faces park.

## DOWNTOWN AREA

*Superior*

**LOS ANGELES HILTON** (930 Wilshire Blvd., L.A.). 1230 units. Just off Freeway Interchange.

**HYATT REGENCY HOTEL** (711 South Hope St., L.A.). 500 units. Broadway Plaza, part of Broadway Department Stores, other shops in building.

*Good*

**BILTMORE HOTEL** (515 S. Olive St., L.A.). 1500 units. Near heart of city. Faces park.

## AIRPORT AREA

*Superior*

**INTERNATIONAL HOTEL** (Century & Sepulveda blvds.). 650 units. Directly opposite entrance to L.A. International Airport. Pool, cabana units, men's health club.

**MARRIOTT HOTEL** (5855 W. Century Blvd., Englewood). 1020 units. New, pool. Although ¾ mile from airport, management claims no guest has complained about aircraft noise.

**AIRPORT MARINA HOTEL** (8601 Lincoln Blvd., Englewood).
800 units. Pool.

*Acceptable*
**HOLIDAY INN-INTERNATIONAL AIRPORT** (9901 La Cie-
nega Blvd., Englewood). 403 units. Pool, kennels.
**SHERATON INN-LOS ANGELES AIRPORT** (98th St. & Airport
Blvd., Englewood). 598 units. Pool, sauna, jet swirlpool.

## HOLLYWOOD

*Superior*
**CONTINENTAL HYATT HOUSE** (8401 Sunset Blvd.). 260
units. Rooftop pool.

*Good*
**HOLLYWOOD ROOSEVELT HOTEL** (7000 Hollywood Blvd.).
450 units. Older hotel, acceptable rooms.

## SAN FERNANDO VALLEY

*Superior*
**SHERATON-UNIVERSAL HOTEL** (Universal City. From Hollywood Freeway, exit Lankershim Blvd. to Universal City Plaza, turn
right). 500 units. Pool and lanai. Popular with swinging set.
**SPORTSMEN'S LODGE HOTEL** (12825 Ventura Blvd., North
Hollywood. From Hollywood Freeway, exit Coldwater Canyon Ave.
to Ventura Blvd.). Pool.
**THE CARRIAGE INN** (5525 Sepulveda Blvd., Van Nuys). 185
units. Pool, no pets.

## *Restaurants*

## WEST SIDE

(All restaurants in this area have valet parking.)

**THE BISTRO** (***) (246 North Canyon Dr., Beverly Hills). Food
has Italian flavor. One of the finer restaurants in area. Dinner for
two approximately $30.
**THE BROWN DERBY** (**) (9537 Wilshire Blvd., Beverly Hills).
Continental cuisine. Dinner for two: $30.

**BUGGY WHIP** (\*\*) (7420 La Tijera Blvd., Westchester). English steak and chop house. Dinner for two: $25.

**CHASEN'S** (\*\*) (9039 Beverly Blvd., Beverly Hills). Continental cuisine. Spinach salad great. Very popular. Dinner for two: $35.

**FOX & HOUNDS** (\*\*\*) (2900 Wilshire Blvd., Santa Monica). English inn atmosphere. Has a varied British-oriented menu, steaks and chops. Children's menu. Dinner for two: $30.

**THE ISLANDER** (\*\*) (385 North La Cienega Blvd., Beverly Hills). Seafood menu, also beef and poultry. Features exotic rum drinks. Dinner for two: $30.

**JADE WEST** (\*\*) (2000 Ave. of the Stars, Century City). Opposite the Century Plaza Hotel. Cantonese Chinese food. Try the Peking Duck. Fine service. Dinner for two: $30.

**KIRKEBY CENTER RESTAURANT** (\*\*) (Wilshire & Westwood Blvds., Westwood). Near U.C.L.A. campus. Rooftop restaurant. Varied menu. Excellent food and service. Luxurious surroundings. Dinner for two: $30.

**LA SCALA** (\*\*\*) (9455 Santa Monica Blvd., Santa Monica). Italian-oriented, Continental menu. Be sure to make reservations. Dinner for two: $35.

**LAWREY'S PRIME RIB** (\*\*) (55 N. La Cienega Blvd., Beverly Hills). Prime rib is the single entrée. Children's menu, caters to families. Dinner for two: $30.

**MADAME WU'S** (\*\*\*) (2201 Wilshire Blvd.). Cantonese and Mandarin menu. Restful, delightful oriental atmosphere. Dinner for two: $25.

**MC HENRY TAIL O' THE COCK** (\*\*) (477 S. La Cienega Blvd., Beverly Hills). Varied menu, pleasant atmosphere. Dinner for two: $30.

**MEDITERRANIA RESTAURANT** (\*\*) (134 N. La Cienega Blvd., Beverly Hills). As the name implies, the menu leans toward Mediterranean dishes. Dinner for two: $25.

**OLD VENICE NOODLE CO.** (\*\*) (2654 Main St., Santa Monica). Great pasta. Wine only, no bar. Stained glass windows, antique atmosphere. Fun place. Dinner for two: $12.

**OLLIE HAMMOND'S STEAK HOUSE** (\*\*) (91 N. La Cienega Blvd., Beverly Hills). Features charcoal-broiled steaks, balance of menu limited. Typical California steak house. Dinner for two: $20.

**THE SCUTTLEBUTT** (\*\*) (2001 Wilshire Blvd., Santa Monica). Seafood, live Maine lobster, oyster bar. Also serves excellent steaks. Good service. Dinner for two: $35.

**SENOR PICO** (\*\*) (10131 Constellation Blvd., Century City). Across from the Century Plaza Hotel. Mexican and early California menu. Service tends to be slow. Favorite drink there is called the Grandee Marguerita. Dinner for two: $30.

**STEAR'S FOR STEAKS** (**) (116 N. La Cienega Blvd., Beverly Hills). Another California steak house. Famous for its garlic bread. Dinner for two: $20.

**TRACTON'S** (***) (3560 S. La Cienega Blvd., L.A.). Prime rib, good service. A Los Angeles landmark. Dinner for two: $30.

**YAMATO RESTAURANT** (**) (2025 Ave. of the Stars, Century City). In the Century Plaza Hotel. A fine Japanese restaurant. Private dining area. Dinner for two: $30.

## WILSHIRE AREA

**THE BROWN DERBY** (*) (3377 Wilshire Blvd., L.A.). Tends to be crowded, service sometimes slow. Varied menu. Dinner for two: $30.

**THE COVE** (**) (3191 W. 7th St., L.A., one block south of Wilshire Blvd.). A fixture in Los Angeles. Continental menu, service only fair. Dinner for two: $35.

**DALE'S SECRET HARBOR** (**) (674 S. Normandie Ave., L.A.). Just south of Wilshire Blvd. Fine Continental cuisine. Dinner for two: $40.

**PERINO'S RESTAURANT** (***) (4101 Wilshire Blvd., L.A.). Elegant restaurant with superior food. Choice Continental haute cuisine. Dinner for two: $40.

**THE WINDSOR RESTAURANT** (no star) (7th St. at Catalina Blvd., L.A.). One block south of Wilshire Blvd. A popular, though overrated restaurant. Continental menu, tends toward heavy side. Service sometimes poor. Dinner for two: $40.

## DOWNTOWN AREA

**COOK'S STEAK HOUSE** (**) (645 S. Olive St., L.A.). One of the oldest downtown steak houses. Features Eastern prime beef. Closed Sundays. Dinner for two: $25.

**LES FRERES TAIX** (**) (1911 Sunset Blvd., L.A.). Close to downtown. Provincial French cooking. A long-time family-oriented L.A. institution. Excellent food and service. Nice bar. Dinner for two: $15.

**LITTLE JOE'S** (**) (904 N. Broadway, L.A.). Italian menu plus steaks. Often tends to be crowded. Dinner for two: $20.

**THE ORIGINAL PANTRY** (**) (9th & Figueroa sts., L.A.). Opened in 1924. Open 24 hours a day, no alcoholic beverages. A Los Angeles landmark for steaks, chops, stews, salads. Sit at counter, if convenient, to watch fry cooks. Excellent food and service in plain, clean surroundings. Dinner for two: $10.

**PACIFIC DINING CAR** (no star) (1310 W. 6th St., L.A.). Specialty is steaks, Eastern prime beef. Quality of food is not dependable. Dinner for two: $30.

**PAPA CHOUX** (\*\*) (1925 W. Olympic Blvd., L.A.). Varied menu, good steaks. Dinner for two: $25.

**THE TOWER** (\*\*\*) (1150 S. Olive St., L.A.). Rooftop restaurant, panoramic view. Fine restaurant with French cuisine. Often features specialties from diverse areas of the world. Good service and bar. Dinner for two: $40.

## AIRPORT AREA

Most airport restaurants, particularly those in Marina Del Rey, are overpriced, overrated, serve mediocre food, and are mainly used by businessmen in search of an evening's companionship.

**HOST INTERNATIONAL RESTAURANT** (\*\*) (201 World Way, L.A. International Airport). Suspended from arches 70 feet above the ground in Airport Theme Building. Observation deck. Dishes from 16 nations. Dinner for two: $25.

**HUNGRY TIGER** (\*\*) (6531 S. Sepulveda Blvd., L.A.). Menu features Maine lobster, other seafood, and steaks. Dinner for two: $25.

**LOBSTER HOUSE** (\*\*) (4211 Admiralty Way, Marina Del Rey). Overlooks marina. Good seafood and steaks. Dinner, for two: $30.

**THE WAREHOUSE** (\*\*) (4499 Admiralty Way, Marina Del Rey). Designed as an old warehouse. Overlooks the marina. Informal atmosphere, varied menu, very good food. Dinner for two: $35.

## HOLLYWOOD AREA

**THE BROWN DERBY** (\*\*) (1628 N. Vine St., Hollywood). A popular old-time restaurant with a nice variety of salads and entrées. Dinner for two: $25.

**DON THE BEACHCOMBER** (\*\*) (1727 N. McCadden Pl., Hollywood). Cantonese menu. Dinner for two: $25.

**EDNA EARL'S FOG CUTTER** (\*) (1635 N. La Brea Ave., Hollywood). Varied menu, not distinguished. Dinner for two: $25.

**LA VILLA** (\*\*) (5724 Melrose Ave., Hollywood). Features Spanish specialties; try the paella. Nice Mediterranean atmosphere. Dinner for two: $25.

**SCANDIA RESTAURANT** (\*\*) (9040 Sunset Blvd., Hollywood). Authentic Scandinavian decor. Varied menu, superior food and service, great desserts. Hangout for show biz types. Dinner for two: $45.

**TICK TOCK RESTAURANT** (\*) (1716 N. Cahuenga Blvd., Hollywood). Varied menu, children's portions. Dinner for two: $20.

## SAN FERNANDO VALLEY AREA

**CHURCHILL'S RESTAURANT** (\*\*) (209 N. Glendale Ave., Glendale). A good family restaurant with good, varied menu. Dinner for two: $25.

**THE GREAT SCOTT** (\*\*) (2980 Los Feliz Blvd., Glendale). Varied menu. Dinner for two: $20.

**LA STRADA ITALIAN RESTAURANT** (\*\*) (3000 Los Feliz Blvd., Glendale). Good Italian fare, singing waiters and waitresses, snatches of Italian opera at tableside. Dinner for two: $35.

**THE CASTAWAYS** (\*\*) (1250 Harvard Blvd., Burbank). Polynesian cuisine in restful setting, overlooking beautiful, downtown Burbank. Dinner for two: $30.

**MC GUIRE'S** (\*\*) (8232 De Soto Blvd., Canoga Park). Irish stew is what they call it—corned beef and cabbage. Tends to be noisy, good service, friendly atmosphere. Dinner for two: $25.

**SORRENTINO'S SEAFOOD HOUSE** (\*\*) (4100 Riverside Dr., Burbank). Seafood specialties, American cuisine, varied menu, good service. Dinner for two: $30.

**TOLUCA SMOKE HOUSE** (\*\*) (4420 Lakeside Dr., Burbank). An old-timer in the San Fernando Valley. Chiefly prime ribs. Dinner for two: $30.

**ENCINO SMOKE HOUSE** (\*\*\*) (16830 Ventura Blvd., Encino). Another San Fernando Valley institution. Prime ribs and seafood specialties. Good service, nice atmosphere. Dinner for two: $40.

**SPORTSMEN'S LODGE** (\*\*) (12833 Ventura Blvd., North Hollywood). Varied menu, good food. Dinner for two: $35.

## *Recommended Reading*

LOS ANGELES HANDBOOK ($4.95). Good general guide to restaurants, night life, sight-seeing, hotels.

THE L.A. GOURMET by Jeanne Voltz and Burks Hamner. (Doubleday, $3.95). Actually is a recipe book—but you can pick your favorite dish and choose the restaurant that serves it best.

GUIDE TO RESTAURANTS OF SOUTHERN CALIFORNIA by Paul Wallach. ($6.95). Has over 800 restaurant listings.

# MIAMI

Miami has been called many things—brash, ugly, vulgar, nouveau riche—but never, never dull. Blessed with an overabundance of sun and sand, Miami has been called the "Los Angeles of the East," but natives dismiss the comparison. In spite of tremendous growth in population, sprawling miles of light industry and commercial property, no smog smears the clear blue skies. And while it is very much a city, Miami has remained a tropical resort, and has a suitable pace.

But the town has come a long way since the turn of the century when Henry Flagler brought his railroad to South Florida, built the Royal Palm Hotel (now the site of the Dupont Plaza Hotel), and predicted that Miami "will never be more than a fishing village for my hotel guests."

By 1912 the city had 5,000 residents. Across Biscayne Bay, the present-day Miami Beach was only a sandbar, a breeding place for gnats. The principal attraction was a crocodile pool with a sign advising "caution."

But since 1921, when Carl G. Fisher discovered what could be done with a suction dredge, 396 hotels and over 3,000 apartment houses have been built on this island dredged from Biscayne Bay. With 85,000 permanent residents, Miami Beach is now a city within a city.

While the Beach prospered, the city of Miami itself deteriorated. Crime mounted. Urban decay spread. Big business moved to the suburbs. Fortunately, Fidel Castro changed all that: with the huge influx of energetic Cubans, downtown Miami has been reborn into a Little Havana, a lively colorful area of broad-beamed women and corner coffee shops.

There are about 300,000 Cubans in Miami, and they control more than 8,000 businesses, including a few multimillion-dollar corporations, several banks, a few dozen furniture factories, a score of garment manufacturing firms, more than 250 restaurants, and three out of every five gas stations. Along the main drag of Southwest 8th Street, *Calle Ocho* shopkeepers display "We speak English also" signs.

Not all the rejuvenation is Cuban-inspired, however. There has been a new spurt of office construction. A new financial district is under construction along Brickell Avenue between the downtown section and the Causeway leading to Key Biscayne. Banks, insurance companies, and major listed companies are building glass and steel high-risers fronting on Biscayne Bay. You remember Biscayne Bay, of course. It surrounds Key Biscayne, made famous by a former resident who happened to become President of the United States for a while.

There are plenty of people who come to Miami and never stray more than a few feet from their hotel pool, soaking up as much of a tan as possible before returning to the frozen North. And there are, of course, many retirees who prefer to take things easy. But unlike some Caribbean resorts where there is little else to do except sit on the beach and listen to your skin sizzle, Miami has everything in the way of **active sports.** There are 90 municipal tennis courts and 29 municipal and 13 private golf courses (try to get a member to invite you out to the Jockey Club).

There are free beaches at Haulover, Crandon, and Matheson Hammock Parks, as well as those of many hotels. There is excellent fishing and boating available. A glass-bottom boat trip is practically a must. For a few dollars you can go out on a group snorkeling boat with twice-daily departures. If you prefer setting your own schedule, rent a 50 h.p. 18-ft. skiff for about $30 a half-day. Catamarans are available at most hotels for a modest hourly rate. Also, at quite moderate cost, you can board a "head boat" and fish for mackerel, king, or red snapper. More serious anglers can charter boats.

If you like more sedentary sports, Miami has **horse and dog racing** year-round, and **Jai Alai** during the winter.

A short distance south of the Rickenbacker Causeway leading to Key Biscayne is a world far removed from Middle America—Miami's Coconut Grove. This Bohemian center is best seen by walking or renting a bike. You'll see leather, woodworking, and art shops, European clothing stores, T-shirt shops, and long-haired, blue-jeaned residents who have beaten the system and manage to survive without a nine to five routine.

Most visitors to Miami never get beyond the city, Key Biscayne,

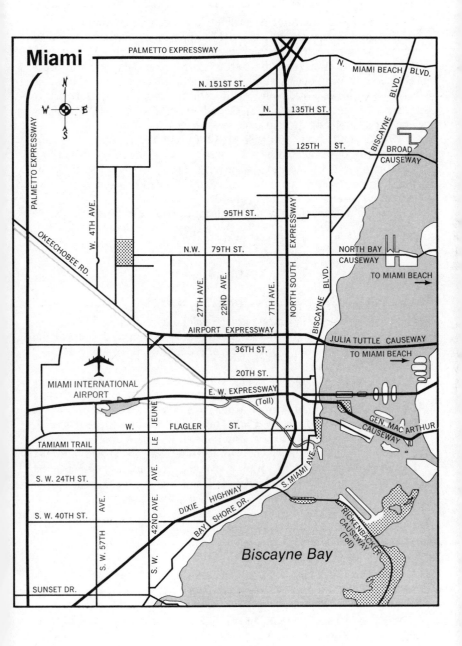

# Miami

N · W · E · S

PALMETTO EXPRESSWAY

PALMETTO EXPRESSWAY

N. MIAMI BEACH BLVD.

N. 151ST ST.

N. 135TH ST.

BISCAYNE BLVD.

125TH ST.

BROAD CAUSEWAY

95TH ST.

N.W. 79TH ST.

OKEECHOBEE RD.

W. 4TH AVE.

27TH AVE.

22ND AVE.

7TH AVE.

NORTH SOUTH EXPRESSWAY

BISCAYNE BLVD.

NORTH BAY CAUSEWAY

TO MIAMI BEACH →

AIRPORT EXPRESSWAY

JULIA TUTTLE CAUSEWAY

TO MIAMI BEACH →

36TH ST.

20TH ST.

E. W. EXPRESSWAY (Toll)

MIAMI INTERNATIONAL AIRPORT

LE JEUNE AVE.

W. FLAGLER ST.

GEN. MAC ARTHUR CAUSEWAY

TAMIAMI TRAIL

S. W. 24TH ST.

57TH AVE.

42ND AVE.

S. W. 40TH ST.

DIXIE HIGHWAY

BAY SHORE DR.

S. MIAMI AVE.

SUNSET DR.

RICKENBACKER CAUSEWAY (Toll)

Biscayne Bay

Coconut Grove, or Miami Beach, but those who do should include
Coral Gables, a charming Spanish-style residential community.

It is pretty easy to get around Miami, and if you drive it makes
sense to rent a car. The highways are good, clearly marked, and
easy to follow. You really have to try to get lost. And, you will probably be venturing out from your hotel often, so your own wheels can
save you a lot of time. Note: Wait until you reach the airport before
you rent a car. The Great Car Rental Price War may still be raging
and it pays to shop around once you arrive.

If you don't drive, you will probably find the city transit system
adequate—supplemented by an occasional cab ride. The system is a
bit complicated because of the physical layout of the city. It is virtually impossible to commute from Key Biscayne to the convention
center on Miami Beach, for example.

Note: The airport is not a long distance from the major hotels. So
if you don't drive yourself, take the airport limousine (bus, that is).

## Hotels

Miami is tourist-oriented and operates by seasons—high and low,
winter and summer. Contrary to the calendar, winter in Miami usually runs from December 15 to April 1 and summer is the rest of the
year—and that's how hotel rates are determined. Winter rates of
many hotels are sky-high.

Location is, of course, a key consideration when selecting your
hotel. But if you don't have to bed down on the strip along Collins
Avenue, the **Coconut Grove Hotel,** the **David Williams** in Coral
Gables, the **Doral Country Club Hotel,** the **Key Biscayne Hotel &
Villas,** and the **Sonesta Beach Hotel** are all excellent choices.

Along Collins Avenue, the **Doral Hotel on the Ocean** and the
**Flamingo Club Hotel** are well above the competition. Other good
choices are the **Carillon Hotel,** the **Deauville,** or the **Miami Beach
Hyatt** (formerly the **Playboy Club**). The **Americana,** up in Bal Harbour, is the best convention hotel in town.

Alas, the once-famed **Eden Roc** and the **Fontainebleau** just ain't
what they used to be.

## Restaurants

For a resort area, Miami has more-varied and higher-quality cuisine than one would expect—probably because of the high percent-

age of New Yorkers who winter here, and who expect the same kind of food and service they get in Gotham. Prices are not bad—by New York or Chicago standards. Dinner for two, including wine, can usually be had for about $30.

If you like French food, the best restaurant in the city is the **Café Chauveron,** a direct import from New York. It serves haute cuisine in the classic manner. **Voisin** likewise will more than satisfy the Francophile. **Chez Vendôme** is another excellent French restaurant, if a bit gaudy.

You shouldn't pass up Cuban food, and the best place for it is **Centro Vasco,** which is practically a local institution. Another old favorite for ribs and barbecued chicken is the **Embers.**

**Hugo's,** in the Miami Beach Hyatt House, is the current darling of the Beautiful People. **Horatio's** is the place for that seafood dinner.

## Potpourri

Night life is plentiful around Miami. And the place to start is the hotels. Many feature star performers. The **Fontainebleau,** although a slightly faded lady in the hotel category, still heads the list, with headliners like Paul Anka, Ann-Margret, and the Fifth Dimension. The dinner and beverage policy for these shows has been dropped —you now pay a per-person cover charge. The Fontainebleau also has entertainment in the Boom Boom Room and in the elegant Club Gigi, which also has dance music.

The **Deauville Hotel,** meanwhile, offers legitimate theater. Up the road at the **Diplomat Hotel,** the Café Cristel features the likes of Dionne Warwick, Liza Minnelli, and Mac Davis during the winter season. The **Americana** in the Bal Harbour section features a French-style, semi-nude review staged by Barry Ashton.

The action at the hotels slows off-season (April–December) but lounges along Motel Row have some very funny, if somewhat raunchy, comics.

One of the better earthy shows in town is at Harry Ridge's **Place Pigalle** in lower Miami Beach. Pearl Williams makes sailors blush.

There are also a number of private nightclubs, many of which are centered away from the Beach. They charge about $10 to $50 annual membership—worth it if you spend more than a few days here. Clientele is late twenties to early fifties. Best include the **Mutiny** and **My Other Place.**

Two other private clubs, the **Jockey** and the **Palm Bay** (both off Biscayne Boulevard and fronting on the Bay) attract singles at the bars and have hotel accommodations for members (or members' guests).

Of course, if you seek gamier activity, Miami has that, too, although periodic police roundups in the area around 163rd and Collins Avenue (Motel Row) slow the skin trade for a few nights. Higher-priced hookers work the bars at the larger hotels in the forties on Collins Avenue.

The city has its more cultural side, too. There is a vigorous local opera association that annually imports some of the world's best operatic talent. The **Greater Miami Philharmonic** was recognized internationally as one of the up-and-coming symphonies in the world until it lost its angel, Maurice Gusman, and French conductor Alain Lombard resigned.

For theater, there's the **Coconut Grove Playhouse,** which hosts road shows. The **Museum of Science and Natural History** is definitely worth a visit—it is one of the best in the country.

Miami is, of course, a **football** town. Loyalty to the Dolphins borders on mania. Dolphin shirts, Dolphin shields, Dolphin memorabilia are everywhere. Even the city's transit system has the same color scheme as the Dolphins.

## *Nitty Gritty*

## HOTELS

*Superior*

**COCONUT GROVE** (2649 S. Bayshore Dr.). On Sailboat Bay. Definitely in with the younger crowd. Beautifully decorated new property with complete resort facilities. Service still needs improvement.

**DAVID WILLIAMS** (700 Biltmore Way, Coral Gables). The elite's elite. Beautiful rooms. Good, unobtrusive service. Patronized by wealthier younger natives.

**DORAL COUNTRY CLUB** (4400 N.W. 87th Ave.). Near the airport and expressways leading to every sector of town. Ideal for golfers with its 18-hole championship course and a par-three for a round after an appointment in town. Excellent service, dining room, nightclub, and bar. Doubles only. Expensive.

**DORAL ON THE OCEAN** (4833 Collins Ave.). Best of the "millionaire" hotels. Highest occupancy rate on the strip, year-round. Fine ocean beach, excellent service, rooftop dining room.

**FLAMINGO CLUB** (58th and Collins Ave.). Probably one of

the best-kept secrets in town. Formerly an annex to the private Bath Club, now open to the public. Beautifully decorated suites and rooms, tennis courts, marina, private beach. Excellent service, convenient location. Double rates only, high in winter.

**KEY BISCAYNE HOTEL & VILLAS** (701 Ocean Dr., Key Biscayne). Hard to get to because of traffic over the Causeway. Strictly resort property, quiet, well appointed. Patronized by the over-forty crowd during the winter season. Housekeeping apartments available. Winter rates are high.

**SHERATON FOUR AMBASSADORS** (801 S. Bayshore Dr.). Combines the best of a commercial and a resort hotel. Convenient location. Fronts on a wide expanse of Biscayne Bay. All rooms are suites because the property was originally designed as an apartment-hotel. Excellent dining rooms and bars.

**SONESTA BEACH** (350 Ocean Dr., Key Biscayne). Super for vacationers but seven traffic-filled miles out of town. Caters to families and small convention groups. Private beach, pool, good dining facilities. Expensive.

*Good*

**AMERICANA** (Bal Harbour). Caters to convention crowds, so check-in-or-out can take an hour. Neiman-Marcus is across the street. Fairly expensive.

**CARILLON** (6801 Collins Ave.). Not quite as spiffy as it was fifteen years ago, but still in good shape. Right on the ocean. Service has slipped a bit. Caters to Midwest repeat crowd which complains, but keeps coming back. Expensive.

**DEAUVILLE** (6701 Collins Ave.). Problems with service. Caters to seniors. Winter rates are high.

**DUPONT PLAZA** (300 Biscayne Blvd. Way). On the Miami River overlooking Biscayne Bay. Large groups may delay check-in, but service and amenities have been maintained. One of the better downtown hotels with good dining room, busy bar. Swimming pool and garage on premises.

**MARRIOTT** (1201 N.W. LeJeune Rd.). A five-minute ride from the airport. Pool, tennis, swinging bar, self-parking, two restaurants with the rooftop open 24 hours.

**MIAMI BEACH HYATT** (5445 Collins Ave.). Formerly the Playboy Club Hotel, and before that the Hilton. Not cheap, but a beautiful property on the ocean. Lobby bar attracts younger crowd. Service is fair to better than it used to be. Rooms are exceptionally spacious and well decorated.

**MIAMI SPRINGS VILLAS** (500 Deer Run). Two miles from the airport. Accommodations range from standard hotel rooms to motor inn rooms to two- and three-bedroom villas with kitchens and hotel service. Popular with airline stewardesses and crews. Good food and service. All-year rates which are moderate for Miami.

**NEW EVERGLADES** (Biscayne Blvd. at N.E. 3rd St.). Handy to downtown. Good service. Decor has been upgraded. Bar is popular, coffee shop open from 6:00 A.M. to 2:00 A.M. Heated rooftop swimming pool. Moderate rates.

*Acceptable*

**ALGIERS** (2555 Collins Ave.). Once a beautiful property. Needs a face-lift badly. Food and service seem to need the same kind of help.

**BISCAYNE TERRACE** (340 Biscayne Blvd.). Well located for the man who wants to walk to an appointment downtown. One of the older hotels, it is filled with Latin travelers and service improves if you speak Spanish. Busy, commercial, inexpensive.

**COLUMBUS** (Biscayne Blvd. and Flagler St.). Commercial, impersonal. Popular with Latin businessmen and families. Cocktail lounge attracts business crowd. Service sometimes sloppy. Rates moderate year-round.

**DI LIDO** (on beach at Lincoln Rd.). One of the old-timers that keeps its following in spite of a minimum of upkeep. On the ocean.

**EDEN ROC** (4525 Collins Ave.). Has changed hands three times in as many years and it shows. Last owner put a quarter of a million dollar chandelier in the lobby, but apparently ran out of money before he redecorated the rooms. Service is poor and Harry's, a long-time favorite bar, has gone gay.

**FONTAINEBLEAU** (4441 Collins Ave.). Still doesn't have a sign outside, but the 1,275-room structure is hard to miss. Once the top hotel in the U.S. Huge sums have been spent on the lobby but towels are threadbare. Carpeting in the older wing needs to be replaced. Service is poor and the old gal just ain't what she used to be.

**VAGABOND MOTEL** (7301 Biscayne Blvd.). Located in a high-crime area, it has made a few headlines through no fault of the management. Well appointed, busy bar. Doubles only.

# RESTAURANTS

**ASTI'S** (**) (468 Arthur Godfrey Rd.). A five-minute taxi ride from the Fontainebleau. Seafood with an Italian accent. Loaded with kitsch—a splashing waterwheel, stone walls, and wine casks—but food is above-average. Dinner for two: approximately $30.

**BERNARD'S RESTAURANT** (**) (In the Carriage House at 54th and Collins Ave.). Quality has slipped since Mr. Bernard and his chef departed. Patronized by locals. Service is good, but not up to opening rave notices. Luncheon favorite for ladies. Dinner for two: $50.

**THE BETSY** (**) (Flamingo Club Hotel, 58th and Collins Ave.). Whimsical decor, changed with the seasons; unfortunately, the menu isn't. Lots of chatter during lunch. Piano music softens the dinner crowd. Still a favorite dining spot of the Miami carriage trade who adore the crisp Armenian bread, *lahvash,* and the strawberry or coffee ice cream cakes. Dinner for two: $50.

**BILBAO** (*) (5910 S.W. 8th St.). Popular lunch and dinner meeting spot of Cubans. Americans are more impressed with the Basque decor and waiters garbed in traditional jai alai outfits than they are with the spicy foods. Dinner for two: $25.

**CAFÉ CHAUVERON** (***) (Bay Harbour Island). Overlooks Indian Creek. One of the last bastions of great dining. Run by father-and-son team of Roger and Andrew Chauveron of New York. Food is classic French and service is for patrons who enjoy being pampered. Expensive, but excellent. Dinner for two: $65.

**CASA SANTINO** (**) (110th St. and Biscayne Blvd.). Italian. Overpriced, even if you get to dine in one of the private "caves" off the wine cellar. Lots of statuary, crystal, and pasta. Dinner for two: $70.

**CENTRO VASCO** (***) (2235 S.W. 8th St.). In the heart of the Cuban section. Moved from Havana to Miami without suffering any transplant shock. Same owners, same menu, and many of the same clients from pre-Castro days. Superb Basque food. Dinner for two: $30.

**CHEZ VENDOME** (***) (700 Biltmore Way). Miami's answer to Maxim's. Excellent service and French food with red velvet walls and lots of crystal. Overpriced, but  . . . Dinner for two: $85.

**CYE'S RIVERGATE** (***) (444 Brickell Ave.). Where the action is. Great food and service. Broad, leafy verandas overlook the Miami River. Butcher-block bar curves around the room, bedecked with curvy singles. A la carte, expensive. Rock-pop-jazz groups. Dinner for two: $80.

**EL CAPITAN** (**) (490 Alton Rd.). Down at the south end of Miami Beach. Large glass walls overlook Biscayne Bay and the fishing fleet. Seafood, Mexican-style. Try the crab enchilada. Checkered tablecloths, simple service. Dinner for two: $20.

**EMBERS** (***) (245 22nd St.). A Miami Beach institution for more than twenty-five years. Ribs and chicken are barbecued before you. Hangout for Miami politicians. Fair service but the food is always good. Dinner for two: $20.

**THE FAMOUS** (**) (671 Washington Ave.) You don't have to

be Jewish to enjoy gefilte fish, kreplach, blintzes, and, of course, homemade chicken soup. But it helps if you speak a little Yiddish. Dinner for two: $20.

**THE FORGE** (***) (Arthur Godfrey Rd.). Beautifully decorated. Bar attracts swingles into the wee hours. Quality food, extensive wine cellar, service almost too fast. Dinner for two: $45.

**GAUCHO STEAK HOUSE** (***) (Americana Hotel). The Place for steak. Service with baked potatoes, crisp salad, and talkative waiters. Dinner for two: $50.

**HUGO'S** (***) (Miami Beach Hyatt House). Newest haunt for the Rolls-Royce crowd. Reservations sometimes two weeks in advance. Excellent service, nice decor. Strolling violinists. Candlelight. Wine corners for two. Dinner for two: $60.

**HORATIO'S** (***) (Coconut Grove Hotel). One of the better nautical-type restaurants. Twentieth floor view of Sailboat Bay. Mood is French. Excellent service, and quality food. Young wealthy crowd. Dinner for two: $55.

**INSIDE** (**) (1009 Kane Concourse, Bay Harbour Island). New owner has kept the French bistro flavor. Popular for lunch. Dinner for two: $18.

**JAMAICA INN** (**) (320 Crandon Blvd. on Key Biscayne). "Veddy" British. Lots of foliage and good service. Food could be better. Dinner for two: $25.

**JAPANESE STEAK HOUSE** (***) (Miami Springs Villas). Succulent steaks cooked to order by Kimono-clad Japanese girls while you're sitting on the floor. Great drinks. Dinner for two: $45.

**JOE'S STONE CRAB** (**) (227 Biscayne St.). Established before Miami Beach became a city in 1913, and still under the same ownership. Excellent stone crabs and other seafood. Impersonal service unless you happen to know Jessie Weiss, whose father opened the restaurant. Dinner for two: $40.

**LES VIOLINS** (*) (1751 Biscayne Blvd.). A favorite with Miami Latins but Americans find it noisy, crowded, and overplayed by waiters who double as entertainers. They sing when you want your coffee. Dinner for two: $50.

**MARCELLA'S** (**) (13866 W. Dixie Highway). Set aside three hours for the prix fixe dinner ($12.50). Nine courses with no choices, which depend on the chef's mood. No menu. An experience in Italian showmanship. Dinner for two: $35.

**NEWPORT PUB** (*) (167th St. and Collins Ave.). One step above a quick-service restaurant. Food is plentiful, service without frills. Dinner for two: $20.

**OMAR'S TENT** (**) (Arthur Godfrey Rd.). Typically Lebanese. Incense burners, Oriental carpets, and superb pita and feta cheese.

Well patronized by Israeli residents. Service is very Arab, which means slow. Dinner for two: $18.

**THE RONEY PUB** (**) (23rd St. and Collins Ave.). For people who don't mind standing in line for more food on their plates than they can eat. Service is in keeping with mass feeding. Most people leave with a doggy bag. Good value. Dinner for two: $20.

**RUSTY PELICAN** (*) (entrance of causeway to Key Biscayne). Beautiful view of Miami, but has gone downhill since a local TV station did an exposé on kitchen cleanliness. Lively crowd still hangs out around the bar. Dinner for two: $35.

**STUDIO** (*) (2340 S.W. 32nd Ave., Coral Gables). Has changed hands and is not up to its former reputation. Interesting grill work, splashy paintings, but service and food quality leave much to be desired. Dinner for two: $25.

**TONY'S FISH MARKET** (*) (79th St., Causeway). Lowered the level of service and quality since opening a cafeteria in the rear. Lost a lot in recent years. Dinner for two: $20.

**VOISIN** (***) (5151 Collins Ave.). What the rich folks like. Decor is Miami Beach-baroque. Dignified service. Food well prepared. Drinks are generous. Dinner for two: $45.


### *Recommended Reading*

FLORIDA CLOSE-UP by Harris H. Mullen. (Trend House, $4.95). Some keen insights and novel views of the people of the Sunshine State.

FLORIDA GOLD COAST GUIDE TO GREATER MIAMI ($1). A good, cheap guide to the city and environs. Pick one up at the airport.

FLORIDA RESTAURANTS—GOLD COAST EDITION by Robert Tolf. (Trend House, $1.95). Better than your average dining guide.

YESTERDAY'S MIAMI by Nixon Smiley. (E. Seamann, $10). Part of the Cities Series.

# MONTREAL

Montreal, Canada's premier city, is so French it doesn't seem to belong in North America. In fact, Montreal has more French-speaking citizens than any other city in the world except Paris. About two-thirds of the city's population of 2.5 million are French-Canadian.

But it is fortunate indeed for North America that Montreal is where it is. This Continental jewel has more élan and joie de vivre than most cities on the Continent, and is unique in North America. A visit there for business or pleasure is bound to be memorable.

It will pay to brush up on your French before visiting the city, and even halting Franglais will be appreciated by Montrealers. But you will get along fine if you speak only English. Some 70% of the French-Canadians know English as well as French, and feelings toward Americans—if not "Anglos" (English Canadians)—are probably warmer than anywhere else in Canada.

Located at the juncture of the Saint Lawrence and Ottawa rivers, Montreal is an island city, built around a mountain. And it is two-tiered. The lower level takes in all of "Le Vieux Montréal," as well as the financial district and court houses, shipping, and city government buildings. A short steep grade separates the lower from the upper—or Sherbrooke Street—level. These two levels, with jutting Mount Royal as a background, give Montreal a spectacular skyline.

Montreal is, of course, an old city by North American standards, and to truly appreciate the city, you should know some of its colorful history.

The young, adventuresome sailor Jacques Cartier was the first white man to set eyes on what is now Montreal, in the year 1535. What he found was a pleasant "island of trees" dominated by a regal outcropping of rock, which he dubbed Mont Réal (Mount Royal). Nestled at its foot, near today's McGill University, was the stockaded Indian village of Hochelaga.

Samuel de Champlain, founder of Quebec City, sailed upriver in 1611, but found no trace of the Hochelaga village. He set up a fur trading post he called Place Royale.

It remained for Paul de Chomedey, sieur de Maisonneuve, in 1642 to found the first permanent settlement. His mission: to Christianize the Indians of New France. Known first as Ville-Marie de Montréal, it was incorporated as the city of Montreal in 1833.

For more than a century, the growth of the city revolved around the spot where Maisonneuve had landed, the area known today as "Le Vieux Montréal," or Old Montreal.

Iroquois hostility ran high, and for the first half-century there were frequent skirmishes and an occasional massacre. The French and Iroquois finally made peace in 1701.

But as trouble with the Indians cooled down, it flared up with the British. Finally, in 1759, General James Wolfe led the British in the successful capture of Quebec City. The capital of New France moved to Montreal, until it, too, capitulated the following year, thus bringing an end to French rule in North America.

Fifteen years later the emerging Americans gave it a try. Ethan Allen and his Green Mountain Boys were captured trying to win over Montreal to the side of the rebelling colonies. But later that year General Richard Montgomery led an American army into Montreal —and took it without firing a shot. The city remained under American control for seven months. The Americans fled after their defeat trying to take Quebec City. In both cases, the Yanks had counted too heavily on being able to get French-Canadians to side with them against King George III.

Still aiming at the British, the Yankees again tried invading Canada during the War of 1812, again unsuccessfully.

Seventeenth-century Montreal was a base for missionaries, traders, and New World explorers. Among the most famous of the latter: Cavelier de la Salle, of Chicago fame; Greysolon du Luth, who ranged as far as Lake Superior and gave his name to the Minnesota city on its shore; de la Mothe Cadillac, founder of Detroit, and the le Moyne brothers, two of whom founded New Orleans and Louisiana.

Throughout the eighteenth century, the city's economic life was dominated by the fur trade, which was taken over and reshaped by the British after 1760. Instead of the Indians bringing their skins to Montreal, the traders began sending out their own "coureurs de bois" and "voyageurs" to scour the wilderness. Competition was deadly, so in 1784, to unite their efforts, several canny Scotsmen organized the North-West Fur Company, which was the kingpin of Montreal's commercial life for almost half a century. Its intrepid trappers left their mark throughout Northern Canada, completing the explorations

of their French predecessors. They certainly earned the raucous res-
pite they enjoyed at the high-spirited celebrations they held as members of Montreal's renowned Beaver Club.

The supremacy of fur, however, did not last long. In 1821, after
years of severe competition, the North-West Fur Company was taken
over by its older rival, the London-based Hudson's Bay Company.
With posts close to shipping points on James Bay, the trappers no
longer needed to make the long overland haul to Montreal.

Montreal, meanwhile, had developed as a major port—the gateway
for both people and goods headed for "Upper Canada," Ontario (up
the St. Lawrence, even though down on the map). This traffic picked
up heavily following the American Revolution, as fleeing loyalists
moved to the still-English colonies to the north.

The port, today Canada's second busiest, brought with it other
industry. Montreal today is a transportation and financial center.
Petrochemicals are the biggest industry in dollar volume, textiles and
the garment industry the biggest employer. Five of the country's
ten chartered banks are headquartered in Montreal, as well as several
large insurance companies, the two transcontinental railroads, the
biggest airline, and the largest communications companies.

If you fly into the city, you'll arrive at Dorval International Airport,
13 miles from downtown. Limousines to the major hotels ply the
route frequently, and cabs are plentiful. When you depart, remember
to leave an extra 15 minutes or so to pre-clear U.S. customs and pay
a call at the duty-free shop.

Getting around the city is easy, even in bad winter weather. Taxi
stands are conveniently scattered around the city, and the Montreal
Metro runs north-south along Boulevard St.-Denis, east-west on
Boulevard de Maisonneuve.

The financial district, in the lower old town, is within walking
distance of centrally located Place Ville Marie.


## Hotels


For all its other charms, Montreal is painfully shy of good hotels.
Until the 4,000 rooms being built in preparation for the Olympics
become available in early 1976, the situation will remain tight. With
both convention and tourism booming, you'd better reserve a room
well in advance.

The best hotel in town is the **Bonaventure,** atop Place Bonaventure,

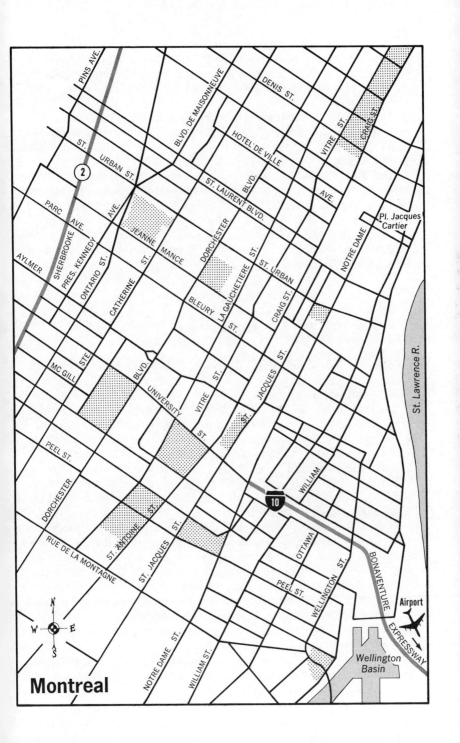

Montreal

a shopping and business arcade. Every room looks out on the interior gardens, in the old Continental manner, but there are touches of modern comfort, too—such as a heated pool that stays open in the winter.

The **Château Champlain** is also a good choice. Local wags refer to it as "the big cheese grater" because of its architectural style—but there is nothing cheesy about the service in this fine Canadian Pacific Hotel.

The **Ritz Carlton** is another good alternate. This dignified, conservative hostelry has managed gracefully to live down the infamy of being the spot where Liz and Dick Burton tied the knot some years ago.

But beyond these few hotels, it's strictly accommodations you'll get, with the possible exception of the **Queen Elizabeth,** as long as it isn't handling a convention.

## *Restaurants*

This is what Montreal is all about to many visitors. If you like Continental cooking, you'll have a lot of trouble leaving this city. Some gourmets insist it has the best restaurants in North America.

Indeed, Montreal has some 5,000 restaurants—most of them good—that cater more to locals than visitors. French-Canadians, unlike English-Canadians, dine out often, and their discerning palates dictate outstanding cuisine at reasonable prices. They get it, too. French-Canadian and fine French cuisine you'd expect, but in Montreal you'll also find superior Italian, Japanese, Portuguese, Russian, Indian, Austrian, Greek, Pakistani, Spanish, Mexican, Chinese, Dutch—even Vietnamese.

French-Canadian cuisine is not simply French food in Canada. In fact, it is something altogether different. Its roots are in French bourgeois cooking, but French-Canadians lay a robust table piled high with dishes made from the ingredients available to the early settlers. Typical French-Canadian dishes include tourtière (meat pie), ham cooked in maple syrup, thick rich split pea soup, pig's feet, and desserts made with maple sugar or syrup. Though it's not as delicate as *haute cuisine française,* a hearty French-Canadian meal can be just as much of a gastronomic adventure.

The most popular dinner hour in Montreal is 8:00 P.M., but most restaurants start serving at 6:00, and continue until quite late. A smattering are closed Sundays.

## *Potpourri*

After five, Montrealers who don't scurry on home love dearly to relax over a drink. The liveliest area of town is up and down Crescent, Mountain, and Stanley streets, between St. Catherine and Maisonneuve. **George's** (2045 Crescent) and **Dominique's** (1455 Stanley) are popular with the credit-card set. **The Boiler Room** in the **Sir Winston Churchill Pub** (1455 Crescent) is friendly, as is the **Friar's Pub** down the block at 1445 Crescent. **La Sexe Machine** (1469), with its Clockwork Orange Milk Bar decor, has gotten très expensive, but is still fashionable. **Casa Pedro** (1471 Crescent) and **Chez Bourgetel** (1458 Mountain St.) are more conventional gathering places.

On Fridays, **Le Carrefour** in Place Ville Marie is, in the words of a recent visitor, "the biggest marketplace I've ever seen." **Alti-thèque 727** bills itself as the "jet-set disco in the sky." Take the high-speed elevator from the ground floor.

**The Golden Hind** in the Queen Elizabeth packs in the homebound crowd before they take the train from Central Station, below the hotel.

In Le Vieux Montréal, **Le Baldaquin** (424 St. Paul East) is very chichi. **Marquis de Sade** (36 St. Paul East) is all done up like the Marquis's original French château. In the same area, **Le Cercle** is lively, too. Most of these places are restaurants and/or discotheques as well as early evening meeting places.

There is a **Playboy Club,** at 2015-A Mountain Street, but it never really caught on.

The poshest nightclubs in town are **Le Caf'Conc'** at the Château Champlain and the **Ritz Café** at the Ritz Carlton. The **Salle Bonaventure** at the Queen Elizabeth attracts a mildly swishy set. The **Portage Lounge** at the Hotel Bonaventure is a more conventional cabaret.

There are scores of little clubs, many with live entertainment and/or dancing, again in the Crescent-Drummond-Mountain-Stanley area, or in Old Montreal.

On the cultural side, Montreal's showcase for the performing arts is **Place des Arts.** Home of the Montreal Symphony Orchestra, the **Salle Wilfred-Pelletier** also draws big-name performers and attractions like the National Ballet of Canada. **Maisonneuve** and **Port-Royal** theaters are also part of the Arts complex.

As international as it may be, Montreal is still in Canada—and in

Canada the national passion is **hockey.** The NHL Canadiens play at the Forum, but getting a ticket without connections is impossible. Note: The mayhem on the ice definitely does not infect the spectators, as sometimes happens in other cities. You applaud politely at the Forum, and are not even permitted to smoke in your seat.

Other home teams are easier to get to see: the Canadian **Football** League Montreal Alouettes at the Autostade, or **baseball's** Montreal Expos at Jarry Park. It's strange to hear America's national pastime being called in French.

An evening of **harness or thoroughbred racing** at Blue Bonnet raceway can be most pleasant. Richelieu Park, with thoroughbred racing in season, is a smaller version at the eastern tip of the island.

No matter how short your stay, weather permitting, take an hour's walking tour of Old Montreal. Pick up a map, and start at Place d'Armes, the site of the first encounter between the founders of Ville-Marie and the Iroquois. Nearby are the **Bank of Montreal Museum;** the **Bonsecours Market; Château de Ramezay,** a historical museum; **Jacques-Cartier Square**, a popular gathering place for young French Canadians on summer evenings; **Notre Dame Church,** mother church of Montreal; **Notre Dame de Bonsecours** church, better known as the Sailors' Church, with its superb view of the harbor.

Out of Le Vieux Montréal, other worthwhile sights include:

**Man and his World** (Île Ste.-Hélène). Son of Expo '67. The 300-acre island that hosted the '67 Fair is now a permanent international cultural and entertainment center with some two dozen pavilions open each summer from mid-June through Labor Day. It also contains the La Ronde amusement area.

**Dominion Square** (St. Catherine & Peel sts.). A lovely central square surrounded by old landmarks. You can get a horse-drawn carriage here for a tour of the city.

**McGill University.** Montreal's top English-language university is in the center of town, beneath the southern slope of Mount Royal.

**Montreal Museum of Fine Arts** (Sherbrooke & Crescent sts.). Founded in 1860, Canada's oldest art institution, it has a good but small collection of modern art, and some interesting Canadiana.

**Mont-Royal Park.** In a city with almost 10% of the total area given over to parks—one of the few things on which the French and English have always agreed—Mont-Royal Park is the largest. Walking up is good for a few months' worth of exercise. The little train (free) runs up and back frequently. Model boats and ducks ply artificial Beaver Lake, the setting for open-air concerts in summer. In winter there are facilities for skating and skiing. If nothing else, go up just to look around. There's a restaurant at the top.

**Old Fort** (Île Ste.-Hélène). Dating from 1822, the Fort today houses the Military and Maritime Museum. Two eighteenth-century military companies recreate battles—down to the bayonet charges, cannon and musket firings, and highland music—daily, May through October.

**Place Ville Marie** (Dorchester Blvd. & University St.). A striking cruciform building rising from a plaza three times larger than Rockefeller Center Promenade; houses sixty stores, five restaurants, two movie theaters. It's a landmark in urban planning.

## Nitty Gritty

## HOTELS

*Superior*

**BONAVENTURE** (Place Bonaventure). Luxurious rooms, all facing interior gardens. Heated outdoor pool.

**LE CHATEAU CHAMPLAIN** (Place du Canada). One of Canadian Pacific's finest hotels. Grand views and excellent restaurants. Superior service.

**RITZ CARLTON** (1228 Sherbrooke St. W.). Elegant Continental hotel. Black marbled formal lobby a bit haughty. Excellent restaurants.

*Good*

**MONTREAL AEROPORT HILTON** (12,505 Côte de Liesse Rd., Dorval). Sprawling but homey, has a pool. Long walks to rooms, but it's quiet. Good food.

**BERKELEY** (1188 Sherbrooke St. W.). Good location. Plenty of zip for an old hotel.

**LAURENTIEN** (1130 Peel St.). Aging, not quite gracefully. Good family hotel with moderate rates.

**QUEEN ELIZABETH** (900 Dorchester Blvd. W.). Excellent location, across from Place Ville-Marie. Bustling convention hotel. Popular with Quebec politicians.

**SHERATON-MONT-ROYAL** (1455 Peel St.). A bit tattered, but still trying hard. Good service, excellent location.

**WINDSOR** (1170 Peel St.). Old but serviceable. Where Mayor Jean Drapeau's restaurant flopped.

*Adequate*

**CONSTELLATION** (3407 Peel St.). Until recently the Sonesta.

**DE LA SALLE** (1240 Drummond St.). Serviceable.

**HOLIDAY INN, DOWNTOWN** (420 Sherbrooke St. W.). Strictly the lodgings of last resort.
**HOLIDAY INN, CHATEAUBRIAND** (6500 Côte de Liesse Rd., Dorval). Airport vicinity.
**QUALITY INN MONTREAL** (410 Sherbrooke St. W.). Qualified quality. Good location.
**SEAWAY MOTOR INN** (1155 Guy St.). Often a room when no one else has one.
**SKYLINE** (6600 Côte de Liesse Rd., Dorval). Competent airport hotel.

# RESTAURANTS

**A L'AMPHITRYON** (*) (364 Notre Dame St. E.). Small, simply decorated cellar rooms in Old Montreal. Warm, cozy, crowded. French and Belgian cuisine. Beef dishes best. Try the caramelized apple crêpes. Dinner for two with drink and half-bottle of wine: $35.
**AU VIEUX FORT** (**) (120 Chemin St. Jean, La Prairie). Restored 300-year-old country building. Excellent French-Canadian fare, including tourtière, baked beans with maple syrup, pig's feet, pea soup. Dinner for two: $25.
**BEAVER CLUB** (**) (Queen Elizabeth Hotel). Favorite lunch spot of transportation executives. Unhotel-like restaurant decked out in trappings of the fur trade. Pool-size martinis. Service unobtrusive, expert. Example: a pencil and small pad on every table. Roast rack of lamb Provençale is a particular specialty. Pastry cart. Feel free to take more than one; the waiter will probably encourage it anyway. Lunch for two: $35.
**BURGUNDY ROOM** (*) (Constellation Hotel). Specialty is beef. Ask for the unlisted lemon parfait for dessert. Lots of champagnes on the wine list. Dinner for two: $35.
**LE CAFE DE PARIS** (***) (Ritz Carlton Hotel). Excellent dining in Continental style. Service leisurely though expert. Extensive wine list, many vintages imported directly from the George V in Paris. Try the Filets de Sole à la Ritz (stuffed with mushrooms, in white wine sauce, topped with caviar), a sample of the award-winning chef's capabilities. Dinner for two: $45.
**CAFE MARTIN** (**) (2175 Mountain St.). Graceful nineteenth-century townhouse split into three dining rooms. Downstairs most intimate. Classic French cuisine. Veal and poultry best. Dinner for two: $35.
**CASTEL DU ROY** (**) (3070 Drummond St.). Old brownstone. Main floor dining room; Colony Bar downstairs has cozier atmo-

sphere. Special gourmet dinners Thursday through Sunday. Excellent house wine. Dinner for two: $25.

**LE CASTILLON** (***) (Hotel Bonaventure). Heavily ornamented room atop Place Bonaventure, overlooking the terrace, streams, and fountains of the hotel's garden. Extensive menu, well handled. Attentive service, strong on showmanship—like the oyster-stuffed steak flambéed in whiskey. Piano and violin. Dinner for two: $45.

**LE CAVEAU** (*) (2063 Victoria St.). Cozy, ideal for tête-à-tête. Once a favorite of McGill students. Fine Filet Mignon Grand Veneur —in venison sauce with cream of chestnuts. Dinner for two: $25.

**LE CHASSEUR** (**) (Berkeley Hotel). Dark, walnut-paneled room serves fine Austrian food. Game dishes a specialty. For dessert, try the pancake stuffed with chestnuts, jam, and sour cream. Dinner for two: $30.

**CHEZ BARDET** (***) (591 Henri Bourassa E.). Hidden away in an undistinguished building at the north end of the Metro line. Serves some of the very best French cuisine in Canada. One of the best wine cellars in the country. His best known specialty: escalope de veau à la crème aux morilles. For an appetizer try the snails à la mode de Saulieu, and for dessert the Chantilly or Grand Marnier soufflé. Service is polished. Dinner for two: $45.

**CHEZ FANNY** (**) (1729 St. Hubert St.). Rustic dining room right out of a Mediterranean village, complete with pétanque court. Provençale cooking. Strolling accordionist. Dinner for two: $30.

**CHEZ LA MERE MICHEL** (***) (1209 Guy St.). Rustic French atmosphere. Limited but excellent menu. "Ce soir" dishes best choice, or try the coq au vin à la Dijonnaise. Homemade apricot pie can't be topped. Attentive service. Good burgundy cuvée reserve de patron. Dinner for two: $35.

**CHEZ PAUZE** (**) (1657 Ste.-Catherine St. W.). Montreal's oldest seafood house. Always hectic, always good. Chowders are excellent. Dinner for two: $35.

**CHEZ PIERRE** (**) (1263 Labelle St.). The food's the thing here. Try the canard à la Diane, duck soaked for days in venison marinade, flambéed in Calvados at your table, and served with apples cooked in butter. Dinner for two: $25.

**CUCKOO NATURE FOODS RESTAURANT** (*) (2055 Bishop St.). Pleasant change of pace. Vegetarian, part of a natural foods store. Uses only fresh produce. Unlicensed. No credit cards. Self service. Dinner for two: $10.

**EL MATADOR** (*) (1933 Ste.-Catherine St. W). Fine dark-timbered Spanish restaurant. Great roast suckling pig. Also superb: the mussels à la marinière. Have the house cake for dessert. Dinner for two: $30.

**L'ESCAPADE** (\*) (Le Château Champlain). Extensive buffet for lunch or dinner, with small à la carte menu evenings. Sensational views. On a clear day you can see the Adirondacks or the Green Mountains of Vermont. Dancing. Dinner for two: $45.

**L'ESCARGOT** (\*) (Pl. Ville-Marie). Regular menu unexciting. Select one of fourteen snail dishes. Bistro atmosphere, with outdoor tables in summer. Lunch for two: $25.

**LE FADO** (\*\*) (423 St. Claude St.). Haute cuisine in well-preserved seventeenth-century building in Old Montreal. Superb rack of lamb, with all nine bouquetière vegetables. Helpful host. Excellent wine list. Dinner for two: $45.

**LA FENICE** (\*) (6877 St. Hubert St.). Italian, three-roomed affair with singing guitarist. Owner-chef Luigi de Zorzi on hand. Try his fettucini du chef, with tomatoes, mushrooms, prosciutto, parmesan, and cream. Dinner for two: $30.

**LE FESTIN DU GOUVERNEUR** (\*) (Old Fort, Île Ste.-Hélène). Authentic French-Canadian feast in seventeenth-century setting. Platters of food, flagons of wine, cornball entertainment. Touristy, good for families. Dinner: $15 a head.

**LES FILLES DU ROI** (\*\*) (415 St. Paul St. E.). One of the oldest houses in Old Montreal. Solid French-Canadian cuisine: tourtière, ham in maple syrup. Try the trempette for dessert: fried maple-soaked bread in cream. Service not always spry. Dinner for two: $30.

**GIBBY'S** (\*\*) (298 Pl. d'Youville). Comfortable steak house in restored stables on historic Youville Square in the old city. Scampi also good. Small wine list. Pleasant service. Dinner for two: $25.

**GUINGETTE LES TROIS** (\*\*) (273 St. Paul St. E.). Well restored, sophisticated. Stone walls and pinewood floor. Stick to the simpler dishes. Quail a house specialty. Wine list small but good. Dinner for two: $35.

**L'HABITANT** (\*\*) (9656 Gouin Blvd., Pierrefonds). Two hundred-year-old stone farmhouse overlooking Rivière-des-Prairies. Très romantic. Steaks very good, especially the pepper steak flambé. Crêpes Suzettes a fitting dessert. Wine list small, well selected. Dinner for two: $35.

**LES HALLES** (\*\*\*) (1450 Crescent St.). Ask for Jacques or Jean-Pierre. Excellent veal dishes, or try the salmon in chablis cream sauce. Dinner for two: $40.

**HÈLENE DE CHAMPLAIN** (\*\*) (Île Ste.-Hélène). City operated. Overlooks Man and His World, the successor to Expo '67. The round, high-ceilinged dining room specializes in Quebec delicacies (Gaspé salmon, lobster from the Madeleine Islands). No liquor, but good wine list. Dinner for two: $20.

**KYOTO JAPANESE STEAK HOUSE** (\*\*) (2055 Mansfield St.).

Decorated with eighteenth-century Japanese folk art. Communal tables. Try the hibachi sirloin. Dinner for two: $30.

**MARITIME BAR** (***) (Ritz Carlton Hotel). Where the elite meet for superlative seafood. Lobster Thermidor as good as you'll find. Ask waiters about seasonal specialties. Also pleasant for cocktails. Dinner for two: $50.

**LE NEUFCHATEL** (**) (Le Château Champlain). Opulent, elegant dining room. Oysters Rockefeller not on the menu, but superb in season. Classic Continental menu. Maître d' Jacques as polished as they come. Wine list should be better. Dinner for two: $40.

**LE PAVILLON DE L'ATLANTIQUE** (*) (1454-A Peel St.). Lively nautical room. Consistent seafood. Steamed lobster among the best in town. Extensive wine list. Moby Dick Bar & Lounge a popular watering hole. Dinner for two: $30.

**PICKWICK RESTAURANT** (**) (1414 Drummond St.). Paneled dining room in the downtown medical building. Only eleven tables, chamber music. Small but good menu. Service excellent. Chef brings you his creations himself. No credit cards. Dinner for two: $30.

**LE PLAT D'ARGENT** (**) (1790 des Laurentides Blvd., Vimont, Laval). A lovely little just-out-of-town place, warmed by white brick fireplace. All entrées bouquetière, special dishes on 24-hour notice. Dinner for two: $35.

**RITZ GARDEN** (***) (Ritz Carlton Hotel). Open June to September. Serviced by same kitchen as Le Café de Paris. Most attractive little café, far from city traffic. Pleasant for tea. Dinner for two: $40.

**LE SAINT-AMABLE** (***) (188 St. Amable St.). This narrow, red-draped dining room in a restored eighteenth-century house in Old Montreal is one of Canada's best restaurants. Try the seafood crêpe, tournedos opera, or roast quail. Wine list a classic. Dinner for two: $45.

**LA SAULAIE** (***) (1161 Marie Victorin, Boucherville). Manor house, twelve miles out of Montreal. Huge crackling fireplace in winter. Grand cuisine française is as it should be. Desserts exotic. Wine list is good. Dinner for two: $40.

**TOKYO SUKIYAKI** (**) (7355 Mountain Sights). Serene Oriental hideaway. Screened off rooms open on the garden. Your waitress cooks your food in front of you—and serves men first. Dinner for two: $25.

**TROIKA** (**) (2171 Crescent St.). A corner of Tsarist Russia with strolling musicians and Cossack waiters. For a show, try the flaming skewered shashliks. The Café Raspoutine comes cold, with Tia Maria and ice cream. The Cossack Bar is pleasant in the wee small hours. Dinner for two: $40.

**LE VERT GALANT** (***) (1423 Crescent St.). Elegant, intimate.

Try to get a chair; the narrow banquettes can get uncomfortable. Try the paupiettes de veau à ma façon. Winning wine list. If you can plan 48-hours ahead and order a special menu for four, it will be worth the effort. Dinner for two: $35.

**WILLIAM TELL** (\*\*) (2055 Stanley St.). Swiss specialties, but best known for fondues—bourguignonne and chocolat are best. Entertainment in Piano Bar. Dinner for two: $30.

## Recommended Reading

The best guide to what's going on in town is MONTREAL CALENDAR MAGAZINE, distributed only to households. Their office is in Old Montreal at 300 Place d' Youville, and if you want to stop by they'll be happy to sell you a copy for 50 cents.

Next best is CURRENT EVENTS, a monthly distributed free at most hotels.

THE HISTORY OF QUEBEC by Leandre Bergeron. (North Carolina Press, $1.50). Popular history.

GUIDE TO DINING OUT IN MONTREAL   (The Montreal Star Ltd., $2.95).

THE MONTREAL BUDGET GOURMET by Haskel Frankel. (Pocket Books, $1.95).

MONTREAL PEOPLE'S YELLOW PAGES   (Egg Yellow Publishing Co., $2.). What to do and where to go, with map.

VOYAGES FROM MONTREAL ($20.) A newly edited edition of Alexander Mackenzie's diaries. Magnificent, but not Montreal.

# NEW ORLEANS

There are plenty of places with a more suitable climate for the Super Bowl than New Orleans, yet the city has played host for this football frenzy twice. There are many other locations in the U.S. more convenient for conventioners to reach, yet New Orleans attracts much more than its share of business meetings. And there are places, too, where Old-World ties are more recent and much stronger than those of New Orleans, but the area is the only one in North America that still stages a Mardi Gras. Why? Let's face it—this is one swinging city, and the people who live there love to party as much as visitors on holiday do. Al Hirt's girth is as much a symbol of the city's sybaritic nature as is the multimillion-dollar Superdome, as stately a pleasure dome as has graced the skyline of any city.

It is a city that loves to eat. Making the most of its Franco-Hispanic-Acadian-Afro-Celtic-Italian-Indian-German origins, New Orleans has developed its own unique cuisine. Coffee with chicory, creole cream cheese, grillades, chaurice and andouille (sausages), po boy sandwiches, gumbo, beignets (square doughnuts), and absinthe frappé are but a few of the local inspirations. And everywhere, there are oysters, shrimp, and crawfish (clams and mussels are not to be found anywhere).

To wash that all down, there is plenty to drink—and plenty of time to do it in. The bars along Bourbon Street close only for a quick sweeping. What to do in the bars? Jazz, man. Even today the city pulses with it. And you should, too. "If you ain't gonna shake it, why bring it?" say the locals.

New Orleans is also easy on the eyes. Much of its past is evident, especially their French Quarter (which has a decidedly Spanish flavor), and the Garden District. And, of course, there is the swift-flowing Mississippi, which picks up a new rhythm as it slides by this Crescent City, and you are likely to, also.

## Hotels

If you can, reserve a room in the **Saint Louis Hotel,** in the old French Quarter. It is small, luxurious, and near everything downtown. You won't even need a taxi to get around. There are also quite a number of small hotels and guest houses in the Quarter that you might find charming. But better make reservations in a larger hotel first, and inspect them after arriving.

There are four major hotels that cater to business visitors. The 1,000-room **Marriott Hotel** on New Orleans' main drag, Canal Street, has all the modern conveniences. The **Royal Orleans** and the **Royal Sonesta** are both in the heart of the French Quarter. The **Downtown Howard Johnson's Motor Lodge** is convenient, near City Hall.

If you prefer to be off the beaten path a bit, try the quaint **Pontchartrain Hotel,** on St. Charles Avenue.

The **Fairmont Hotel** (formerly the Roosevelt), **Braniff Place** (formerly the Jung Hotel), the **Monteleone Hotel** in the French Quarter, and the **International Hotel** three blocks from the Mississippi River on Canal Street are frequent hosts to conventions, and might suit your needs. The Marriott likewise attracts its share of conventions.

## Restaurants

It's about as difficult to get a bad meal in New Orleans as it is to find a sober person during Mardi Gras. But there are some truly outstanding places worth seeking out.

**Brennan's,** of course, is the place for breakfast—some claim it was invented here. What can happen to eggs here is *formidable*. At lunchtime it is a businessman's hangout.

**Antoine's** is probably the most famous dining spot in town, but it may be a disappointment unless you go with a local friend who is a regular. There are upstairs and downstairs sections—one for the tourists, one for the regulars. Locals refer to downstairs as "the Barber Shop," where the out-of-towners get clipped. Waiting in line for a table for two up to two hours (reservations aren't accepted downstairs) is not likely to put you in the best mood for dining. But the food is superb.

The **Andrew Jackson** is small, rather expensive, and specializes in local cuisine. It is very popular with locals, not yet a mecca for tourists. A fine place to sample New Orleans specialties.

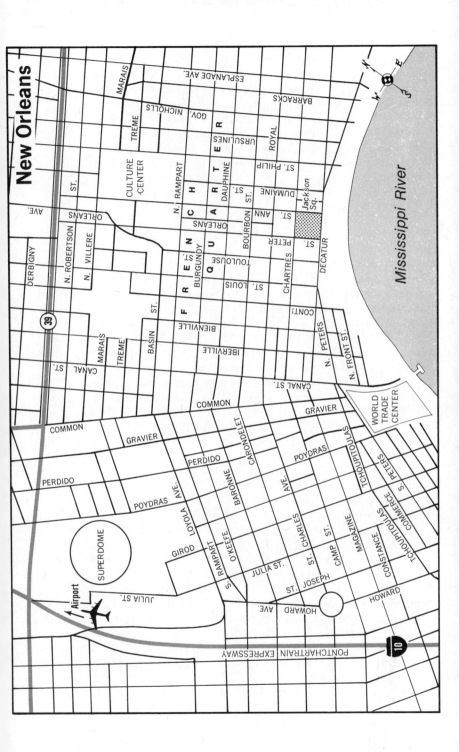

**Galatoire's** is another very popular dining spot, with natives and visitors alike, and it has worn its fame well. The service is still as good as the almost legendary cuisine. It isn't all that expensive, either. But you'll have to wait—no reservations are accepted.

The **Caribbean Room** of the Pontchartrain Hotel can be a memorable experience. It's a little out of the way, but worth it—and probably not so crowded. Local dishes are the specialties.

**Le Ruth's,** across the Mississippi in Gretna, is small, intimate, Victorian, and fantastic. It's New Orleans food, with uptown touches.


## *Potpourri*


There are so many places where it is happening in New Orleans that the easiest thing to remember is where NOT to go, and that is Decatur Street's tough-looking bars. Avoid, too, the obvious B-girl joints along Bourbon Street. Local police try to curb their shenanigans —but it is all but impossible. These girls can be very cutesy. A recent visitor was awakened at 7:00 A.M. by a knock on his hotel room door, and a comely lady of the very-late-evening begged entry—she was being pursued by an angry, drunken suitor, she said. The startled visitor (a pseudo-savvy New Yorker) admitted her, and called the hotel desk for the police. While he was doing so, his ring, airplane ticket, and traveler's checks vanished. So did the girl. (*Mirabile dictu,* the police nabbed the girl the next night—she thought the visitor would take off as scheduled, but he went cruising around with the police looking for her.)

With that said, have a good time. Your first stop is likely to be Bourbon Street, and **Al Hirt's Club** or **Pete Fountain's French Quarter Inn.** Check in advance to make sure that those performers are there—they are sometimes on the road. The **Blue Angel** on Bourbon is another good stop, where George Finola and his Chosen Few perform.

If you are staying at or near the Fairmont Hotel, you might want to take in the Tuxedo Brass Band in the **Fairmont Court.**

You might also make a visit to **Preservation Hall** on St. Peter's Street. There's no liquor license, and only hard benches to sit on, but there's great jazz played by old-timers who might otherwise be out on the street. Also along Bourbon Street is the **Jazz Museum** (at Conti Street). Besides some relics of the jazz greats like Armstrong, Bix Beiderbecke, and others, the museum has recorded jazz programs that you can listen to.

The **Absinthe House,** on Bourbon, is a must stop for a drink, even though you can no longer order an absinthe (it's illegal, since its main ingredient, wormwood, causes brain damage). The building dates back to 1805, and is said to be the place where Andrew Jackson planned the Battle of New Orleans. **Charley's Corner,** in the Château Le Moyne Hotel, is another good watering hole. And for a nightcap, have an Irish Coffee at the **Esplanade Lounge** at the Royal Orleans Hotel.

To end the evening, have coffee and beignets (those square doughnuts) at the **Café du Monde** on Decatur Street. Or, if you have an appetite, head for **Brennan's** and a legendary breakfast.

If you are free in the daytime, a walking tour is a must. If time is short, stroll through Jackson Park, featuring art shows and impromptu guitar concerts by young longhairs. On one side of the park is the **Cabildo,** seat of government during the Spanish rule (from 1763 to 1803, during which time one of the Spanish governors was Don Alexander O'Reilly). Nearby is the **Presbytère,** a former French courthouse now part of the Louisiana State Museum. There are charming female guides to show you around.

From there, wander down Royal Street, in the French Quarter, where the shops offer everything from toy soldiers to excellent prints and boutique fashions. There are plenty of junk shops around, too.

Other sights to see: The **Mississippi waterfront** (if you have time on a Saturday take the steamer *President* on its weekly jazz-filled cruise) and the **Garden District** where Americans built their spacious homes apart from the Creoles in the 1830s and 1840s. Nearby is the **Irish Channel,** named for the immigrants who settled there in the early nineteenth century, many of whom died digging the city's canals.

If time permits, **Lake Pontchartrain** and a tour of some of the **plantations** near the city can also be enjoyable.

## *Nitty Gritty*

## HOTELS

*Superior*

**SAINT LOUIS** (730 Bienville St.). Small, elegant luxury hotel in the heart of the French Quarter. Excellent service. Close to downtown. Relaxing atmosphere, popular with businessmen.

*Good*

**BRANIFF PLACE** (1500 Canal St.). Formerly the Jung Hotel, this old-timer still caters to the conventions in a big way, hooking up with Braniff Airlines. The convenient location makes it popular with business types.

**CHATEAU LE MOYNE** (301 Dauphine St.). Small, cozy, efficient, with a good bar.

**DOWNTOWN HOWARD JOHNSON'S** (339 Loyola Ave.). Overlooking City Hall, the State Office Building, and the new Superdome. Caters to businessmen. Roomy, comfortable.

**FAIRMONT** (University Pl.). Once the city's finest as the Roosevelt, it is on the way back after an extensive refurbishing and building program. Long a convention favorite. Home of the famous Blue Room, a popular entertainment spot.

**MARIE ANTOINETTE** (827 Toulouse St.). Actually a small motel, cozy and convenient.

**MARRIOTT** (Canal & Charles sts.). Massive, dominates the skyline, well located for businessmen and conventioners. Service is good —but elevators slow.

**MONTELEONE** (214 Royal St.). Aging hotel that is undergoing modernization. Location, only a block from Brennan's fine restaurant, makes it a winner.

**PONTCHARTRAIN HOTEL** (2031 St. Charles Ave.). Small, deluxe hotel with Continental service and absolutely great food in the Caribbean Room. A bit off the beaten path, but worth it.

**ROYAL ORLEANS** (621 St. Louis St.). Location has been a prime factor in this hotel's continuing popularity. Businessmen find it relaxing. Two blocks from Bourbon Street.

**ROYAL SONESTA** (300 Bourbon St.). Smack dab on Bourbon Street, this hotel specializes in luxury at a bargain price.

*Acceptable*

**INTERNATIONAL** (300 Canal St.). New. Capitalizes on its location across the street from Rivergate Convention Center and is within easy walking distance of the French Quarter.

# RESTAURANTS

**ANDREW JACKSON** (**) (221 Royal St.). A central location in the heart of the French Quarter and a taste of luxury complement the great food ladled out by this kitchen. Try the lump crab meat Lafitte hollandaise or the veal King Ferdinand VII. Dinner for two: approximately $25.

**ANTOINE'S** (***) (713 St. Louis St.). Expensive but certainly worth it. This restaurant is a "must" for every visitor. Try the chicken sauce Rochambeau. Dinner for two: $50.

**BRENNAN'S** (***) (417 Royal St.). Specializes in long, leisurely breakfasts that stretch into the afternoon. Dinner tops is the buster crabs Béarnaise with a mixed oyster dish. Oysters Rockefeller, Bienville, and Roffignac not far behind. Dinner for two: $25.

**CARIBBEAN ROOM** (***) (2031 St. Charles Ave.). The trout Veronique is magnifique; the oysters en brochette you won't forget. For dessert try the mile-high ice cream pie. The lone drawback is the taxi ride to get there. Dinner for two: $40.

**ELMWOOD PLANTATION** (**) (5400 E. River Rd.). Noted for game, much of it raised on premises. Authentic old plantation. Dinner for two: $25.

**GALATOIRE'S** (***) (209 Bourbon St.). Everyone is a king at this unusual restaurant—all line up outside the small dining room waiting their turn at eating excellent cuisine. Recommended highly is the trout Marguery. Dinner for two: $25.

**LE RUTH'S** (***) (636 Franklin St., Gretna). It will take a $5 taxi ride to get to this imperial eating house, but the meal will be worth the trip. Operation is small, but owner Warren Le Ruth scores with his personal touch. Dinner for two: $35.

**MASSON'S** (***) (7200 Pontchartrain Blvd.). French haute cuisine, some local fare. Try the rack of lamb or the roast duckling. Dinner for two: $30.

## Recommended Reading

There are excellent guide books on this exciting, extraordinary city. Here are some of the best:

NEW ORLEANS by Carolyn Kolb. (Doubleday and Co., Inc., $3.95).

THE NEW ORLEANS UNDERGROUND GOURMET by Richard H. Collin. (Simon and Schuster, $2.95).

NEW ORLEANS by Sarah Searight. (Stein and Day, $8.95).

NEW ORLEANS, A PICTORIAL HISTORY by Louis V. Huber. (Crown Publishers, Inc., $12.95).

FABULOUS NEW ORLEANS by Lyle Saxon. (Robert L. Crager and Co., $12.50).

# NEW YORK

As every schoolchild knows, the Dutch bought New York City for $24 worth of trinkets. Critics have been crying "Give it back to the Indians" ever since.

Indeed, Gotham can be hostile to the unwary visitor. Ask any native and he will tell you that it is a great place to live, but he wouldn't want to visit there. New York is so big, so diverse, so fast-paced, and so loaded with assorted nuts that the new arrival is easily bewildered. It is impossible to get your arms around the city without a long stay or a lot of homework.

But obviously, New York can be a fascinating and enjoyable city. It is unique in North America—no matter what your interest, appetite, virtue or vice, you needn't walk away unsatisfied.

New York does demand one important thing from the visitor—planning. The city is simply too vast to wander around and just happen across what you want. Unplanned stays in the Big Apple can be very lonely—and for the businessman, less than wholly productive.

The history of New York City is fascinating, but so few vestiges of it remain that it is largely academic. The two most significant remnants from the Dutch era in the seventeenth and eighteenth centuries are the word "stoop" (brick steps leading into a house) and a liking for Dutch beer (Heineken). The only traces from the days when Nieuw Amsterdam became anglicized into New York are the names "Stuyvesant Town" and "Peter Cooper Village," two middle-income housing developments.

There are but few relics still around from Revolutionary days—most notably Fraunces Tavern on Water Street, which present-day revolutionaries tried to blow up.

The nineteenth century saw the city grow enormously with the huge influx of Irish, German, Italian, and other immigrants; but history has obliterated most of the remnants of that era, save some of the old tenements built to house them. Now these buildings are occupied by poor Blacks and still another generation of new arrivals from Puero Rico, Cuba, and Greece (New York now has the largest population of Greeks west of Athens).

The city Landmarks Commission has been able to save some splendid late-nineteenth-century mansions from the wrecker's ball, as well as some skyscrapers. And, of course, the famous brownstone, usually blackstone these days, is still very much on the scene, in many cases lovingly restored by energetic, slightly crazy New Yorkers.

But the artifacts are pitifully few for a city as big and as historically rich as New York. Both Philadelphia and Boston have far more reminders of the Colonial era; the nineteenth century left more footprints in Washington than in Gotham. New York is simply not a nostalgic city. It is rude to its past. Nothing is built with the idea that it should last. The old joke that New York will be a great place when they finish it is almost true. The city almost works properly. But there is always one kind of crisis or another—power, water, telephone, transportation, fiscal, social, moral, spiritual, etc.

Something is always happening, but a lot of it is positive. On the upper East Side, for example, young and youngish people from all over the world pay exorbitant rents for tiny apartments just so they can be in the Big Apple, try their hand at a career, and live among like-minded types who don't want to save up their lives—or their dollars—for tomorrow.

Greenwich Village is still a mecca for the intellectuals and intellectually inclined, but now they are hopelessly outnumbered by oglers. Many of the artists have retreated south to SoHo (South of Houston Street), effecting yet another transformation in the city. Old abandoned lofts become studios for a sculptor who works in steel, an abstract expressionist, a pianist. Ask any of them where they will be next month, and they will be stuck for an answer.

You have to go to the suburbs to find stability in New York, or along Park and Fifth Avenues, where money insulates the rich New Yorkers from what the rest of the city is doing.

New York is, of course, the financial and business capital of the country. More corporate headquarters are located here than anywhere else, despite widespread publicity about those relative few who have fled the city, usually to bedroom communities in Westchester, New Jersey, and Connecticut, where the chief executives live. And Wall Street, of course, is where all the important money deals take place, from floating a new stock issue to arranging for the Russian purchase of wheat.

The pace of business is, like everything else in the city, hectic and dedicated to getting things done now, if not sooner. You can get a lot done in New York in a very short period of time. People usually don't small-talk much. They get right down to business. And because so many companies are crammed into the midtown area, you can usually walk or take a short cab ride between appointments.

Because most businessmen live in distant suburbs and have long commutes, they are often late to work and early to depart. Schedule appointments between 10:00 and 4:00. Breakfast meetings are not as common as elsewhere. And a drink after work is usually just that. After 6:30, trains to the "sticks" become few and far between.

If you entertain or are entertained over lunch, it can be long (except downtown in the financial district). The long lunch is probably the reason why every New York businessman totes an attaché case around with him, even if he only gets to work on its contents on Saturdays. And remember that despite the fact that there are hundreds of restaurants in the midtown area, most are crowded at noon. Always make reservations, even as late as noon itself. Again, because of long commutes, don't expect your contacts to ask you out for dinner or over to their homes for a brief visit.

Foreign visitors are most likely to find New Yorkers brusque and almost rude in the way they do business. And locals will have no patience if you are struggling with the language. Don't expect too many courtesies. You'll be lucky if you are asked to have a cup of coffee. While this takes some getting used to, it all works in your favor. You can be much more productive in a shorter time. But be prepared to start talking business as soon as you have said hello.

## Hotels

By and large, midtown is where much of New York is happening, and is the logical place to stay. Most of the better hotels are located here for that reason.

Take some time in selecting your hotel—it can make a big difference in how you enjoy your visit. Prices don't differ that much from the very best to the just-mediocre hostelries in the city's midsection.

If possible, try to avoid the big convention hotels such as the **Americana,** the **New York Hilton,** the **New York Sheraton,** the **Waldorf-Astoria** (except the Waldorf Towers), and the **Summit.** Nothing wrong with these hotels—except that they are big and often crowded, and therefore cannot offer personal service. They are fine for big

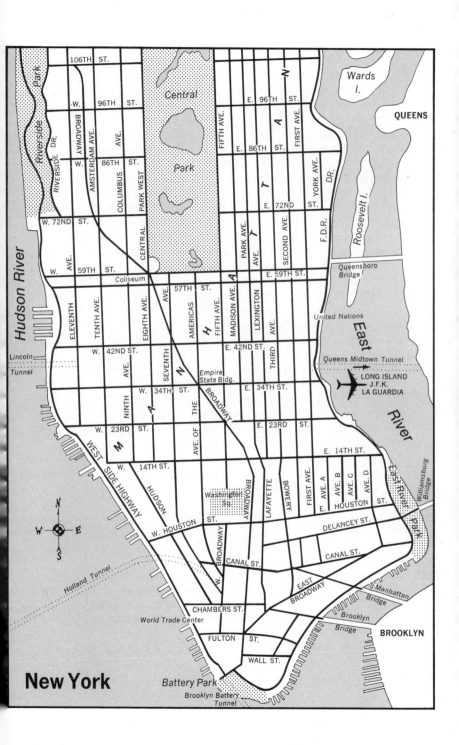

groups and for large meetings, but if you are on your own and have a choice, pick a smaller, quieter hotel where you are not simply a number. Among the best are the **Plaza** (recently refurbished by the Western International chain), the **St. Regis-Sheraton** (proof that chain management isn't always bad), the **Pierre** (a truly international hotel, with lamentably few available rooms), **Delmonico's**, the **Regency**, the **Sherry Netherland**, and the **Park Lane** (gilt and glitter).

Rates at these hotels are high—in some of them you can't get a single room for less than $50. A notch below these hotels are places like the **Barclay**, the **Drake**, and the **Essex House**, but they are a little overpriced. Then there are the former greats that have lost some luster for one reason or another, but still maintain their adherents. The **Algonquin**, the **Barbizon Plaza**, the **Gotham**, the **St. Moritz**, the **Sheraton-Russell** and the **Warwick** will do if you don't want to spend top dollar and want a hotel with some elegance even if it is faded.

Note: If you drive into town, you might prefer a hotel or motel with free parking. The **City Squire,** across the street from the Americana, has free parking smack on Broadway. Farther west, the **Skyline Motor Inn** is in a raunchy area, but has free parking and very comfortable rooms at reasonable prices. Most other motor inns with free parking are awkwardly located.

When making reservations at any of New York's hotels, try to do it yourself. Call the hotel—not a reservations system number. There are enough hotels in New York in every category so that you should not have to settle. You can get what you want in the right price range if you just stay with it a bit. Ironically, New York's largest, loudest hotels are often full or close to full when more charming, often less expensive hostelries have rooms open. So when you call a large hotel and are told there is no room at the inn, don't panic—there are plenty of other places to stay.

## *Restaurants*

When it comes to food, New York can drive you nuts. "Where to eat" is a life-long game New Yorkers play with great skill, yet sometimes they make horrible mistakes. New Yorkers are experimenters, as is borne out by the many different types of cuisine available. All of which is very good for the visitor.

French, of course, is the première cuisine, and is accorded unusual status in New York, even though the city has only a tiny French population—most of whom run restaurants. In a recent court case, for example, a New York judge ruled against an apartment dweller who sued a fashionable French restaurant, **La Goulue,** for emitting cooking odors he deemed obnoxious. The judge fumed that the apartment dweller must indeed be in the minority to find such odors repugnant. He added that good French restaurants were signs of a civilized society.

There are a handful of superb, if very expensive, French restaurants in New York, and an unusually large number of good, inexpensive ones. And there are too many mediocre, high-priced ones.

If money is no object, **Lutèce** offers the best classic French cuisine, with suitable Gallic service. It is the bastion of the gourmet, the oenophile, and, alas, the phony. One public relations executive had a table there permanently. He would only call if he did *not* plan to show up for lunch each day. He used the restaurant to impress—and wasn't all that keen on the cuisine. His favorite dish was actually mutton chop, which would never find its way into Lutèce. Dinner for two at Lutèce can easily soar over $100, higher if you get fancy with the wine. But it is a dining experience. Beware: you will get a raised eyebrow from the captain in Lutèce if you order a martini as an aperitif (it kills your palate—stick to kir), or if you laugh out loud or light a cigarette between courses.

Francophiles might put **La Grenouille, La Caravelle, Lafayette, La Côte Basque** or **Le Perigord-Park** in the same league with Lutèce —I won't quibble. Certainly they are in the same league as far as price goes. And that's really going some.

Fortunately, there are a number of bistro-type French places that have less ambitious menus. They can serve excellent dishes, at much lower prices. By and large, they are family-run operations, located in lower-rent districts—but perfectly safe and not too inconvenient. **A La Fourchette, Britanny du Soir, Les Pyrénées, Le Chambertin, René Pujol, Du Midi, Pierre au Tunnel, Georges Rey, Café de France, La Mangeoire,** are standouts in midtown.

Best value of all, however, in terms of price and quality is the ineptly named **Crepes Suzette.** It serves no crêpes; no one there is named Suzette. No credit cards are accepted. But the quality of the Provençale cooking—especially the seafood specialties (baby salmon meunière, for example)—is extraordinary for the price.

Italian restaurants abound in Gotham, but only a few are worth mentioning. **Orsini's** is where the beautiful people partake of pasta. **Romeo Salta** is just up a bit—in distance as well as in the variety of its menu. **Giordano's** is where real Italians eat in midtown if money is no object. **Giambelli's, Amalfi's, San Marino, Louise Jr's.,** and the **Italian Pavillion** have their adherents, too.

But the most colorful Italian restaurants are not in midtown. They are in Little Italy, Greenwich Village, and the boroughs. Closest to midtown is **Angelo's** in Little Italy.

New York now has hundreds of thousands of Greek residents—and you know what happens when Greeks meet. There are literally thousands of small, inexpensive Greek lunch counters and greasy spoon-type restaurants, where Greeks and a few venturesome souls eat. But souvlaki has almost replaced pizza as the eat-on-the-run snack, and is served at Greek snack bars all over town. Even the mighty Italian hero is being replaced with its Greek counterpart, the Gyro.

For Greek food on a higher plane, there's **Mykonos,** and if you like a little dancing in between—American disco style—there's **Dionysus.** Both also feature Greek entertainment.

Oriental cooking is well represented in midtown, although purists will insist a trip down to Chinatown is the only way. Nonetheless, **Szechuan, Sun Lee Dynasty,** and **Pearl's** will satisfy most Caucasians and a lot of Chinese as well.

New York also has good Japanese restaurants, notably **Kamehachi** and **Saito,** as well as a number of Japan-esy **Benihana** restaurants (best is the **Palace**) which offer tasty, hibachi-cooked shrimp, beef, and vegetables. Owner Rocky Aoki knows what Americans really like—American food.

The area of Yorktown, in the East Eighties, still has some good German restaurants, but in midtown there are but few. The **Blue Ribbon** survives, and **Luchow's** down on East Fourteenth Street has some German dishes left, but that's about it.

Spanish restaurants, too, are few—**Fundador** is almost alone. The **Jai Alai** in Greenwich Village is a better choice if you have the time.

If it's simply a steak you hanker for, you can pay up to $20 for it in places like the **Palm, Christ Cella, 21,** and **Manny Wolfe's**—or $15 for it in the likes of **Gallagher's, Kenny's,** or a dozen other places in town where you get just as good a piece of beef. The **Steak and Brews** are strictly caveat emptor.

Note: Many New York communities have outstanding ethnic restaurants, featuring Haitian, Jamaican, Cuban, Thai, Russian, Hungarian, Austrian, Jewish, Scandinavian, Peruvian, Brazilian, you-name-it specialties. If you want to try them out, best bet is to find a Jamaican, Haitian, Cuban, etc., and ask him.

And lest some New Yorkers smother us with mail, there are, of course, a number of good soul food restaurants downtown, in Harlem, and in the boroughs. Ask a brother, if that's your liking.

As rich as other parts of New York are in restaurants, the Wall Street area is pitiful. If you find yourself down there over the lunch hour and cannot wangle an invitation to a private club, here's the next best: **Oscar's** (steaks, canneloni), **Fraunces Tavern** (baked chicken à la Washington), **La Borsa di Roma** (veal Marsala), and **Michael's** (steaks). **Jimmy's Greek American** is an inexpensive Greek kitchen restaurant, always jammed. The **Kabuki** has Japanese. **Massoletti's**, **Sloppy Louie's** and **Sweet's** are the best places for fresh seafood.


## *Potpourri*


Everything is here, from the earthiest to the most ethereal.

First, the former. The town swarms with hookers, whose numbers swell with the temperature and the summer tourists. They traditionally cruise along Lexington Avenue, Broadway, and 7th Avenue, in the Forties and Fifties, and also work the Port Authority Bus Terminal. If you can't spot these cuties by their dress, you might be blind. In which case you will soon learn to recognize their smooth line: "Hey, goin' out?" Don't even think about these girls—they are rip-off artists supreme.

Up a notch, so to speak, are the girls who work the hotels. These girls can't work without the knowledge and cooperation of bartenders, doormen, maids, and bellmen. So you are not taking your life in your hands if you entertain one in your room. But it could cost you $100. Don't worry about finding them—if you are in the market, they will find you and get right to the point. One Canadian was recently returning to his room in the Hilton when a comely blonde smiled and said, "Hi. Are you looking for something? I might be able to help you." Being a curious devil, he replied, "Yes." "It'll cost you one hundred. What's your room number?"

So don't imagine you have engaged a hooker at the bar if she hasn't brought up the subject of money in two minutes or less.

You'll notice quite a few massage and "rap" parlors scattered around town—their locations and names often change—which advertise "massages" or "rap sessions" for a given sum. That is your entrance fee to the parlor. You negotiate anything else with your masseuse or rapping partner at that point. If you must, pick a spot in a decent-looking neighborhood, and don't complain about any aftereffects. Some of these places take credit cards.

If you are more interested in the sport of the chase, and in nonprofessional talent, the city awaits you—and your wallet. You can get lucky, or at least engage in some interesting patter with the fair sex, in virtually any cocktail lounge in the city, especially on Wednesday and Friday evenings as soon as the offices empty. But there are several places in the midtown and upper-East Side areas that are known as swingles hangouts, and whose patrons are usually interested in more than one quick drink and catching the 5:35 to Larchmont.

**Charlie O's** (E. 48th St., between 5th & 6th aves.) is an attractive paneled pub that draws an over-thirty set, mainly advertising and communications types from nearby offices. Irish bartenders and more than a few Irish and Irish-American patrons assure two things: There is a lot of serious imbibing and a lot of chatter. There are occasional "strays" who wander in, including an adventurous hooker now and then (Xaviera Hollander claims she worked the bar on occasion). But mainly it's good conversation here, and some good drinks.

**Rumm's** (E. 50th St., off 3rd Ave.) is dark and dingy, has no entertainment, and doesn't even have a coat room. You can hardly find room to stand on a Friday—which is exactly the point of the place. Patrons are all crowded so close together, it is no problem starting a conversation, like "You're standing on my toe." Serious swingles never go there—too many G.U.s (geographically unacceptables) and dallying husbands (and wives). Crowd age ranges from mid-twenties to whenever the urge to chase stops.

The **Cattleman East** (E. 45th St., off 5th Ave.) used to attract a decent crowd, but has faded somewhat. But on any given night in this town . . .

**Maxwell's Plum** (1st Ave. & E. 64th St.) has maintained its charm despite reams of publicity, the movie *John & Mary,* and an expansion program that makes the place only slightly smaller than Asia. It still attracts a stylish crowd, in their late twenties and up, and remains one of the few mingling places in town where you can also get a very good meal.

Clustered around Maxwell's are a host of other watering holes for singles and would-be singles, most of which attract a younger crowd. **Adam's Apple** (1st Ave. between 61st & 62nd sts.), which is a plastic garden run riot into jungle, does a thriving business, as does the granddaddy of them all, **Fridays** (1st Ave. & E. 63rd St.). This was the prototype of the singles bar: Tiffany-type lamps, old, roughed-up bar, sawdust on the floor, waiters in striped shirts, menu on the blackboard, beer and cheeseburgers, "Do you come here often?" conversations. It's something of a curiosity now, but the younger generation still packs the place.

New York has a huge Irish and Irish-American population, of course, and if that's your thing, the **John Barleycorn** (E. 45th St. off 3rd Ave.), the **Billymunk** (E. 45th St. off 2nd Ave.), **Danny Boy's**

(2nd Ave. & 50th St.) and **Jimmy Byrne's** (E. 54th St. between 3rd & 2nd aves.) celebrate St. Patrick's Day virtually every night.

Once you have made an acquaintance, you can head for **P. J. Clarke's** (E. 55th St. & 3rd Ave.) for a late hamburger, or to one of the many piano spots in town. Depending on your pocketbook and style, they range from Bobby Short, who does the Cole Porter thing in the **Hotel Carlyle** (E. 76th St. & Madison Ave.) down to the likes of Skip Ackerly, who moans early Rock and Roll from the keyboard at the **Cattleman East.** Or, if you prefer the frenetic dancing scene, head for **Dionysus** (E. 48th St., off 1st Ave.) or **Hippopotamus** (E. 54th St., off Park Ave.) and dislocate a hip.

If you prefer a quieter evening, there is Broadway, Off-Broadway, concerts, opera, ballet. If you know specifically what you want to see in advance, it's best to write for tickets ahead of time. You can usually get last-minute tickets for hard-to-see shows, for the Metropolitan Opera, or for a "sold out" concert, but not without paying for them. See a ticket agent.

For Broadway and Off-Broadway shows that are starting to fade, remember **Tkts**—it's a theater-supported ticket agency on Broadway and West 45th Street that sells unsold tickets at half price, for shows not already sold out that evening. You can often get two-fers for fading shows, too. These tickets can be redeemed at the box office before each performance, and you get two tickets for the price of one.

If your company is headquartered in the city, or has a large branch, check with the public relations man for all tickets. If he doesn't have them, he should know where to come up with them.

Note: The 7:30 curtain is no longer automatic on Broadway. Check your tickets carefully for curtain time.

Remember, too, if the play, concert, or ballet is in **Lincoln Center,** there are pitifully few good restaurants in the area. Best are **Le Poulailler** (W. 65th St., off Columbus Ave.) and the **Top of the Park,** on the roof of the Gulf & Western Building. If you want something more modest, **O'Neal's Baloon** (W. 63rd St. & Columbus Ave.) is crowded but good.

For **sports** action, again, see your public relations man. Most season tickets to Madison Square Garden Center are sold in blocks to companies. The Garden is home to the Rangers (hockey), Knicks (basketball), the Ringling Brothers Circus, two college basketball tournaments (Holiday Festival and National Invitational). Ticket scalpers make a living peddling overpriced tickets outside the Garden, so if your PR man cannot supply them, plan on watching the game on closed-circuit television in a comfortable bar.

Shea Stadium, in the borough of Queens, is now home to the Mets, Jets, Yankees, and the Giants. As New York is a football town, tickets can be difficult, but they're not impossible as long as a team is not a title contender. Again, check with your PR department or a ticket agent. For the baseball Mets and Yankees tickets are no problem, except for key late-season games in a tight flag race.

If you have never been to the Big Apple before, there are some worthwhile sights, should time permit. The **Statue of Liberty** and the **Empire State Building** are sites New Yorkers never visit, except if dragging visitors around. There is a method to this madness—the Statue is best seen from a distance. And the **Circle Line** runs excursion cruises around Manhattan Island (from the W. 43rd St. Pier) when the weather is warm, which afford great views not only of the Lady but of the entire New York skyline. And even seasoned New Yorkers respond to that. In winter, you can still get a great view of the Statue, and the southern tip of Manhattan, from the deck of the **Staten Island Ferry.** Staten Islanders are immune to the views, but they are awesome.

The Empire State Building a bore? Not really, but many New Yorkers work in high office buildings and get their elevator ride-and-view-trip daily. If you have kids along, they will love it.

Other favored tourist haunts are the **UN Building** (1st Ave. & E. 45th St.), the **Bronx Zoo** (go via subway during non-rush hours—ask the token seller for directions), the **Botanical Gardens** (best reached by train from Grand Central Station), and the museums: the **Metropolitan** (E. 81st St. & 5th Ave.), the **Guggenheim** (E. 88th St. & 5th Ave.), the **American Museum of Natural History** (W. 79th St. & Central Park West), and the **Museum of the City of New York** (E. 104th & 5th Ave.).

All of these museums are short cab rides from midtown hotels—you can easily walk to the **Museum of Modern Art** (W. 53rd between 5th & 6th aves.) and to the **New York Cultural Center** (W. 59th St. & 7th Ave.).

Some of New York's neighborhoods are worth seeing, especially **Greenwich Village, Little Italy,** and **Chinatown.** From midtown, take a cab or ask your not-so-friendly, but savvy, token seller in the subway for directions.

If you've never been, a trip to the **New York Stock Exchange** (11 Wall St.) is an experience. Amazing how billions of dollars in transactions are handled in such a primitive way, with frantic signaling, running around, and shouting by specialists on the floor. One day, they say, a computer will handle it all.

## *Nitty Gritty*

## HOTELS

### *Superior*

**CARLYLE** (Madison Ave. & E. 76th St.). A trifle out of the way from midtown, but if a room is available, grab it. Fine, elegant, expensive establishment now mostly occupied by permanent residents.

**DELMONICO'S** (Park Ave. & E. 59th St.). An old dowager that has been dusted off. Not quite as expensive as others in this group.

**ESSEX HOUSE** (Central Pk. S. between 6th & 7th aves.). Crisply efficient, if a little stiff. Popular with executives. Marriott showcase. A little less expensive than others in this group.

**PARK LANE** (Central Pk. S., between 5th & 6th aves.). New kid on the block (C.P. South), still a little wet behind the ears. Lots of gilt and glitter. Very popular with business types.

**PIERRE** (5th Ave. & E. 61st St.). Recently acquired by Trust-Houses Forte, and much to its credit the old gal has only improved. Old-World charm, with nothing fading. Very expensive.

**PLAZA** (5th Ave. & E. 59th St.). A landmark—officially. Proof that a large hotel doesn't have to be impersonal. It's to be hoped that Western International will spend a few dollars on sprucing up the rooms in this grande dame, which could use it.

**REGENCY** (Park Ave. & 61st St.). Probably has more crystal chandeliers, inch for inch, than any other hotel in the U.S. Nice and quiet. Expensive.

**SHERRY-NETHERLAND** (5th Ave. & 59th St.). Another graceful oldster overlooking the Park.

**ST. REGIS-SHERATON** (5th Ave. & E. 55th St.). Still the favorite of many European travelers. Many rooms filled with antique furnishings. Quiet executive favorite. Has a few moderately priced singles.

**WALDORF-ASTORIA** (Park Ave. between E. 50th & 51st sts.). Magnificent lobby and public rooms. An institution. Has trouble handling check-outs in the morning. Adjoining Towers house permanent guests.

### *Good*

**BARCLAY** (Lexington Ave. & E. 48th St.). Convenient to midtown corporations. Keeps a stiff upper lip in spite of some tawdry goings-on in the neighborhood.

**ALGONQUIN** (W. 44th St., between 5th & 6th aves). Public

rooms and restaurants far outshine upstairs accommodations. Still has cachet for some.

**AMERICANA** (7th Ave., between W. 52nd & 53 sts.). A colossus, designed for big conventions. Large, attractive rooms. But you can grow old waiting for elevators, check-in, check-out at certain times. Dubbed the box the Summit Hotel came in.

**BARBIZON PLAZA** (6th Ave. & W. 59th St.). Prime location. A bit worn around the edges.

**DRAKE** (Park Ave. & E. 56th St.). One of the nobler guardians of the Avenue.

**GOTHAM** (5th Ave. & W. 55th St.). Once a rival to the St. Regis, has suffered from neglect.

**NEW YORK HILTON** (6th Ave., between W. 53rd & 54th sts.). Busy, busy, busy. Comfortable rooms, spotty service. Handles conventions well.

**NEW YORK SHERATON** (7th Ave. & W. 56th St.). Trying hard to upgrade.

**ST. MORITZ** (Central Pk. S. & 6th Ave.). Great view of the Park from front rooms. Not what it used to be.

**SHERATON-RUSSELL** (Park Ave. and E. 37th St.). Very quiet, convenient location. Attractive public rooms, if a bit shopworn.

**SUMMIT** (Lexington Ave. between 51st & 52nd sts.). Businessman's hotel. Efficient. Looks like it belongs in Miami—but it's too long a walk to the beach.

**WARWICK** (6th Ave. & W. 53rd St.). Handy to convention hotels like Hilton and Americana, but much, much quieter.

*Acceptable*

**ABBEY-VICTORIA** (7th Ave. & W. 51st St.). A bit sleazy. Rates are low for New York.

**BELMONT-PLAZA** (Lexington Ave. & E. 49th St.). Better outside than in.

**BEVERLY** (Lexington Ave. & E. 50th St.). In a pinch.

**BILTMORE** (Madison Ave. & E. 43rd St.). Close to Grand Central.

**CITY SQUIRE MOTOR INN** (Broadway & W. 51st St.). Free parking.

**COMMODORE** (E. 42nd St., between Park & Lexington aves.). In Grand Central.

**EXECUTIVE** (Madison Ave. & E. 37th St.). In a pinch.

**HOLIDAY INN** (W. 57th St., between 8th & 9th aves.). If you have to drive.

**HOWARD JOHNSON'S** (8th Ave. & 51st St.). Likewise.

**LEXINGTON** (Lexington Ave. & E. 48th St.). A bit tacky.

**MC ALPIN** (Broadway & W. 34th St.). Way past its prime. Rates are relatively moderate.

**PENN-GARDEN** (7th Ave. & W. 31st St.). Handy to garment district. Relatively moderate rates.

**RAMADA INN** (8th Ave. & W. 48th St.). It'll do.

**ROGER SMITH** (Lexington Ave. & 47th St.). Not the best, but the price is right.

**ROOSEVELT** (Madison Ave. & E. 45th St.). Quite tolerable.

**SHERATON-MOTOR INN** (12th Ave. & W. 42nd St.). Very bad area.

**SKYLINE MOTOR INN** (10th Ave. & W. 49th St.). Comfortable but neighborhood is bad.

**STATLER HILTON** (7th Ave. & W. 33rd St.). Was once a show-case. You could do much worse.

**TAFT** (7th Ave. & W. 50th St.). In an emergency. Moderate rates.

**WELLINGTON** (7th Ave & W. 55th St.). Clean, not bad at the price.

## RESTAURANTS

**ALGONQUIN** (**) (W. 44th St., between 5th & 6th aves.). Still popular with literary types, some of whom date back to Dorothy Parker days. Rose Room now has more cachet than noisier, posher Oak Room. Great salads. Lunch for two: approximately $30. Dinner for two: $40.

**A LA FOURCHETTE** (**) (W. 46th St., between 8th & 9th aves.). Moderate French bistro with limited but good menu. Heavy on sea-food. Handy to theaters. Caution: no credit cards. Dinner for two: $35.

**AMALFI'S** (**) (E. 48th St., between Fifth & Madison aves.). Your basic Italian restaurant, usually crowded. Dinner for two: $35.

**ARTIST & WRITERS** (*) (W. 40th St., between 8th & 9th aves.). Former speakeasy, then private club, then popular with newsmen. Now new garment district-types show off models there. Decent steaks, chops, etc. Dinner for two: $35.

**ASSEMBLY** (*) (W. 51st St., off Fifth Ave.). Steak, thumb bits, and the like. Nothing to rave about. Dinner for two: $40.

**AUNT FISH** (*) (W. 63rd St. & Broadway). Sidewalk café. So-so seafood. Handy to Lincoln Center. Dinner for two: $20.

**AUTOPUB** (*) (Fifth Ave. & 59th St.). Loaded with gimmickry, including a racing car hung over the bar. Hamburger fare, etc. Good swingles bar at cocktail hour. Dinner for two: $20.

**BARBERRY ROOM** (\*\*) (E. 52nd St. between Fifth & Madison aves.). Quiet. Varied menu. Popular for breakfast meetings. Dinner for two: $35.

**BARBETTA** (\*\*) (W. 46th St., between 8th & 9th aves.). Northern Italian cuisine. Atmosphere of faded elegance. Prides itself on imported white truffles. Delightful garden in season. Dinner for two: $50.

**BENIHANA PALACE** (\*) (W. 44th St., between 5th & 6th aves.). Your personal Japanese cook/juggler/magician fries up your un-Japanese steak and shrimp with great flourish. Oh, it tastes OK, too. There are other Benihanas in town—this is the best. Dinner for two: $30.

**BILLYMUNK** (\*\*) (E. 45th St., between 2nd & 1st aves.). Hamburger-and-up-type food, well done. Irish bar. Kitchen open late. Dinner for two: $20.

**BLUE RIBBON** (\*) W. 44th St., between 6th & 7th aves.). Spacious German brauhaus. Great game in season. Masculine ambiance. Best at lunch. Lunch for two: $25.

**BRASSERIE** (\*\*) (E. 53rd St., between Park & Lexington aves.). Modern decor. French cuisine. Open 24 hours. Dinner for two: $30.

**BRUSSELS** (\*\*) (E. 54th St., between Park & Lexington aves.). What a good French restaurant should look like, and almost what it should taste like. Excellent service. Reasonable wine list. Dinner for two: $60.

**BULL & BEAR** (\*\*) (E. 49th St. & Lexington Ave., in the Waldorf-Astoria). Very popular with business types at lunch and cocktail time. Steaks, etc. Dinner for two: $40.

**CAFE ARGENTEUIL** (\*\*) (E. 52nd St. & 2nd Ave.). Comes on strong for a bistro. Very good French cuisine. Dinner for two: $35.

**CAFE DE FRANCE** (\*\*) (W. 46th St., between 8th & 9th aves.). Inexpensive French cuisine—not haute, but good. Ideal for pre- or post-theater. Dinner for two: $30.

**CAFE EUROPA** (\*) (E. 54th St., between 1st & 2nd aves.). Cozy, dark enough for nervous cheaters. Ample and decent food at reasonable prices. Usually crowded. Try the chicken Kiev. Dinner for two: $35.

**CAFE NICHOLSON** (\*\*) (E. 58th St., between 1st & 2nd aves.). Hard to locate. Continental cuisine in a unique setting—you have to see it to believe it. Dinner for two: $40.

**CARLOS** (\*\*) (W. 48th St., between 5th & 6th aves.). Floor-through of a townhouse. Unusual but cozy setting for seafood-cum-creole menu. Good value. Dinner for two: $30.

**CASA BRASIL** (\*\*) (E. 85th St., between 1st & York aves.). An East Side aberration: inexpensive, dinner only, no booze, little choice of fare on menu. Jammed, so early reservations needed. Dinner for two: $30.

**CATTLEMAN** (*) (E. 45th St., between Fifth & Madison aves., and W. 51st St., between 6th & 7th aves.). Cornball turn-of-the-century decor, decent steaks and chops. Very busy swingles bar in East Side branch. Dinner for two: $30.

**CAVE HENRI IV** (*) (E. 50th St., between 2nd & 3rd aves.). It's too bad you can't eat atmosphere, of which there is plenty here—as there isn't much good food. Settle for an omelet. Dinner for two: $30.

**CENTRAL PARK** (****) (59th St., between Fifth Ave. & Central Pk. W., and due north). For couples, weather permitting. Go to liquor store for Gallo Hearty Burgundy, to local deli for French bread, brie, apples. Picnic. Watch governesses and young mommies push baby carriages. Stroll. Kiss her in the zoo, under the Delacorte clock. Lunch: $4.14.

**CHARLES A LA POMME SOUFFLE** (**) (E. 55th St., between Lexington & 3rd aves.). Don't worry, this bistro serves more than potato puffs. Good value. Dinner for two: $35.

**CHARLIE BROWN'S** (*) (E. 45th St., between Lexington & Vanderbilt aves.). After 5:00, the bar is like Grand Central Station —which is where it is. Guzzling commuters miss trains and start divorces here, but the food isn't too bad in the restaurant in back, though they never notice. Dinner for two: $30.

**CHARLIE O'S** (***) (W. 48th St., between 5th & 6th aves.). Irish-style pub with a great bar, good hot sandwich counter, fair-to-middling menu items. Favorite watering hole of communications types in the area. Great for a quick meal. Lunch for two: $20. Dinner for two: $25.

**CHATEAU MADRID** (**) (E. 48th St. & Lexington Ave., at the Hotel Lexington). Entertainers imported from España. They are better than the food. Dinner for two: $40.

**CHEZ RENEE** (**) (E. 49th St., between 2nd & 3rd aves.). Small, busy French bistro. Cozy. Dinner for two: $35.

**CHRIST CELLA** (**) (E. 46th St., between Lexington & 3rd aves.). Steaks, lobster, some good Italian dishes served in undecorated rooms of an old brownstone. Waiters right out of *The Godfather.* Somehow it all works, and it's always jammed with business types. Lunch for two: $40.

**CHRISTO'S** (*) (E. 48th St., between Lexington & 3rd aves.). Decent enough Italian restaurant, with steaks and other fare as well. Dinner for two: $40.

**COPAIN** (**) (1st Ave. & E. 50th St.). Routine French restaurant immortalized—and improved—by *The French Connection.* Dinner for two: $45.

**CREPES SUZETTE** (\*\*\*) (W. 46th St., between 8th and 9th aves.). Hate to mention it, because this could ruin the place. Best bargain for French food in the city—bar none. Menu is simple, but extremely well done. Cozy bistro, with attentive service—and it's dirt cheap. Lunch for two, with full bottle of wine, dessert, espresso: $15, including tip. No credit cards. Who needs them there?

**DANNY BOY'S** (\*) (2nd Ave. at 50th St.). Lovely swingles bar for Irish and would-be Irish. Corned beef and cabbage and the like from the kitchen. Entertainment. Dinner for two: $25.

**DANNY'S HIDE-A-WAY** (\*\*) (E. 45th St., between Lexington & 3rd aves.). Good steaks and the like. Bar popular with celebs. Dinner for two: $45.

**DELMONICO'S** (\*\*) (59th St. & Park Ave., Delmonico Hotel). Smart, old-style elegance. The kind of dancing where you hold on to each other. Food is all right. Dinner for two: $45, plus cover.

**DELSOMMA** (\*\*) (W. 47th St., between Broadway & 8th Ave.). Toothsome Italian food. Celeb hangout sometimes; handy to theater. Dinner for two: $30.

**DIONYSUS** (\*\*) (E. 48th St., between 2nd & 3rd aves.). Greek music, food, and in-the-aisle dancing. Also a discotheque. Dinner for two: $45.

**DORIENTAL** (\*\*) (E. 56th St., between Park & Lexington aves.). Very good Cantonese food. The proof: It has a strong Jewish following. Dinner for two: $30.

**DU MIDI** (\*\*) (48th St., between 8th & 9th aves.). Bistro. Transplanted Frenchmen eat here. Dinner for two: $25.

**DUNCAN'S** (\*\*) (E. 54th St., between 2nd & 1st aves.). Jock hangout with very active bar evenings. Steaks, chops, etc., at reasonable prices. Tucker Frederickson, former N.Y. Giant fullback, lumbers through occasionally. Dinner for two: $35.

**EMPIRE ROOM** (\*\*) (49th St. & Park Ave., at the Waldorf-Astoria). Showcase for name entertainers. Good food. Dinner for two: $45, plus cover.

**FORUM OF XII CAESARS** (\*\*\*) (W. 48th St. at 6th Ave.). Gallic influence overcame Roman when Paul Kovi and Tom Marghatti took over. Decor fit for a Nero, menu for a Latin soph, portions for Lucullus, bill for Croesus. Dinner for two: $LXXX.

**FOUR SEASONS** (\*\*\*) (E. 52nd St., between Park & Lexington aves.). A monument more to architecture than to food, which is no fault of the present owner, Paul Kovi. Continental cuisine with a very heavy French accent, usually very well prepared. Dine alongside an indoor reflecting pool, where the ceiling is so high that clouds form. Occasionally has special menus that are usually fabulous. Dinner for two: $90.

**FRIAR TUCK** (*) (55th St. & 3rd Ave.). If you are in a Robin Hood or Maid Marian mood, this is the place. English-type food, which can never be anything better than fair. Dinner for two: $35.

**GAIETY DELI** (**) (Lexington Ave., between 56th & 57th sts., and W. 47th St., between Broadway & 8th Ave.). When you want a pastrami on rye, a little cole slaw, maybe a little Danish. Lunch for two: $9.

**GIAMBELLI'S** (**) (E. 50th St., between Madison & Park aves.). Northern Italian cuisine, better than most. But service is spotty. Dinner for two: $50.

**GALLAGHER'S** (**) (W. 52nd St., between Broadway & 8th Ave.). As big as Madison Square Garden, and usually as packed. Ad guys, bad golfers, ex-jocks' hangout. Good steak, especially spiced with house sauce. Handy to theaters. Dinner for two: $30.

**GEORGES REY** (**) (W. 55th St., between 5th & 6th aves.). French restaurants are supposed to be awful when they are big—this is the exception. Efficient, good cuisine, fair prices. Voilà. Dinner for two: $30.

**GIORDANO'S** (***) (W. 39th St., west of 9th Ave.). Hard to find, but worth it. Fine Northern Italian cuisine. Rustic decor. Limitless menu—there is none. But you name a Northern Italian dish and they can prepare it. Very popular with Italian-Americans and would-be Italians. Dinner for two: $45.

**GLOUCESTER HOUSE** (**) (E. 50th St., between Madison & Park aves.). Very good seafood, skillfully prepared. Nautical atmosphere that isn't schmaltzy. A bit steep, but the location demands it. Dinner for two: $40.

**GOLD COIN** (**) (2nd Ave. & E. 44th St.). Chinese restaurant popular with UN types. Dinner for two: $30.

**GREEN MAN** (*) (E. 56th St., between Park & Lexington aves.). Cozy bar, veddy informal. Food isn't the thing here (hamburger, etc.). Londoner Larry Carnell is owner and barkeep and lures British types from all over the city. 'Ave an ale and a game of darts or backgammon. Lunch for two: $10.

**GROUND FLOOR** (**) (52nd St. & 6th Ave.). Decent hamburger-and-up food, but a swinging bar. Biggies from Black Rock (CBS) try to make their secretaries here. Dinner for two: $25.

**HAHN KOOK** (**) (E. 48th St., between Fifth & Madison aves.). Authentic Korean dishes—spicy if you like. Decor part Gay Nineties, part Seoul modern. Ah-so, it works. Entertainment after 9:00 P.M. Dinner for two: $35.

**HAYMARKET PUB** (8th Ave., between 47th & 48th sts.). Typical of "earthy" places I'd avoid. Awful food. I'd leave it to the roaches.

**HIPPOPOTAMUS** (**) (E. 54th St., between Lexington & 3rd

aves.). Swinging discotheque. Not for stags. Gunga Din environment. Jocks, show-biz types let it all hang out here. Food is fair.
Dinner for two: $40.

**IRISH PAVILLION** (*) (E. 57th St., between Park & Lexington
aves.). There's a bit of a shop in front, and an attractive bar. Buy a
tweed hat, have an Irish coffee, but don't eat here. Dinner for two:
$30.

**ITALIAN PAVILLION** (***) (W. 55th St., between 5th & 6th
aves.). Popular with publishing types, but staff still hasn't gotten
surly yet. Excellent cuisine. Steak Diane as it should be. Sit in back
in warm months for garden view. Dinner for two: $40.

**JIM DOWNEY'S** (*) (8th Ave. at 44th St.). Irish-American
cuisine. Former struggling actor's hangout, but change of ownership
hurt food quality. Still good for an Irish coffee after the theater.
Dinner for two: $35.

**JIMMY WESTON'S** (**) (E. 54th St., between Park & Lexington
aves.). As big as a couple of basketball courts—Jimmy used to coach
the game. Dimly lit. Jazz combo at night. Over-thirty-five ex-jocks,
ad people, flashy-type gals keep the bar busy. Steaks and the like.
Dinner for two: $40.

**JOE ALLEN** (**) (W. 46th St., between 8th & 9th aves.). Decor
is American Basement—bare bricks, old posters covering holes in
walls, trés old Bohemian. Good steaks, burgers, drinks. It must work
—he has a branch in Paris. Handy to theater. Dinner for two: $30.

**JOE'S PIER 52** (*) (W. 52nd St., between 6th & 7th aves.). Seafood house. Too big, too noisy, too expensive. Takes advantage of
location across from Americana Hotel. Dinner for two: $50.

**JOHN BARLEYCORN** (**) (E. 45th St., between 3rd & 2nd
aves.). If you're Irish, come into this parlor. Jammed most evenings
with swingles, etc. Irish entertainment, food. Don't mention Belfast.
Dinner for two: $30.

**KAMEHACHI** (*) (W. 46th St., between 5th & 6th aves.). If you
like tempura and other real-live Japanese fare. Round-eyes are
usually outnumbered. Dinner for two: $35.

**KENNY'S** (*) (Lexington Ave. between 50th & 51st sts.). Big as a
barn. Decent steak. Recently had a bit of a health problem, which
might mean they will improve service a bit. If you don't care for
frills. Dinner for two: $35.

**KING COLE** (**) (E. 55th St. & 5th Ave., at the St. Regis-Sheraton). Long piece of mahogany, behind which is a huge mural. Popular cocktail spot for couples. Dinner for two: $35.

**LA BIBLIOTHEQUE** (**) (E. 43rd St., between 2nd & 1st aves.).
Overlooks UN Building. Limited but well-prepared menu, nothing

too fancy. Decorated like an open-air library. Popular with couples. Dinner for two: $35.

**LA CABANA** (\*) (E. 57th St., between Lexington & 3rd aves.). Decor is straight out of a Bogie movie, with tiled floor and walls, huge antique bar, wooden ceiling fans, palm-draped piano. Cuisine is Argentine, and could be better. Great spot for a pitcher of Sangria and a salad. Dinner for two: $25.

**LA CARAVELLE** (\*\*\*) (W. 55th St., between 5th & 6th aves.). Very expensive, very chi-chi, very good haute cuisine. Suitable for the VIP, expense-account lunch. Lunch for two: $60. Dinner for two: $90.

**LAFAYETTE** (\*\*\*) (E. 50th St., between 3rd & 2nd aves.). Is underrated for some reason—could be because it won't admit women in pants. Haute cuisine in the best Gallic tradition, excellent service. Fireplace cozy. Dinner for two: $60.

**LA GRENOUILLE** (\*\*\*\*) (E. 52nd St., between Madison & 5th aves.). Faultless. If you ate the fresh-cut flowers on your table, no one would blush. Superb cuisine, trés français. The beautiful people gain by dining here. Dinner for two: $70.

**L'AIGLON** (\*\*) (E. 55th St., between 5th & 6th aves.). Elegant setting. Haute French. Dinner for two: $60.

**LA MAGANETTE** (\*) (E. 51st St. and 3rd Ave.). As big as Tuscany. Italian food, nothing special. Dinner for two: $35.

**LA MAISONETTE** (\*\*) (E. 55th St., between 5th & Madison aves., at the St. Regis-Sheraton). Intimate spot popular with couples. Continental cuisine, nicely done. Entertainment. Dinner for two: $40, plus cover.

**LANDMARK** (\*\*) (W. 46th St., at 11th Ave.). Very old bar (circa 1850) lovingly restored by the O'Neal Bros. Hamburger-and-up fare, good to very good. Best at lunch. Very far west of things. Dinner for two: $25.

**LA TOQUE BLANCHE** (\*\*) (E. 50th St., between 2nd & 1st aves.). Country French decor, menu. Has quite a following. Dinner for two: $40.

**LAURENT** (\*\*) (E. 56th St., between Park & Lexington aves.). French and Continental cuisine. Furnished like a drawing room. Excellent service. Tables not too close together. Ideal spot for an important business lunch. Dinner for two: $50.

**LE CHAMBERTIN** (\*\*\*) (W. 46th St., between 8th & 9th aves.). Very good French cuisine at decent prices. If you heed maître d's advice on ordering, you'll probably have a super meal. The hot pâté en croute and the pajorski (when available) are superb. Good wine list. Dinner for two: $35.

**LE CHANTECLAIR** (\*\*) (E. 49th St., between Park & Madison aves.). Good French fare served as well as crowded quarters permit. Not for important luncheon discussions, but otherwise fine. Lunch for two: $25. Dinner for two: $35.

**LE CHEVAL BLANC** (\*\*) (E. 45th St., between Lexington & 3rd aves.). More like someone's apartment than a restaurant. Simple but good French dishes. Very good value for the location. Dinner for two: $30.

**LE CYGNE** (\*\*\*) (E. 54th St., between Madison & Park aves.). Excellent haute cuisine. Garden-like setting. Dinner for two: $60.

**LE MADRIGAL** (\*\*\*) (E. 53rd St., between 3rd & 2nd aves.). Very good French menu; excellent service. Popular with publishing and show-biz types. Outdoor garden. Dinner for two: $65.

**LE MANOIR** (\*\*) (E. 56th St., between Park & Lexington aves.). Not currently held in high favor by the beautiful people, but a fine French restaurant with charming decor. Special pre-theater menu. Dinner for two: $55.

**LE MARMITON** (\*) (E. 49th St., between 3rd & 2nd aves.). You simply cannot mass-produce French cuisine, or expect people to suffer haphazard service. But the place thrives. *Incroyable.* Dinner for two: $45.

**LEOPARD** (\*\*\*) (E. 50th St., between 3rd & 2nd aves.). Somewhat overshadowed by its neighbor Lutèce, but an excellent spot for an intimate lunch or dinner. Limited Continental menu, usually excellent. Pampering service. One master stroke: good wine, included in meal price, is poured as you require—red, white, or both. Dinner for two: $60.

**LE PERIGORD** (\*\*\*) (E. 52nd St., between 1st Ave. & FDR Dr.). Cheery atmosphere for very fine French cuisine. Popular with beautiful people for lunch. At dinner, they prefer the uptown version. Dinner for two: $60.

**LE PERIGORD—PARK** (\*\*\*) (Park Ave. at 63rd St.). More elegant setting, same high-quality cuisine as midtown branch. Dinner for two: $80.

**LES PYRENEES** (\*\*) (W. 51st St., between Broadway & 8th Ave.). A sleeper. Good French food, okay service, great prices. Dinner for two: $30.

**LE VERT-GALANT** (\*) (W. 46th St., between 6th & 7th aves.). Living proof that a small, successful bistro can't go big-scale. Plush, professional but the food is mass-produced. Dinner for two: $50.

**LONG RIVER** (\*\*) (W. 45th St., between 5th & 6th aves.). Your basic Chinese restaurant. Cheap considering the location. Dinner for two: $50.

**LOUISE JR.** (\*\*) (E. 53rd St., between 2nd & 1st aves.). Good

Italian food, and you'd better be hungry. Complimentary plate of appetizers is a meal alone. Always amusing to watch first-timers ogle at unordered heaps of shrimp, artichoke hearts, pimentos, etc. Entrées up to par. Dinner for two: $45.

**LUTÈCE** (\*\*\*\*) (E. 50th St., between 3rd & 2nd aves.). If you haven't heard the name, don't bother. The flagship of New York's houses of French haute cuisine. Still has a full head of steam. Food as an art form, service as a ballet. *Après Lutèce, rien.* Dinner for two: $100.

**MAMA LAURA** (\*) (E. 58th St., between 3rd & 2nd aves.). Pleasant spot; attentive service. Good Italian fare. A bit steep. Dinner for two: $60.

**MAMMA LEONE'S** (\*\*) (W. 48th St., between Broadway & 8th Ave.). Living Italian camp. The Godfather would have loved it—there's enough room for the entire "family." Calls itself the biggest Italian restaurant in the world. Who knows? But it's one big meatball. Great if you are in a fun mood, and one of the few places in town where you aren't embarrassed to dine alone. No one will notice. Dinner for two: $35, and bring a doggy bag.

**MANNY WOLF'S** (\*) (E. 49th St. & 3rd Ave.). For a big place that is supposed to cater to steak-loving, martini-guzzling executives, it should be ashamed. Service can be impossible, food doesn't make up for it. Dinner for two: $50.

**MARIO'S VILLA BORGHESE** (\*\*) (E. 54th St., between Park & Madison aves.). Better-than-average French and Italian food, pleasant setting, good service. Dinner for two: $60.

**MAUD CHEZ ELLE** (\*\*) (W. 53rd St., between 5th & 6th aves.). Sounds very chi-chi, right? Food would be French, close to elegant, right? Attract beautiful people, right? Yes, yes, yes, but somehow it doesn't come off—probably because too many advertising types nurse ulcers there. Dinner for two: $60.

**MIKE MANUCHE** (\*\*) (W. 52nd St., between 6th & 7th aves.). THE place for you if you are: (*a*) an incurable N.Y. Giants fan and love Wellington Mara, the owner; (*b*) an indifferent eater who settles for a steak; (*c*) Irish Catholic. Dinner for two: $50.

**MONK'S COURT** (\*\*) (E. 51st St., between 3rd & 2nd aves.). Like eating in a monastery, to the strains of Bach. Waiters cloaked in robes. Very effective. Spell continues when free bread, cheese, and apples are served. Unfortunately, the kitchen is medieval, too, and very ordinary food emerges. Dinner for two: $40.

**MUSEUM OF MODERN ART** (\*) (W. 53rd St., between 5th & 6th aves.). Go ahead, you might meet HER there, after all. World's most intellectual cafeteria. Bring eyeglasses, preferably shades. Lunch for two: $5.

**MYKONOS** (\*\*) (W. 46th St., between 8th & 9th aves.). Discover why the Turks can push the Greeks around—the sons of Homer are having too much fun. All the stuff you ever wanted in grape leaves, lots of good wine, dancing on tables, in aisles, etc. Dinner for two: $50.

**NANNI'S** (\*\*) (E. 46th St., between Lexington & 3rd aves.). Better-than-average Italian food. Jammed at lunch. At times reservations have been ignored in favor of regulars. Dinner for two: $35.

**NATHAN'S** (\*) (W. 43rd St. & Broadway). You don't have to be Jewish, or unemployed. It IS a good hot dog, dammit. Lunch for two: $3.50.

**NEARY'S PUB** (\*\*) (E. 57th St., between 2nd & 1st aves.). Where the Irish elite meet. Good bar, fair food. Dinner for two: $30.

**NEW YORK HILTON** (W. 53rd St. & 6th Ave.). All the restaurants are served by a common kitchen—which is awful. Only under penalty of death. Dinner for two: $50 at the kitschy Old Bourbon Steak House, $45 at the Grill.

**OAK ROOM** (\*\*) (5th Ave. & E. 59th St., in the Plaza Hotel). Paneled room with grand old paintings Western Hotels wanted to give away as a tax deduction. New Yorkers booed them out of it. Great room. Dinner for two: $40.

**ORSINI'S** (\*\*\*) (W. 56th St., between 5th & 6th aves.). Svelte New Yorkers who have stayed on their diets go there to show off and have fettucine. Very attentive service, handsome decor. She'll love it. Dinner for two: $60.

**OYSTER BAR** (\*\*) (59th St. & 5th Ave., at the Plaza Hotel). Is one oyster worth $1? Yes, when it is served here. The only place in town where Oysters Rockefeller are a credit to our V.P. Lunch for two: $35.

**OYSTER BAR—GRAND CENTRAL** (42nd St. & Park Ave.). Brody Corp. just took it over, and has made believers of cynical commuters who traipsed by for years without a stop. One of the extensive fish menus in town—definitely worth a lunch. Even New Yorkers go there. Lunch for two: $25.

**PALM** (\*\*) (2nd Ave. between E. 44th & 45th sts.). Very plain, very good steak, very high prices. Very popular. Very peculiar. Dinner for two: $60.

**PALM COURT** (\*\*) (59th St. & 5th Ave., at the Plaza Hotel). F. Scott loved it. Holden Caulfield would have. Your grandmother does—and you'll probably see her there. Tea and pastries for two: $15.

**PALM TOO** (\*\*) (2nd Ave. between E. 44th & 45th sts.). Across from Father Palm, Junior is a little bit less in all except prices. Dinner for two: $60.

**PAPARAZZI** (\*\*) (2nd Ave. & E. 51st St.). Sidewalk tratorria, safely enclosed so your soup doesn't get dirty before you eat it. Italian. Has a great salad. Great for people watching. Reasonable. Dinner for two: $25.

**PARK ROOM** (\*) (Central Pk. S., at the Park Lane Hotel). Menu tends to be French. View of Central Park. Service still somewhat inept. Wine list not nearly what it should be. Dinner for two: $50.

**PATSY'S** (\*\*) (W. 56th St., between Broadway & 8th Ave.). Better than average Italian restaurant, usually crowded with B'way types. Dinner for two: $35.

**PEACOCK ALLEY** (\*\*) (Park Ave. & 49th St., at the Waldorf-Astoria). Great spot for a business breakfast—attractive, cheerful, crisp service. Breakfast for two: $12.

**PEARL'S** (\*\*\*) (W. 46th St., between 5th & 6th aves.). Madame Pearl's new location is right out of *A Clockwork Orange*. A bit noisy and always crowded. But lemon chicken, steamed sea bass, and other Chinese dishes as good as you'll find in town. No reservations for lunch, no credit cards (too many experiences with those Time, Inc.-ers?). Dinner for two: $40.

**PERSIAN ROOM** (\*\*) (59th St. & 5th Ave., in the Plaza Hotel). Plush nightclub, top entertainers. Celeb hangout. Decent food. Dinner for two: $40 plus cover.

**PIERRE AU TUNNEL** (\*\*) (W. 48th St., between 8th & 9th aves.). Cutesy bistro. French menu, homey service. Good pre- and après theater. Dinner for two: $30.

**PIERRE'S** (\*\*) (E. 53rd St., between Madison & Park aves.). Expensive, popular with executives. More relaxed than most high-priced French restaurants. Dinner for two: $60.

**P. J. CLARKE'S** (\*\*) (3rd Ave. & E. 55th St.). Where celebs go for a beer and a damned good hamburger. Scuzzy-looking bar, tables in rear. Worth a stop anytime. Dinner for two: $20.

**PRESS BOX** (\*) (E. 45th St., between Lexington & 3rd aves.). Press guys can't afford to eat here, unless being entertained by PR men. High, considering. Dinner for two: $40.

**RAINBOW GRILL** (\*\*) (Rockefeller Plaza, atop RCA Bldg.). Best rooftop roost in town. Name entertainers. Dinner for two: $40, plus cover.

**RAINBOW ROOM** (\*\*) (Rockefeller Plaza, atop RCA Bldg.). Same great view, more-formal dining room. Great wine list. Continental cuisine. Dinner for two: $40. Note: You can reserve a dining room under the Rainbow, on the 64th floor, for lunch or evening meetings.

**RATAZZI** (\*\*) (E. 48th St., between 5th & Madison aves.). Basically good Italian restaurant. Caters to ad types. Gets greedy and permits small parties, which are too noisy if you want to talk business. Dinner for two: $45.

**RENE PUJOL** (\*\*) (W. 51st St., between 8th & 9th aves.). Inexpensive bistro with some nice Continental touches. Dinner for two: $30.

**ROGER'S** (\*\*) (E. 57th St., between 2nd & 1st aves.). Spacious two-tiered dining room, attractive bar. Pianist knocks out show tunes. Conglomerate cuisine. Dinner for two: $40.

**ROMEO SALTA** (\*\*\*\*) (W. 56th St., between 5th & 6th aves.). Elegant Roman restaurant with extensive menu, attentive service, and usually excellent food, especially pasta, veal and seafood. Try clams posillipo (clam soup) as an appetizer. Dinner for two: $60.

**ROSE'S** (\*) (W. 52nd St., between 5th & 6th aves.). Bar always busy with communications types. Toots Shor camps out here now. Food is OK, tends toward Italian. Dinner for two: $40.

**ROYAL BOX** (\*\*) (W. 52nd St. & 7th Ave., in the Americana Hotel). Showcase for name entertainers. Dinner for two: $40, plus cover.

**RUSSIAN TEA ROOM** (\*\*) (W. 57th St., between 6th & 7th aves.). Decor is overdone; diners rise to the occasion. Ideal for post-Carnegie Hall or City Center. Lures celebs. Dinner for two: $35.

**ST. REGIS ROOF** (\*\*) (E. 55th St. & 5th Ave.). Showcase for name entertainers. Dancing. Dinner for two: $50, plus cover.

**SALLY'S** (\*) (W. 55th St., at 7th Ave.). One of the few bars in town where you can go alone, see some decent (if not name) entertainment, and not be hassled. Decent food. Dinner for two: $30.

**SAN MARCO** (\*\*) (W. 55th St., between 5th & 6th aves.). Good Northern Italian fare. Dinner for two: $30.

**SAN MARINO** (\*\*\*) (E. 53rd St., between 3rd & 2nd aves.). Northern Italian cuisine as it should be. Dinner for two: $45.

**SARDI'S** (\*\*\*) (W. 44th St., between 7th & 8th aves.). Only in New York could you have a show-biz hangout where the food is basically Italian (try the canneloni). Reserve your table downstairs. Best after theater. Dinner for two: $50.

**SEA FARE OF THE AEGEAN** (\*\*) (W. 56th St., between 5th & 6th aves.). Expensive seafood house. Dinner for two: $45.

**SHEPHEARD'S** (\*\*) (Park Ave. & E. 56th St.). Egyptian discotheque, nicely done. Entertainment. Dinner for two: $35, plus cover.

**SHUN LEE DYNASTY** (\*\*\*) (2nd Ave. & E. 48th St.). Excellent Chinese food, mainly Mandarin and Cantonese. Don't pass up the appetizer tray. Will prepare Peking Duck if you order a day in advance. Dinner for two: $35.

**STEAK & BREW** (\*) (practically everywhere). Variations:

Burger & Brew, Roast Beef & Brew. Decent, inexpensive. Chain operation. Dinner for two: $20 including all the lousy Schlitz beer you can stomach.

**SUN LUCK** (*) (W. 49th St., between 6th & 7th aves., and other locations). Once-popular chain of Chinese restaurants has slipped, though still a bargain. Dinner for two: $20.

**SWISS PAVILLION** (**) (W. 49th St., between 5th & 6th aves.). Pleasant, modern decor. Interesting Swiss food. Dinner for two: $40.

**THURSDAY'S** (**) (W. 58th St., at 6th Ave.). Swingles bar done in Tiffany modern. OK kitchen. Dinner for two: $35.

**TOP OF THE SIXES** (W. 53rd St. & 5th Ave.). Good view from top, but food is dreary. Dinner for two: $35.

**TRADER VIC'S** (**) (59th St. & 5th Ave. at the Plaza Hotel). One of the best of the entire chain. Kooky pseudo-Polynesian drinks, so-so food. Very effective atmosphere. Nice and dim for cheaters. Dinner for two: $40.

**TWENTY-ONE** (***) (W. 52nd, between 5th & 6th aves.). A place to be seen. Show biz celebs are outclassed by very big-business types. Downstairs is "in." Cuisine is Continental. Make reservations from out of town. Dinner for two: $60. Note: several upstairs dining rooms are available for business meetings. The Remington Room, with original oils of the Western artist, is best.

**WALLY'S** (**) (W. 49th St. between Broadway & 8th Ave.). Very good if somewhat dingy steak house. Smack in theater district. Dinner for two: $40.

**WIENERWALD** (*) (W. 48th St. & 8th Ave., and elsewhere). Chain of German-type restaurants. Ample, if unimaginative, food. Dinner for two: $20.

## *Recommended Reading*

THE COMPLETE NEW YORKER by Howard Hillman. (McKay, $5.95). If your stay will be long or if you are relocating, it can save you a lot of grief.

INSIDER'S NEW YORK    (Random House, $4.95). One of the Pan Am city-by-the-cards series. Comprehensive, but awkward to use despite the intention.

MICHELIN GUIDE TO NEW YORK CITY    (Michelin, $3.50). Leave it to the French to put New York into proper perspective—and between the covers of a well-mapped guide.

MYRA WALDO'S RESTAURANT GUIDE TO NEW YORK CITY    (Collier, $3.95). Ratings on 800 restaurants, some open to question. Only five get top ratings—one of which has a menu item named after the author.

NEW YORK AT-A-GLANCE by Howard Hillman. (McKay, $2.50). Best pocketbook guide to the city and its restaurants. Unfortunately, needs updating.

NEW YORK IN FLASHMAPS by Toy Lasker. (Flashmaps, Inc., $1.95). Revised annually, "An Instant Guide to Every Place in Town." Unique mine of information, including understandable subway and bus maps, address finder, major shops, and skyscrapers and best views.

SOCIAL GUIDE TO NEW YORK BARS by Evan Broadman. (Collier, $1.50). Describes where "singles, separated, divorced and one-nighters go." Indeed.

WORD OF MOUTH by Jim Quinn. (J. B. Lippincott, $2.95). Precious descriptions of restaurants supposedly only you can judge.

There are two good magazines worth picking up:

NEW YORK MAGAZINE    Has listings and reviews of shows, movies, exhibitions, and frequently has buying tips, restaurant reviews, etc. 60¢ at newsstands.

THE NEW YORKER    Far more urbane, and doesn't even think the Big Apple is the center of the universe. Has very complete listings. 60¢ per copy at newsstands.

# PHILADELPHIA

For the nation's fourth largest city, Philadelphia is still a small town. Critics—most Philadelphians—complain that it is provincial and will always be hopelessly overshadowed by the behemoth to the north. Probably so. But there is a lot bubbling beneath the quiet grace and charm that is Philadelphia.

For one thing, Philadelphia is still growing from the inside. Suburbanites are actually moving back into town, renovating eighteenth- and nineteenth-century townhouses around Rittenhouse Square and in Society Hill. Businesses are looking downtown again, too. Several new concrete and glass office buildings have shot up recently, and there are more on the drawing boards.

A small pond Philadelphia may be, but it offers lots of polywogs a chance to look big. You frequently find thirty- and forty-year-olds occupying the top offices of banks, brokerage firms, and burgeoning corporations. Not that Philadelphia's old guard has turned over all the reins to the new breed. The social register is the only phone directory in many homes and membership in the Union League Club is still the sine qua non of full respectability.

No one would call Philly a swinging town. But times, they are a-changing. Streets are not rolled up at 10:00 P.M. anymore. The polite clubs and intimate "at-homes" are giving way to a growing number of atmospheric little restaurants and bars that are springing up almost weekly.

You will find Philadelphia very comfortable to work in, or to live in. You aren't overpowered. Buildings are on a human scale. Streets are not overcrowded. By a tradition as binding as law, no building is taller than the height of William Penn, who stands atop historic City Hall at 537 feet. You can stroll the streets without throngs of escapees from high-rise office buildings walking on the backs of your shoes.

While the city area is actually broad, encompassing "the great northeast" and "west Philadelphia" (location of University of Pennsylvania and Drexel University), only two square miles constitute "center city." In this hub between the Delaware and Schuylkill Rivers and South and Vine streets, lies most of the office space and after-hours entertainment for in-towners as well as those from the bedroom communities of Chestnut Hill and the Main Line.

Venerable City Hall is at the intersection of the city's axes: Market Street, running east-west, and Broad Street, running north-south. The southern quadrants hold most of the action.

Most of the banking and financial business is carried on between JFK Boulevard and Walnut, from Broad to 19th streets. Down around Independence Hall (6th and Chestnut) is another business center encompassing several brassy new office buildings. Some big companies have fled to suburbs like Valley Forge and City Line areas.

In the center city, your feet are your best means of getting around during business hours. Traffic is usually choked on the three main drags: Market, Chestnut, and Walnut.

For longer runs, you'll find busses and trolleys fairly frequent in case you can't flag a cab. (Note: yellow cabs are usually available at cabstands by hotels; only occasionally can you flag one on the street.) Two subways run the lengths of Market and Broad streets. They are usually very crowded, but fast.

If you must have a car, don't park illegally. Police and private companies make a sport—and a bundle—out of towing.

## *Hotels*

The small, gracious **Latham,** at 17th and Walnut, is the best in town. The Not-Quite-Cricket downstairs is a cozy, discreet late-night bar that frequently features live music.

On Rittenhouse Square, the **Barclay** is the quintessence of quiet, Old-World elegance. Service is excellent and the dining room unsurpassed. The old grand dame the **Bellevue Stratford,** at Broad and Walnut, is right in the heart of things.

**Holiday Inns** have literally sprung up all over town. The one at 18th and Market sports its series of fine eateries and bars. Popular with wandering executives, it also draws visiting college and professional sports teams.

Out on City Line Avenue, the **Marriott Hotel** is a virtual resort in itself, containing five good-to-excellent restaurants, bars, and swim-

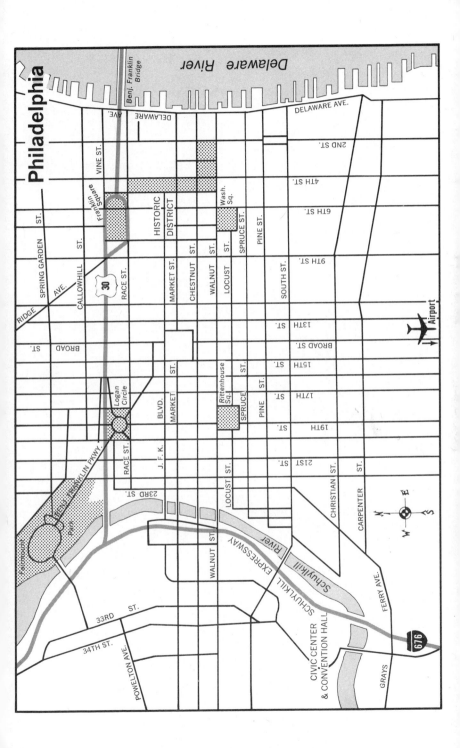

ming pools. Across the street is another **Holiday Inn** featuring a glass-enclosed restaurant and bar on top.

Twenty-five minutes from town, near Valley Forge, is a glittery **Hilton,** popular with conventioneers, businessmen, and tourists. It has a pool and health club. For strobe-light fans, the Magic Twanger discotheque also swings there.

The **Valley Forge Sheraton,** which looks like a mini-UN building, has plenty of diversions, including several restaurants, two movie theaters, and a swinging discotheque. This Sheraton is miles above its center-city cousin.

## Restaurants

**Le Bec-Fin** is the best in town, although **La Panetière** comes in a close second. The latter has a more elegant dining room, but the formality and pretension can be discomfiting.

**Helen Sigel Wilson's** rates high marks for consistently good food and service. **Frog,** nestled in a townhouse on 16th near Spruce, offers imaginative French cooking.

Society Hill boasts quite a share of the city's night life. The **Parson's Table, Le Champignon,** and **Lautrec** are among the more popular troughs. What they may lack in culinary mastery, they make up for doubly in ambiance.

## Potpourri

Nighttime swinging in Philadelphia is still a little lame, but the town is working on it. Hotel bars, particularly the **Not-Quite-Cricket** and those of the Holiday Inns, are usually a good bet. The **Magic Twanger,** in the Hilton, and **Cahoots,** in the Valley Forge Sheraton, are likewise quite frisky.

**Arthur's Steak House** at 1512 Walnut features downstairs entertainment. The **Penthouse** at 15th and Locust and the **Empire Room** of the Holiday Inn at City Line offer the best city views.

**Casablanca,** at 20th and Spruce, is a bar and discotheque. **Cafe Etranger,** a glamorous old movie house, has been converted into a restaurant/bar/discotheque that's worth a visit.

Downtown, a little slip of a street called Bank Street is aglow with stage lamps and the glare of four or five joints that have seen better days. Don't bother, unless you're homesick for Bayonne, New Jersey.

If you're in the neighborhood, poke into the **Middle East**—a slightly tacky, Middle Eastern restaurant that features belly dancing—by both professionals and ouzo-inspired diners. Over at 2nd and South, **Konstantinos** rocks till 2:00 A.M. with Greek bouzouki and dancing.

Across the river in Cherry Hill, New Jersey, the **Latin Casino** hosts a stream of top-name entertainers. A cab will take you there and back. And make a reservation.

Note: the B-girl joints on the Locust Strip, between 12th and 9th, aren't particularly risky—or rewarding.

Philadelphia is blessed when it comes to theater. It is on the circuit for many Broadway-bound shows, and it also hosts touring companies or indigenous theater companies at the Walnut, Shubert, or Locust Street theaters. Smaller, straw-hat theater proliferates quietly in the neighborhoods.

**Annenberg Center,** at 3680 Walnut, has been getting some good literary plays, including several of Joseph Papp's. Central City Ticket Office (1422 Chestnut) or the Philadelphia Theater Ticket Office (1413 Locust) are two good ticket brokers.

The **Academy of Music** is unfailingly excellent, attracting big names in ballet, opera, and orchestra, when Philadelphia's own Eugene Ormandy isn't conducting.

For **sports** fans, Philadelphia has its share of teams—though not its share of winners. The 76'ers dribble to empty seats and the Flyers play hockey to sellout crowds at the Spectrum in South Philadelphia. Try to get a member to wine and dine you at the Blue Line Club there.

Veterans Stadium hosts the baseball Phillies and the Eagles football team. The Broad Street subway is probably your best bet, as cabs there are practically nonexistent.

If your wife is along, there are enough art museums to occupy her for weeks. The **Philadelphia Museum of Art,** the impressive Greek edifice at the end of the Parkway, has one of the best Americana collections in the U.S. The **Rodin Museum,** halfway between the museum and center of town, houses an impressive array of Rodin's sculpture.

Center City has the **Peale House Gallery** and the **Academy of the Fine Arts** (Broad and Cherry). Try **The Print Club** (1614 Latimer Street) for contemporary graphics and the **University Museum** at Penn (34th and Spruce) for ancient art.

If your kids are along, a tour of the **Independence Hall area** is probably in order. Guides will show you the Liberty Bell, the Betsy

Ross House (239 Arch), and the rest, while the **American Wax Museum,** the **Mint,** and the **Atwater Kent Museum** should also be part of your tour. And don't forget **Valley Forge.**

For shopping, your wife might enjoy the boutiques all along Walnut from Broad to 20th. **Nan Duskin,** at 18th and Walnut, stands out for fashion—and price. **John Wanamaker** (13th and Chestnut) and **Strawbridge & Clothier** (9th and Market) are fine old family establishments.

## *Nitty Gritty*

## HOTELS

### *Superior*

**LATHAM** (17th and Walnut sts.). Small, quiet, and elegant, with liveried doormen. Computerized bar caddies in the rooms.

**BARCLAY** (E. Rittenhouse Sq.). Decorous beyond reproach. A few of Philadelphia's dowagers have taken up permanent residence here.

### *Good*

**HOLIDAY INN PENN CENTER** (18th and Market sts.). Your basic Holiday Inn with a few refinements. A bit off the beaten track.

**MARRIOTT** (City Line Ave. & Monument Rd.). Rather commercial. You'll probably never have time to enjoy all its restaurants, bars, and facilities.

**VALLEY FORGE HILTON** (Route 202, King of Prussia). Glassy and brassy. Popular with the out-of-town executive and tourist trade.

**VALLEY FORGE SHERATON** (Route 363, King of Prussia). Not your typical Sheraton. Grand and luxurious, though the service needs work.

### *Acceptable*

**BELLEVUE STRATFORD** (Broad and Walnut sts.). Gets a tremendous amount of hurly-burly traffic as it is right in the heart of town. Top luncheon spot for City Hall crowd.

**WARWICK** (17th and Locust sts.). Garish, but rooms are comfortable if you can fight your way through the stewardesses and traveling salesmen around the front door.

**BEN FRANKLIN** (9th and Chestnut sts.). One of Philadelphia's oldest, it boasts a large, blue-neon bust of Ben on the roof. Popular with the convention crowd.

The **PENN CENTER INN** (20th & Market sts.) and the **ADEL-PHIA** (13th & Chestnut sts.) are a couple of other acceptable old Philadelphia sleepers. Not great, but if you need them, they are there.

*Not Recommended*
**SHERATON** (17th St. & JFK Blvd.). Philadelphia's rendition of Grand Central Station. Even its blinding new orange and turquoise carpeting can't help this baby.

# RESTAURANTS

**LES AMIS** (\*\*) (1920 Chestnut St.). Canard à l'orange and chicken breast with tarragon and wine rate high marks here, as does the modern decor. Lunch and prix fixe dinner. Dinner for two: approximately $40.
**ARTHUR'S STEAK HOUSE** (\*) (1512 Walnut St.). A convenient spot for the not-too-demanding. Try the cheesecake. Lively downstairs features weekend music and bar. Dinner for two: $30.
**BARCLAY DINING ROOM** (\*\*) (18th St. and Rittenhouse Sq.). Some of the city's best Continental fare in a quietly elegant dining room, complete with crystal chandeliers and fresh flowers. Service is excellent. Dinner for two: $20.
**LE BEC-FIN** (\*\*\*) (1312 Spruce St.). Best French dining in town. It seats thirty in each of two sittings. Food and service superior. Skip lunch and plan to spend four hours for dinner. Dinner for two: $60.
**BOGART'S** (\*) (17th and Walnut sts.). Beneath wooden fans and posters of Humphrey, this discreetly dark enclave dishes up rather ordinary fare. Mood and service are almost worth the $25 for two.
**OLD ORIGINAL BOOKBINDERS** (no star) (125 Walnut St.). Far from what it used to be. Lobsters and oysters Rockefeller are tempting—but not at those prices. Dinner for two: $35.
**BOOKBINDER'S SEAFOOD HOUSE** (\*) (215 S. 15th St.). Brought to you by the real Bookbinder family. A huge rambling place, it offers an extensive seafood and grill menu. Broiled bluefish is a good bet. Dinner for two: $20.
**LE CHAMPIGNON** (\*) (122 Lombard St.). Named for Philadelphia's famous mushroom, this cozy little bistro offers rather unimaginative fare that is erratic. Dinner for two: $25.
**FRANKIE BRADLEY'S** (\*) (Juniper and Chancellor sts.). Passable steak house popular with the downtown business crowd. Dinner for two: $30.
**FROG** (\*\*) (264 S. 16th St.). Friendly, hip bistro nestled in a center-city townhouse. Creative French menu, which changes daily

at the chef's whim and usually succeeds. Dinner for two: $25.

**GAETANO'S** (**) (727 Walnut St.). A popular Northern Italian spot. Try the veal Bolognese. Dinner for two: $25.

**HELEN SIGEL WILSON'S** (**) (1523 Walnut St.). Reminiscent of a ladies' luncheon club. Favorite luncheon and dinner spot for downtown businessmen. Don't miss the carrot blini appetizer (with caviar). Quality is high. Dinner for two: $30.

**KONSTANTINOS** (*) (2nd & South sts.). Lively Greek dining spot with some exotica, including octopus and grape leaves. Bouzouki players and the locals kick up the dust here on weekends. Dinner for two: $25.

**LAUTREC** (*) (408 S. 2nd St.). A stylish little café down on historic Head House Square. Heavy on the cheese and omelets. Dinner for two: $15.

**LICKETY SPLIT** (*) (401 South St.). One of the more up-beat eateries in town. But its eclectic menu is pretty reliable. Dinner for two: $20.

**LONDON** (**) (2301 Fairmount Ave.). A fun, pub-like affair offering relaxed, informal dining. Menu is not exceptional, but it is well prepared and served. Chicken in pineapple and raisin sauce is a winner. Dinner for two: $20.

**THE MAGIC PAN** (*) (1519 Walnut St.). A good spot, centrally located, for a quick, light crêpe or two. Part of a chain. Dinner for two: $15.

**MIDDLE EAST** (*) (126 Chestnut St.). A somewhat garish, family-owned establishment whose major claim to fame is its live belly dancer (usually a family member). Dinner for two: $20.

**LA PANETIÈRE** (***) (1602 Locust St.). Probably has the most elegant dining room in town. The fare, though costly, is excellent. Panetière lost its famous chef to the Bec-Fin, and some say it dropped to second place as a result. Dinner for two: $60.

**PARSON'S TABLE** (*) (26 S. Front St.). Classic black-and-white decor, with single red carnations on the Parson's tables, gives this a certain cachet. The light crêpes stuffed with cheese and meat are a treat. Also serves light suppers to late-nighters. Dinner for two: $35.

**SALOON** (*) (750 S. 7th St.). Hidden on a colorless South Philadelphia street corner, but sparkling Victorian inside. Fare is saucy Italian. Go by car, as you can't find a cab back. Dinner for two: $25.

**LA TERRACE** (*) (3436 Sansom St.). If you find yourself in West Philadelphia with a couple of hours to spare, stop in at this lively café where university types mix with the downtowners. Food is variable, but generally good. Try the filet of sole with cream sauce and oysters. Dinner for two: $20.

**THREE THREES** (*) (333 S. Smedley St.). A cozy little townhouse lends itself to a rather uninspired, though reliable, Italian and mixed-grill menu. Dinner for two: $15.

## Out-of-Town Restaurants

If you're staying outside town, or feel like a drive in the country, you might want to try:

**L'AUBERGE** (**) (Spread Eagle Village, Wayne, N.J.). Owned and run by the Wilsons, former owners of Helen Sigel Wilson's. Food is variable, but you can't go wrong with the lamb chops or French pancake supreme. Dinner for two: $30.

**COVENTRY FORGE INN** (***) (Coventry Rd., off Route 23, Coventryville). This famous eighteenth century country inn is deemed by many to offer the finest dining in the area. Dinner for two: $50.

**KOBI** (*) (Valley Forge Hilton). A Japanese steak house where your chef cooks your meal at table. The steak or shrimp are tasty enough to make it worth one trip. Dinner for two: $30.

**KONA KAI** (*) (At the Marriott). A huge, plastic-Polynesian affair with all the gimmicks—a bridge, waterfall, hanging vines. Food and atmosphere, though touristy, are fun. Dinner for two: $30.

**TOWNE HOUSE** (**) (South Ave. and Baltimore Pike). Lively, active, featuring Italian-American cooking. Great for the kids. Dinner for two: $20.

## Recommended Reading

INSIDE PHILADELPHIA, THE COLLEGIATE GUIDE (Hadley Group, $2.95). Re-written annually, it gives the latest on dining, entertainment, and shopping in witty, concise prose, with capsule summaries and unambiguous opinions.

THE PHILADELPHIA MAGAZINE'S GUIDE TO PHILADELPHIA by Nancy Love. ($2.95). Clever and amusing, it discusses Philadelphia by areas, noting restaurants and activities within the text. Also outlines walking tours.

A GUIDE'S GUIDE TO PHILADELPHIA by Julie P. Curson. (Curson House, Inc., $1.95). Aimed at the tourist with kids in tow. Good historical sketches.

PHILADELPHIA MAGAZINE A monthly, this is the best guide to what's happening daily. Ads for restaurants and stores are plentiful. Listings include area concerts, plays, and movies for the month.

# PITTSBURGH

Pittsburgh still has a lingering reputation as "the smoky city." Alex Karras recently referred to it on national television as "the only town I ever played football in where the birds cough." Well, that reputation is about 25 years out of date. The smoke was cleaned up long ago, and today Pittsburgh's air-quality problems are no more serious than those of most other large cities. In fact, on clear days, it's actually pretty, with its dramatic hills and impressive rivers.

Unfortunately, Pittsburgh's other reputation—"the Renaissance City"—is also out of date. The famous renaissance of the early 1950s, spurred by a coalition of political and business leaders, has pretty much come to an end. Many attribute its demise to two circumstances: The death of industrialist Richard King Mellon, its prime architect, and the election of Democratic Mayor Peter Flaherty in 1969. Flaherty was reluctant to undertake major projects, such as a rapid transit line and a convention center, which the business community wanted.

Pittsburgh is a headquarters city. The number of major corporations housed there is far out of proportion to the city's size or population. As a result, the city—particularly in the suburbs—abounds in middle-management types. But there is a dearth of smaller entrepreneurs—men who own their own foundries, or tool and die shops, or other small businesses, and make between $35,000 and $80,000 a year. This distribution has adverse affects. Cultural organizations devoted to drama, ballet, or opera have a hard time supporting themselves, and either depend on the very rich or founder.

For years, Pittsburgh has been known as a "shot and a beer" or "blue collar" town, and there are statistics to back that up. A disproportionate share of the city's workers earn between $10,000 and $15,000 a year, with fewer below and fewer above that range than in other cities. One effect of this has been to make Pittsburgh a town of sports fanatics. The Pittsburgh Steelers—a dramatically improved ball club in the last few years—had no trouble drawing respectable crowds throughout most of the 1960s to watch them play distinctly mediocre football.

Pittsburgh's downtown—its famed "Golden Triangle"—is especially compact. You can walk the distance from its tip (where the Allegheny and Monongahela rivers join to form the Ohio) to its base in less than 15 minutes—taking time out to pull up your socks a few times.

All the major corporations are clustered together within a stone's throw of one another. While an accident of geography may have brought them that close together, it's said that the private Duquesne Club is the real glue. The Club is far more central to the daily life of Pittsburgh executives than exclusive men's clubs in other cities. In fact, it is rumored that more than one local chief executive has scotched plans to build new headquarters structured in the inviting acreage surrounding Pittsburgh because "it would be too far away from the Club." Many assume there is something slightly sinister about all this, and that it has to do with the power of the monied interests. But it probably has more to do with the power of Nicholas Colletti. He's the Duquesne Club's chef, and in a town that is not distinguished by its fine restaurants, the food at the Duquesne Club is reason enough to remain loyal to the institution. Many other private luncheon clubs thrive for that same reason.

Pittsburgh is an early-rising, hard-working town. By the time the average New York copywriter finds his way to his desk in the morning, the typical Pittsburgh cost accountant is thinking about where to have lunch. This has something to do with the town's Presbyterian heritage. Andrew Carnegie was Presbyterian, and so were the Mellons. As a result, Presbyterianism is more or less the establishment religion in Pittsburgh, holding the position that Episcopalianism enjoys in most other cities.

## Hotels

To take advantage of Pittsburgh's compactness, you'll probably want a hotel right in the downtown area. One good choice in the city is the **HoJo's at Chatham Center.** It's like an island unto itself, with restaurants, meeting rooms, a swimming pool, exercise facilities, a movie theater, and even a grocery store right in the building. And it's good that it is, because unless you have business at the nearby

Civic Arena, which houses the exhibits for most shows and conventions in Pittsburgh, you may find Chatham Center a bit out of the mainstream.

The **Pittsburgh Hilton Hotel** has been a focal point of Pittsburgh's Gateway Center since 1960. It's a chain hotel, of course, with all that that implies, but it features a good restaurant, The Rifle and Plow, where wild game and venison are frequently on the menu. Its location is a bit of a disadvantage after 6:00 P.M., when all the nearby offices close and leave the Gateway area desolate.

If you haven't been to Pittsburgh for a while, try the **William Penn,** overlooking Mellon Square, right in the heart of things. This older hotel, formerly known as the Penn-Sheraton, was in a decline until it was bought by a subsidiary of Alcoa a few years ago (the Alcoa headquarters are just across the street). Since then, it's undergone a multimillion-dollar face lift, with all of its 800 rooms refinished. It combines the best of the old and new. The refurbished Palm Court, in the central lobby, recaptures the height of 1930s elegance.

## *Restaurants*

Pittsburgh does not have the quality or variety of restaurants found in cities like Cleveland or St. Louis. A good wine list in a Pittsburgh restaurant is rarer than a public advocate of Japanese steel, and the nearest authentic French restaurant is over two hours away, in Frostburg, Maryland.

Nevertheless, there are some very good restaurants in Pittsburgh, but you have to know where to find them. Don't leave it to chance. Downtown, Alex Tambellini's **Woods Restaurant**—while frequently crowded and not particularly opulent—consistently offers the best seafood available in Pittsburgh, although **Klein's,** just around the corner, has loyalists who would argue. For first-class hotel dining, there's the **Candlelight Room** in the Carlton House Hotel, plush and elegant, with an inventive menu.

Mt. Washington, overlooking downtown Pittsburgh, offers one of the best views available in any American city—a fact not lost on the local restaurateurs, who armwrestle one another for cliffside space there. Among the handful of restaurants perched atop the mountain, the finest may be **Christopher's,** an elegant affair on the top floors of a new, high-rise apartment building. Its fans swear it is the best in town. The menu is diverse and Continental, the wine list impressive, the service efficient, the atmosphere romantic, the view stunning.

Also well worthwhile on Mt. Washington is the **Tin Angel,** which

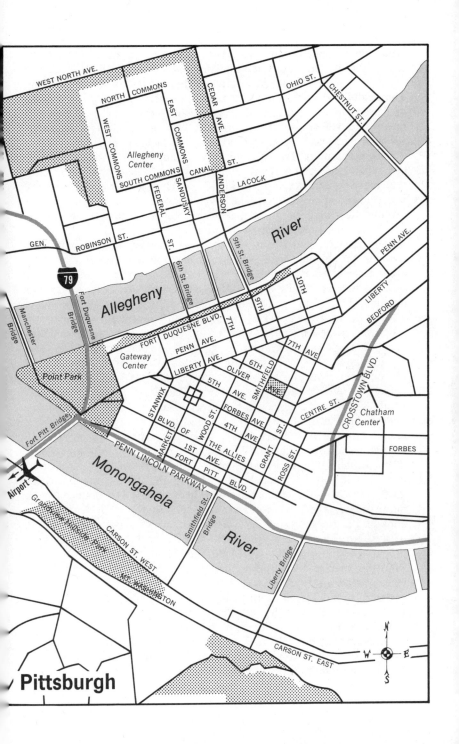

also offers a spectacular view. The entrées are straightforward but superbly prepared, and much imagination is put into the side dishes.

Without a view, but with a kitchen that makes up for it, is **Louis Tambellini's.** Because there was once a prolific Tambellini, there are at least seven restaurants that go by that name, and you have to make sure you've got the right one. This one is at 160 Southern Avenue. The specialty is seafood, and the menu is extensive.

There are more Italian-American restaurants in Pittsburgh than any other kind, but they are almost invariably pedestrian. The only real place for Italian food is **The New Meadow Grill,** in the East Liberty section of the city. The neighborhood's a bit rough, but the inventiveness and energy of the owner chef more than make up for it. The second most common category of restaurant in Pittsburgh is Middle Eastern, and two establishments just past the university district vie for first place in Arabian food. One is **Samreny's** and the other is **Omar Khayyam's.** They're across the street from one another, they both have family-owned atmosphere, they're both housed in immense, converted residential dwellings. Which one you choose has a lot to do with what side of the street you happen to be driving on.

It used to be difficult to recommend Chinese restaurants in Pittsburgh, because the suggestions hinged on the quality of the chef, and the few good ones were constantly rotating. Things settled down a bit, however, with the opening of two restaurants where the owners personally oversee the kitchen. One is **The Great Wall,** opened by a young Formosan engineer, which specializes in Mandarin cooking. Peking duck is the house specialty, and there are no clichés on the menu. The other is **Anna Kao's,** where the emphasis is on strictly authentic ingredients, a varied menu, and no cutting corners.

Pittsburgh's one-time pride and joy, the **Park Schenley** restaurant in Oakland, fell from the heights during the 1960s, but in recent years, thanks to the enthusiasm of a new chef, it has bounced back impressively. The beef dishes are a special source of pride. **Sgro's** is another Pittsburgh restaurant where the owner is the chef. Nothing tricky here. The entrées are simple and direct, but always very well prepared. **Nino's,** another Oakland restaurant, combines a Mediterranian ambiance with an adventuresome menu. It's almost impossible to get a bad meal here.

To refresh yourself during downtown meanderings, stop at the **Oyster House Café** in Market Square, which can trace its beginnings to 1827. It's a local landmark, both officially and by popular choice. With pictures from all the Miss America contests adorning its tile walls, and 3000 customers a day tramping over its tile floors to wolf down mammoth butterfly filet of whitefish sandwiches, stuffed oysters, and glasses of buttermilk or draught beer—on tap, side by side—it is surely one of the more distinctive cafés remaining in the United States.

## *Potpourri*

Night life in Pittsburgh is, somewhat surprisingly, a bright spot. The compact downtown area is not only easy to walk around in, it is also very safe at night. Suburbanites can frequently be found there, having a good time, and there's nothing like that to give a city a sense of vitality.

And for some obscure reason, Pittsburgh is a true jazz center. The quality of the music is extraordinary, and frequently, it's just for the price of a drink. Very few months in the year go by without a major jazz talent appearing at one of the Pittsburgh clubs.

The center of activity downtown is Market Square, just beyond Gateway Center. The Square is filled with singles bars, sing-along bars, bars with live entertainment, topless bars, and plain old bars.

The focal point is **Walt Harper's Attic,** featuring jazz by Pittsburgh pianist Walt Harper and his group, dancing on a stainless-steel dance floor, and food (don't go out of your way to eat there, however). The Attic is frequently host to big-name jazz artists.

Avant-garde saxophonist Eric Kloss—one of the best in the country —holds forth at **Sonny Dayes Stage Door.** For some very good trombone, it's Harold Betters at the **Encore II.** If you're single, or so inclined, try **Buddies.** For authentic bluegrass music, as pure as any you'll hear in the hills of Appalachia, take a taxi to **Walsh's,** in the East Liberty section of the city.

If you just want a drink in a convivial atmosphere, two bars right downtown can meet your needs: **Mahoney's** and **The Top Shelf.** The music is generally soft, the conversation is friendly, and the drinks ample.

Pittsburgh has three old-fashioned, down-to-earth supper clubs scattered out along the Pennsylvania Turnpike. They are the **Holiday House,** the **Harmar House,** and the **Twin Coaches.** At any time of the year, you can expect to catch acts like Milton Berle, Phyllis Diller, Trini Lopez, or the Lettermen. Prices for a dinner-and-show package are extremely reasonable. Pittsburgh also specializes in private after-hours clubs. If you have a friend who can show you the ropes, some of these can be very rewarding.

Pittsburgh can boast of an outstanding new theater: the completely renovated **Heinz Hall** for the Performing Arts. It's the home of the

**Pittsburgh Symphony.** Pittsburgh's legitimate theater is the **Nixon,** which hosts most of the touring companies.

If you're a **sports** fan you can, depending on the season, watch the NHL Pittsburgh Penguins play some rather routine hockey at the Civic Arena at the base of the Golden Triangle, or watch the Pirates or the Steelers play some first-class ball at the dazzling new Three Rivers Stadium across from the point of the Golden Triangle.

If you only have a bit of free time, you might stroll down to the 36-acre **Point State Park** and take in a couple of relics of the pre-Revolutionary War era: the remains of Fort Duquesne, and the Fort Pitt Blockhouse, amplified by a small museum.

If you plan to take in the view from Mt. Washington, get up there by one of the two remaining **inclining railroads** that creak straight up and down the side of the mountain. The funicular cars are antique, and the sensation is distinct.

For art, the **Frick Art Museum** in Point Breeze features a limited but impressive collection of Renaissance masters. The Museum of Art at the **Carnegie Institute,** with a new wing, offers a rounder collection. The **Frick Fine Arts Building,** across from the Carnegie, is a curiosity. It displays 22 copies of famous Italian paintings, all executed by the Russian painter, Nicholas Lochoff.

If your wife comes along and has some free time, she might be interested in some shopping. There's a **Gimbel's** in Pittsburgh, and a **Saks** in Gimbel's. Also, have her try the local department stores, **Joseph Horne Co.** and **Kaufmann's.** Better, suggest she take a cab to Walnut Street, in the Shadyside section of the city. There are shops and boutiques of every stripe, intriguing little galleries and crafts shops, and some nice places to have lunch. That should take the better part of a day.

If you both have some time, rent a car and drive out to **Falling-water,** the home Frank Lloyd Wright designed over a waterfall for Edgar Kaufmann, the department store executive.

Speaking of Frank Lloyd Wright, he once delivered a speech to a group of leading Pittsburgh citizens, and afterwards one of them asked him what they might do about their city. "Abandon it," he suggested.

Pittsburghers like to tell that story themselves, primarily because they would never think of taking the suggestion seriously. While they may not have a center-of-the-universe complex, Pittsburghers like their town, and they are consistently upbeat about it.

## *Nitty Gritty*

## HOTELS

*Good*

**CHATHAM CENTER** (Across from Civic Arena). Newish, loaded with extras, but a bit inconvenient for walking to downtown office buildings.

**HILTON** (Gateway Center). It's a Hilton, there's no doubt about that, but it's right next door to the major office buildings and it has a good restaurant.

**WILLIAM PENN** (Mellon Sq.). An old hotel brought up-to-date without sacrificing its venerable charm. The best-located of the downtown hotels.

*Acceptable*

**CARLTON HOUSE** (Grant St.). Primarily a residential hotel, but it still takes an interest in transient trade. It features a good location and an outstanding restaurant. No suites for overnight.

**WEBSTER HALL** (Oakland). Cozy and informal, it's the best place to stay if your business is in the university area. Five minutes from downtown.

## RESTAURANTS

**CANDLELIGHT ROOM** (\*\*\*) (Carlton House Hotel). Elegant and plush, featuring a menu a far cry from Pittsburgh steak-house fare, the Candlelight Room should be valued for its appetizers, its salads, and both its crab and lamb dishes. Dinner for two runs about $26.

**CHRISTOPHER'S** (\*\*\*) (Grandview Ave., Mt. Washington). Here, at last, claim its devotees, is a Pittsburgh restaurant to be proud of. The Continental menu is not quite French, but more Belgian. It is hard to know which to rank higher: the service, the food, the decor, or the view. Dinner for two: $38.

**GREAT WALL** (\*\*) (2735 Saw Mill Run Blvd.). Velvet chicken, Peking duck, beef with hot ginger sauce, and Mandarin pancakes are some of the things to try here. The menu is arranged so that you can have a broad sampling. Dinner for two: $20.

**ANNA KAO'S** (\*\*) (1034 Freeport Rd., O'Hara Township). The Chinese menu is dazzling in its variety and refreshing in its authenticity. Chicken stuffed with shrimp and fried in walnut batter and ginger, and steamed spareribs in black bean sauce are sure to please. Dinner for two: $22.

**KLEIN'S** (**) (4th Ave., Downtown). A bustling family operation incapable of misbroiling a piece of fish, and entirely capable of some very ambitious seafood dishes. Dinner for two: $22.

**NEW MEADOW GRILL** (**) (420 Larimer Ave., East Liberty). Pittsburgh's only real Italian restaurant distinguishes itself with its shellfish, pasta, and veal dishes. A plea to the eccentric owner, "Alex, let me eat," brings forth dishes that promptly transfer the establishment into the three-star category. Dinner for two: $24.

**NINO'S** (*) (214 N. Craig St., Oakland). Italian specialties and seafood, invariably well prepared, make it a worthwhile stop. But try to be seated in the main dining room rather than the somewhat tacky room off the bar. Dinner for two: $24.

**OMAR KHAYYAM'S** (*) (Baum Blvd., Oakland). Middle Eastern fare, served in an authentic atmosphere. Ask for one of the upstairs rooms. Dinner for two: $16.

**PARK SCHENLEY** (**) (Bigelow Blvd., Oakland). After a few years of decline, this once-outstanding Pittsburgh restaurant is now on the rebound, thanks to the energies of a new chef. The beef dishes here are probably the best available in Pittsburgh. Dinner for two: $35.

**RIFLE AND PLOW** (*) (Hilton Hotel, Gateway Center). Venison, pheasant, and occasionally, rabbit are on the menu here. Be sure to try the spinach salad with a hot dressing. Dinner for two: $30.

**SAMRENY'S** (*) (Baum Blvd., Oakland). Middle Eastern specialties such as salad with lemon and mint, raw kibbee, and humus are featured. Ask not to be seated in the new addition at the front; it's strictly a dinette. Dinner for two: $18.

**ALEX TAMBELLINI'S WOODS RESTAURANT** (**) (213 Wood St., Downtown). Many say the best seafood in town is available here, and some others say that it offers the best food period. Either the seafood or the beef is excellent. Dinner for two: $22.

**LOUIS TAMBELLINI'S** (**) (160 Southern Ave., Mt. Washington.) A popular seafood place, where you can expect to wait for your table on weekends. The fish is superb, the Caesar salad is very nice, but steer clear of Italian entrées as ambitious as saltimbocca. Dinner for two: $21.

**THE TIN ANGEL** (*) (Grandview Ave., Mt. Washington). Good beef, interesting side dishes, and a stunning view are the chief attractions. A bit expensive for what it offers, however. Dinner for two: $30.

**SGRO'S** (**) (Campbell's Run Rd., off Parkway W.). The straightforward entrées, prepared under the watchful eye of the owner-chef, are enhanced by the attention paid to the garnishes, appetizers, and side dishes. Dinner for two: $28.

*Not Recommended*

**LE MONT** (Grandview Ave., Mt. Washington). This plush and well-known Pittsburgh restaurant is still capable of outstanding meals, especially with its beef dishes, but is also entirely able to serve perfectly wretched food. In addition, the immense dining room gives the place all the ambiance of an amphitheater.

**TOP OF THE TRIANGLE** (U.S. Steel Bldg.). This is a Stouffer operation with exceptional prices out of line with the routine food. For some reason, the decorator went out of his way to capture the flavor of a rathskeller—62 stories above street level.

## Recommended Reading

A WALKING TOUR OF PITTSBURGH    (Pittsburgh Council for International Visitors, 408 Bruce Hall, University of Pittsburgh, Pittsburgh, Pa. 15213, 50¢). A 22-page guide, with descriptions, explanations, and photographs of various noteworthy sights.

GILBERT LOVE'S GO GUIDE    (Pittsburgh Press, $2). Provides information on areas around the city to go for vacations, weekend trips, etc. Found on newsstands.

PITTSBURGH AREA NEWCOMER'S GUIDE    (Thomas O'Keefe and Associates, Inc., $1.75). Lists communities and areas around the city, including information on schools, homes, taxes, cultural activities, etc. Available at many newsstands.

PITTSBURGH TODAY    (Convention and Visitors Bureau, Gateway Center, Pittsburgh, Pa., 15230). Contains 95 pages of color photos of main points of interest, with information on restaurants, shopping, etc.

PITTSBURGH: THE STORY OF AN AMERICAN CITY by Stefan Lorant. (Doubleday and Co., $12.50). Few cities have such a dedicated and talented biographer, whose affection for Pittsburgh is sincere—and contagious.

# ST. LOUIS

There is something nostalgic about St. Louis. It's the birthplace of the ice cream cone and the hot dog, the home of the Stan Musial Cardinals, the namesake for Lucky Lindy's plane (he raised the cash there), the barn for Budweiser's Clydesdales, and the place to meet Louie.

Indeed, St. Louis does have a rich history—dating back well over 200 years. In 1764 a French fur trapper named Laclede founded a trading post on the banks of the Mississippi, and that started it all. Lewis and Clark came by a little later and began their trip west from here up the nearby Missouri River. When the Riverboat ruled the rivers, St. Louis was in its prime.

But the twentieth century hasn't been so kind to the "dowager of the Mississippi." Like many major cities, St. Louis has had its share of urban decay. However, the city fathers are doing all they can to reverse that pattern. Certainly, it is still a thriving business center, and a hub for rail, water, truck, and air transportation. Within a radius of 500 miles there are a market of over 83 million people and 3,000 manufacturing plants.

The most conspicuous thing about St. Louis—aside from the mighty ole Miss—is the Gateway Arch, which symbolizes the city as gateway to the West. True enough. But Wisenheimers quip that the 630-ft. monument—the nation's tallest and weirdest—gives St. Louis the dubious distinction of being the only city in the country with a handle on it.

But because it is an old city, getting a handle on St. Louis isn't all that easy for the first-time visitor. There is a downtown, of course, but the city spills out unchecked from there. And the airport is a good 45 minutes by cab from downtown, more in rush-hour traffic. Best bet: rent a car. You will need one to get around, and it will also come in handy if you have any time for sight-seeing. And make sure you know which sections of the city you will be doing business in beforehand, so you can select an appropriate hotel.

## Hotels

Fortunately, there is ample hotel and motel space in all areas of the city.

Downtown, you have two good choices in the **Stouffer's Riverfront Inn** and the **Bel Air East,** both near the Gateway Arch. Midtown, near Forest Park, there is the venerable **Chase-Park Plaza. The Cheshire Inn & Lodge** and the **Bel Air West** are in the same league, should the Chase-Park be full—which it often is.

In Clayton, central St. Louis County, the **Clayton Inn** and the **Colony Hotel** are more than suitable. In South County, stay at the **Breckenridge Ramada Inn;** in West County make it the **Sheraton West Port Inn.** If you are staying near the airport, the **Marriott Motor Hotel** is your best choice.

## Restaurants

St. Louis is a good city to eat in—and has some unexpected pleasures. The beef you can count on, sure, but Italian and German cuisine? Catfish that's delicious?

Of course, there are the floating restaurants, the pseudo-sternwheelers and the like, and you've got to eat in at least one. **Al's** has an elegant riverboat atmosphere, if not the river itself, and very good Continental cuisine. **Bayou Belle** is an actual sternwheeler, although it has been moved inland. The antebellum atmosphere might overshadow the food, however, although the Cordon Bleu and steaks are fine. **Becky Thatcher Paddlewheeler Restaurant** is the real McCoy, docked at the riverfront at Showboat Landing. It also has entertainment. The seafood and steaks are good. But best of all is the **Robert E. Lee,** where the steaks and seafood match the environment. No working riverboat could ever have been appointed as elegantly as this one in retirement, so . . . we pretend a little bit.

If you like Italian food, you're in luck. **Tony's** is one of the best Italian restaurants anywhere. They serve other specialties as well, and no matter what you order, it should be excellent. Don't miss it, even though you will have to wait for a table. Other fine Italian restaurants include **Kemoll's, Rich & Charlie's, Lombardo's** (which also serves French), and **Al Baker's.**

You can get an excellent steak in an elegant fin de siècle setting at the **Tenderloin Room** of the Chase-Park Plaza, with service to match. **The Cheshire Inn** is done in olde English, and serves fine prime ribs and roast duck.

Don't laugh—**Catfish & Crystal** is a great spot for prime ribs, steaks, and, of course, catfish. You Yankees stop scoffing and try some, hear? If you're chicken, there are more conventional seafood dishes served in **Nantucket Cove,** very New England.

## *Potpourri*

This is no place to fool around after the sun sets—not that it's all that dangerous, certainly no more than any other major city. Exception: East St. Louis, Illinois. That's your basic tough neighborhood. There just isn't that much to do. Periodically someone breathes life into Gaslight Square, but it really isn't much. Besides, with the city so spread out, as a stranger you'll spend half the night finding the isolated spots that do jump. For that reason, the hotels often have very good entertainment—stay there and relax after dinner.

For **sports** fans, there are several ball teams, of course. The baseball Cardinals are consistently worth watching. The football Cardinals have to be seen to be believed (ask a contact for ducats). The Hockey Blues surprised a lot of people with their good play. Soccer is also popular—the Stars play where both Cardinal teams do, Busch Stadium.

If you like sight-seeing, there is plenty to see. Most obvious is the mighty **Mississippi.** Many excursion boats offer 60-minute guided tours, or, you can take a cruise aboard the steamer *Admiral,* the world's largest river excursion steamer.

Downtown, besides the Gateway Arch and its museum, there's the **Old Courthouse,** scene of the famous Dred Scott Case and now a museum to the nation's history of westward expansion; the **Old Cathedral,** oldest west of the Mississippi; the **home of Eugene Field,** the famous children's poet; **Campbell House,** with original furnishings of the Victorian era; **Chatillon-DeMenil Mansion,** one of the finest examples of Greek Revival architecture. On the southern edge of downtown is **Ralston Purina**'s great research center, involved in improving the world's food supply, and **Anheuser-Busch**'s "World's largest" brewery, which offers free tours—and samples. And, there's the riverfront, with its boats and the Goldenrod Showboat for "old tyme melodrammers."

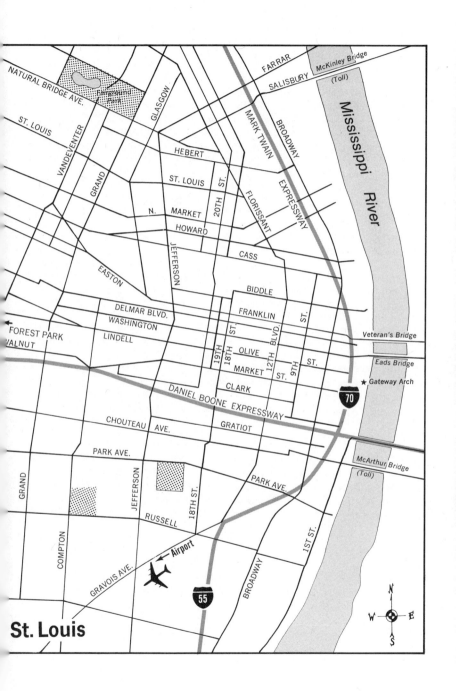

The city is also famous for the world's largest and finest equipped zoo, occupying 83 acres in 1,400-acre **Forest Park.** The park also has the fine St. Louis Art Museum; the Jefferson Memorial Museum (housing the Lindbergh trophies); a Municipal Opera, boasting a magnificent summer outdoor theater; the renowned McDonnell Planetarium; the Jewel Box, a unique floral conservatory; and the Missouri Historical Society, with its exhibit of western America.

Three miles south of Forest Park is the **Missouri Botanical (Shaw's) Garden,** one of the largest exhibition and experimental gardens of plant life in the Western Hemisphere. Here, too, is the world famous geodesic-domed Climatron with its large collection of plants in a tropical environment.

A short drive west of Forest Park is the **Museum of Science and Natural History.**

In suburban St. Louis attractions include the **Museum of Transport** and **Grant's Farm,** a 281-acre tract which includes land once owned by Gen. Ulysses S. Grant and which was turned into a zoo and game preserve by the August A. Busch (brewery) family.

For history buffs, in nearby Florissant, there's old **St. Ferdinand's,** where Mother Duchesne, beatified by the Catholic Church, worked and where Father DeSmet, the Indians' "Black Robe," was ordained. The main street of **St. Charles,** site of Missouri's first capitol, has been restored.

In nearby Illinois, on Hwy. 460, eight miles east of St. Louis, is the **Shrine of Our Lady of the Snows,** largest outdoor shrine in the country. On Alternate 40, about 9 miles east of St. Louis, are the **Cahokia Mounds,** remnants of a great pre-Columbian city, covering 4,000 acres. Between A.D. 800 and A.D. 1500 this city had about 35,000 inhabitants. Much of it has been restored by archeologists.

A 35-minute drive from St. Louis is **Six Flags Over Mid-America,** a great 200-acre theme park, open from Memorial Day through Labor Day.

As for that Big Handle. Yes, you can ride to the top of it. And on a clear day, you can see . . . St. Louis.


## *Nitty Gritty*

## HOTELS

*Downtown*

**BEL AIR EAST** (4th & Washington). Superior. Just north of Gateway Arch.

**DOWNTOWNER MOTOR INN** (12th & Washington). Acceptable.

**JEFFERSON HOTEL** (415 N. 12th). Acceptable.
**MAYFAIR HOTEL** (806 St. Charles). Acceptable.
**RAMADA INN** (U.S. Highway 40 at Grand Blvd.) Acceptable.
**RODEWAY INN** (Jefferson & Market). Good.
**STOUFFER'S RIVERFRONT INN** (200 South 4th). Superior.
Excellent view overlooking Gateway Arch.

*Midtown—Near Forest Park*
**CHASE-PARK PLAZA** (Lindell & Kingshighway). Superior.
**BEL AIR WEST** (4630 Lindell Blvd.). Good.
**CHESHIRE INN & LODGE** (6300 Clayton Rd.). Good.
**FOREST PARK HOTEL** (4910 W. Pine Blvd.). Good. Inexpensive.

*Clayton—central St. Louis County*
**CLAYTON INN** (7750 Carondelet). Superior.
**COLONY** (7730 Bonhomme). Superior.

*Airport*
**MARRIOTT MOTOR HOTEL** (I-70 at Airport). Superior.
Indoor-outdoor pool, sauna, etc.
**HILTON AIRPORT INN** (10330 Natural Bridge). Good. Soon
to be operated by Musial & Biggie's.
**SHERATON AIRPORT INN** (4201 N. Lindbergh). Good.
**RODEWAY INNS OF AMERICA** (10232 Natural Bridge). Good.

*South County*
**BRECKENRIDGE RAMADA INN** (800 S. Highway Dr., across
from Chrysler Plant). Superior. Has name entertainment.

*West County*
**SHERATON WEST PORT INN** (Page & I-270). Superior. Newest
and one of the finest with its own entertainment complex.

## RESTAURANTS

**AL BAKER'S** (***) (8101 Clayton Rd.). Italian and gourmet specialties. Ask for specialties; many are not on the menu. Well known.
Dinner for two: $30.
**AL'S RESTAURANT** (***) (1st & Biddle). Continental cuisine;
specialties include rack of lamb, steak Siciliana. Elegant riverboat
atmosphere of 1850 era. Dinner for two: approximately $30.
**ANTHONY'S** (***) (10 Broadway). Continental menu, superb
decor and service. Crêpes, tournedos, duckling, etc. That league.
Dinner for two: $30.
**BAYOU BELLE** (**) (12341 St. Charles Rock Rd.). Lobster
Cordon Bleu, stuffed Dover sole, prime steaks. Elegant antebellum

atmosphere on sternwheeler moved inland. Entertainment in lounge. Dinner for two: $25.

**BECKY THATCHER PADDLEWHEELER RESTAURANT** (**) (Showboat Landing). Prime steaks and fresh seafoods plus a varied menu. Floating riverboat decorated accordingly. Dinner and entertainment nightly. Dinner for two: $25.

**BEL AIR EAST** (**) (4th & Washington). **Open Hearth** has Colonial specialties. Also **Trader Vic's,** with exotic South Seas atmosphere. Dinner for two: $25.

**BEL AIR WEST** (**) (4630 Lindell Blvd.). Good breakfast-to-dinner menus. Popular after theater. Free bus service to hockey games. Dinner for two: $20.

**BEVO MILL RESTAURANT** (**) (4749 Gravois). Modeled after Old-World windmill. Features German specialties like sauerbraten and wiener schnitzel, plus steaks and seafood. Sauerbraten dinner for two: $11.

**CATFISH & CRYSTAL** (***) (409 N. 11th St.). Fine American dishes, including prime ribs, steaks, delightful fish, especially catfish and corn bread, a rebel's delight. Dinner for two: $12.

**CHESHIRE INN** (***) (7036 Clayton Ave. at Skinker, just west of Forest Park). Authentic olde English setting—fine prime ribs, roast duck, seafood. Dinner for two: $20.

**CREST HOUSE** (**) (Broadway & Chestnut). Good beef and steak. Businessmen's hangout. Dinner for two: $24.

**EBERHARD'S** (**) (117 N. Main, Columbia, Ill.). Authentic German cuisine, German draft beer, finest German wines. With its gemuetlich air, it is worth the 25-mile drive from downtown. Dinner for two: $17.50.

**HOUSE OF MARET** (**) (3811 S. Lindbergh). Fine German fare in an Old-World German Gast Haus. Outdoor Bier Garten from mid-May nightly through mid-September. Dinner for two: $20.

**KEMOLL'S** (***) (4201 N. Grand). Distinctive Italian cuisine, elegant atmosphere. Check for international gourmet nights. Dinner for two: $20.

**LA SALA** (**) (513 Olive Street). Extensive selection of Mexican dishes. Dinner for two: $15.

**LOMBARDO'S** (***) (W. Florissant & Riverview). Excellent Italian and French dishes. Try Vealchops Dianna. Dinner for two: $20.

**MUSIAL & BIGGIE'S STEAK HOUSE** (**) (5130 Oakland Ave.). You may run into Stan the Man, but not the best food. Dinner for two: $20.

**NANTUCKET COVE** (***) (40 N. Kingshighway). Fresh seafood of all kinds; authentic New England fishing village atmosphere. Dinner for two: $20.

**RICH & CHARLIE'S TRATTORIA** (***) (5920 Clayton Ave.). Italian dishes in a cozy bistro atmosphere. Dinner for two: $25.

**ROBERT E. LEE** (***) (100 S. Wharf St.). Riverfront boat restaurant, elegantly furnished. Seafood, steaks, and other dishes. A must. Dinner for two: $20.

**ROSE'S ITALIAN RESTAURANT** (**) (925 Martin Luther King Blvd.) St. Louis' oldest and still a favorite. Dinner for two: $20.

**RUGGERI'S RESTAURANT** (**) (2300 Edwards). One of several good Italian restaurants in the "Hill Section," southwest St. Louis. Dinner for two: $25.

**SCHNEITHORST'S HOFAMBERG INN** (**) (Lindbergh & Clayton rds.). Good German fare in a Bavarian setting. Entertainment nightly in Weinskeller Cocktail Lounge. Dinner for two: $20.

**SEA CHASE** (**) (Chase Park Plaza Hotel, Kingshighway & Lindell). Fishing village atmosphere. Fresh seafood, oysters, clams, shrimp. Special stand-up oyster bar. Dinner for two: $24.

**SHANGHAI INN** (**) (606 Pine St.). Peking and Mandarin dishes; suitably Oriental atmosphere. Dinner for two: $20.

**SLAY'S** (**) (2652 Hampton Ave.). International cuisine. Lebanese every Monday. Dinner for two: $20.

**STOUFFER'S RIVERFRONT INN** (**) (200 S. 4th St.). St. Louis' only revolving restaurant. Steaks, chops, and seafood. Best view of city and Gateway Arch. Dinner for two: $25.

**TENDERLOIN ROOM** (***) (Chase Park Plaza Hotel, Kingshighway & Lindell). Famous for steaks, chops; Victorian decor, crackerjack service. Dinner for two: $30.

**TONY'S** (***) (826 N. Broadway). None better in town. Glorious food, Italian and otherwise, and superb service. No reservations accepted. Allow at least 30 minutes for waiting after 7:00 P.M. Dinner for two: $25.

## Recommended Reading

There are a number of good books available at the St. Louis Visitors Center, 330 Mandion House Center, and at the riverfront by the Gateway Arch. Among the best:

GUIDE TO PLACES IN AND NEAR ST. LOUIS by Rosemary Goodson. ($1). Loaded with facts, figures, admission prices, etc.

ADVENTURES IN ST. LOUIS by Harry W. Hagen. ($2). Suggestions on what to see and do.

THE ST. LOUIS VISITORS CENTER RESTAURANT GUIDE (free). A good list of where to dine.

# SAN FRANCISCO

To the visitor, San Francisco must rank as the nation's most feminine city. It presents a variety of faces—some naughty, others quite dignified, still others warm and comfortable. It can be ugly when caught without makeup. Witness Market Street, once a true open-air market, now a chopped-up road as a result of the construction of BART, the mass transit system that finally arrived in San Francisco, but still isn't debugged.

Along Broadway in North Beach, San Francisco's naughty face blinks in neon, with signs of "Love-In" and barkers beckoning the innocent to a "night you won't forget." Actually, you just might, since topless has been banned. Most locals avoided these rip-off joints anyway, of course, and weren't too alarmed at their demise. There still are a few pasties here and there, however.

A prettier facet of San Francisco is its cultural life. And locals pride themselves on taking full advantage of the ample opera, symphony, and theater offered, and often attend black tie. Not that they are pretentious, however. No one blinked an eye when topless entered the scene (or when it left).

Nor would anyone be too shocked to learn his boss/landlord/mother-in-law smoked "funny cigarettes" every now and then. San Franciscans love to tolerate the bizarre. Men dressed as women, women embracing, or all coming out of the closet at the same time—so what?

But this tolerance is strictly for locals. Enter one tourist, decked out in white belt and shoes and burgundy knit pants asking directions to Telegraph Hill, and he'll probably be pointed straight to the airport. (Such attire is anathema to locals.) A worse offense: Call the city "Frisco." You may have to hole up in your hotel until you leave.

One reason for the local pride evident in so many San Franciscans stems from the city's compact size and the neighborliness that it fosters. You can walk from the Union Square area to the financial district in ten minutes, and from there to North Beach in another ten.

A reason for the city's fickleness may be its Barbary Coast past, which started in the Gold Rush days, and brought gambling, boozing, and whoring to a large section around the financial district and North Beach. Some say the city is still trying to live down those debauched days, while others claim it is still trying to live up to them.

## *Hotels*

San Francisco is, of course, a city of hills and views. And two hotels typify the best of both—the **Mark Hopkins** and the **Fairmont** on Nob Hill. Each has its die-hard supporters; take your pick.

The **Stanford Court** is a newer contender in the area located one door from the Mark Hopkins.

On Union Square, the **St. Francis** is the finest old hotel in town, if that's to your liking. The **Sir Francis Drake** shares the same neighborhood, but not the same reputation, although it, too, is a favorite among old-timers.

Some of the newer hotels in town built for tourists have become tourist spots in themselves—the Portman-designed **Hyatt Regency** in particular, with its huge atrium, complete with cooing birds and sculpture, worth seeing even if you don't stay there. The **Hyatt on Union Square** and the **Westbury,** both near Union Square, are fine, distinctive hotels. The **Clift** is still known as the "personal" hotel in San Francisco, with a faithful, conservative clientele.

## *Restaurants*

When dining, don't try to scrimp in San Francisco, where there are over 2,600 restaurants, offering a wide variety of excellent cuisines. For French, **La Bourgogne** is the best, followed by **Le Trianon, L'Orangerie, L'Etoile,** and **Fleur de Lys.**

For Italian, there's **Doro's, Vanessi's, Ristorante Orsi,** and the many family-style spots in North Beach where the waitress will mother you for the entire meal. For Chinese, the **Mandarin** has the No. 1 spot, though **Kan's** and the **Empress of China** offer fine meals.

Fisherman's Wharf, long touted for its seafood, has turned commercial and tacky. It appears at times to be one huge souvenir shop.

If you still want to venture, however, **Castagnola's** is the best choice. But you could stay downtown and eat at the **Tadich Grill** or **Sam's Grill** and partake of what is really the best seafood in town.

Worth the expense-account-only prices, **Ernie's** is probably the most famous restaurant in the city—with food that rates the reputation.

Don't be leery of word-of-mouth advice from locals. San Franciscans keep a lot of the best places to themselves.


## *Potpourri*

After dinner, San Francisco relaxes a bit and offers a broad range of entertainment options: jazz, theater, opera, sports, and lower forms of amusement.

The Fairmont Hotel's **Venetian Room** has name entertainers. In a more swinging vein, **Earthquake McGoon's** Dixieland jazz club is a fun dancing, dining, and drinking spot. **Basin Street West** offers jazz and supper. The **Finocchio Club** provides very good female impersonators—who look like the girls you never took home to mother.

Despite its swinging reputation, liberated women, and plethora of singles bars, San Francisco can be a lonely town if you are on your own. To be sure, there are tourist traps for those seeking to buy companionship: The **Tenderloin** is known as hooker territory. Polk Street has its gay bars.

But if you just want a quiet drink, and perhaps some friendly conversation in a decent part of town, Union Street is the best and safest bet.

**Perry's** is the most respectable, but there's nothing tawdry about **Thomas Lord's, Slater Hawkins, The Cooperage,** or **Pierce Street Annex** (loud music, dancing).

Downtown the best scenes are found at **Harpoon Louie's, Paoli's, Templebar,** the **Iron Horse, The X Change.**

The raunchiest of raunchy swingles bars is **Ripples,** One Embarcadero, in the financial district.


The **Geary and Curran theaters,** near Union Square, run everything from Shakespeare to Coward. Peruse the local papers for shows by little theater groups, which have a large following in San Francisco. After theater, **David's Delicatessen** or **Pam-Pam East** are fun eateries.

San Francisco has more than its share of **sports.** There are the pros: Seals (hockey team), Golden State Warriors (basketball), 49'ers and

Oakland Raiders (football), and the Giants and A's (baseball).

Stanford and the University of California (Berkeley) offer a great range of college sports events if you are up to a little more traveling to see them.

If the family is in tow this trip, take a day and visit **Golden Gate Park.** Try the de Young Museum, which includes the Brundage collection of Asian art. When the kids weary of the Steinhart Aquarium, the Morrison Planetarium, and the Fleishhacker Zoo, take them to the Japanese Tea Garden for tea and fortune cookies. It's located next door to the de Young.

The park also has a lovely arboretum and Stow Lake where you can rent a boat. Note: The park, however, isn't very safe at night. Plan to leave by sundown.

A favorite half-day trip for all Bay Area residents is the **ferryboat ride** to Sausalito. But avoid the half-hour ride at commuter hour when seats are grabbed quickly and kids are scowled at by harried workers. For a nice lunch at Sausalito, try the **Trident,** a semi-hip, organic place with haute prices, braless waitresses, and a fabulous water view.

A less-mobbed version of Sausalito is **Tiburon,** also reached by ferry. It resembles Portofino, Italy, with its mini-villas, trees, and sailboats. You'll find the local tennis/sailing set sipping gin fizzes at **Sam's Cafe,** an unpretentious, sea-worn afternoon spot. For a good dinner, try the **Dock.**

For a day-by-day rundown of local events, dial 391-2000. The Convention and Visitors Bureau lists the main events for the day.

## *Nitty Gritty*

## HOTELS

*Superior*

**FAIRMONT** (California & Mason sts.). Recently renovated with atmosphere still bustling, due to the hotel's many restaurants and bars. Interesting people-watching lobby.

**MARK HOPKINS** (On Nob Hill, at California & Mason sts,). One of San Francisco's finest and oldest. Recent renovations throughout have only added to its charm. Easy access to most of city.

**ST. FRANCIS** (Powell St., between Geary & Post sts.). A happy combination of old and new, though the older section is a little darker. Tower section affords some of San Francisco's best viewing.

**STANFORD COURT** (California & Powell sts.). Newest addition to the Nob Hill hotel group. Turn-of-the-century theme, carried off with friendly, gracious service. Top location.

## Good

**CLIFT** (Geary & Taylor sts.). Personalized service prime selling point here. Quiet, small, no crowds. Note: don't bring a long-haired son with you. He'll be refused seating in the dining room.

**HYATT REGENCY** (5 Embarcadero Center). Service not yet seasoned enough. Rooms small for the high prices asked. Glamour abounds, but the lobby may be the best part of this hotel.

**HYATT ON UNION SQUARE** (Stockton & Post sts.). Not as bustling as the Regency, but closer to the hub of shopping, theater, and business. Room rates vary with view and floor.

**HUNTINGTON** (1075 California St.). A quiet, dignified hotel on top of Nob Hill. Good address for those who yearn for privacy and quiet.

**MIYAKO** (1625 Post St.). Out-of-the-way location, but fine service. Here's where you can get one of few legitimate massages in San Francisco. Suites have saunas and mats for sleeping.

**WESTBURY** (480 Sutter St.). A new Knott hotel, two blocks from Union Square. Rooms seem to overly compensate for dark locale with the brightest of reds, purples, and yellows. Otherwise, quiet.

## Not Recommended

**JACK TAR** (Van Ness Ave.). If this hostelry is famous outside San Francisco, the locals can't be blamed. For they cast every disparaging word on this place, as it is lacking in any distinguishable character. Noisy and out of the way, too.

# RESTAURANTS

**ADOLPH'S** (\*\*\*) (641 Vallejo St.). Intimate, very cozy, featuring Northern Italian cooking. Try the cappelini. Dinner for two: approximately $30.

**ALEXIS** (\*\*\*) (1001 California St.). Expensive Middle Eastern/ French spot. Dinner for two: $40.

**BLUE FOX** (\*\*) (659 Merchant St.). Once the place to dine, now a bit overrated. Still, an elegant meal, especially its Italian dishes. Dinner for two: $40.

**CARNELIAN ROOM** (\*\*) (555 California St. atop Bank of America Center). One of the city's finest views, followed by average food. Dinner for two: $40.

**CASTAGNOLA** (\*\*) (286 Jefferson St.). The only Fisherman's Wharf restaurant worth going to. Try the abalone or calamari. Order selectively and you can get a good meal. Dinner for two: $20.

**CHO-CHO** (**) (1020 Kearny St.). Great Japanese lunches and dinners. Financial district. Dinner for two: $25.

**DORO'S** (***) (714 Montgomery St.). One of the best lunch spots in the financial district. Elegant, but not flashy. Good Italian menu, though there's Continental too. Try the canneloni or fish dishes. Lunch for two: $12. Dinner for two: $30.

**EMPRESS OF CHINA** (***) (838 Grant Ave.). Great decor, food and view. Lunch and dinner. Dinner for two: $35.

**ERNIE'S** (***) (847 Montgomery St.). San Francisco's big apple. The most in Victorian and red velvet. Very formal, very good. Dinner for two: $45.

**FLEUR DE LYS** (***) (777 Sutter St.). Intimate and French. Dinner for two: $40.

**FOURNOU'S OVENS** (**) (At the Stanford Court Hotel). Fine spot. Rack of lamb a good choice. Dinner for two: $45.

**JACK'S** (***) (615 Sacramento St.). Some French, some seafood. An old tradition in San Francisco dining. Fine service. Lunch and dinner. Dinner for two: $25.

**KAN'S** (***) (708 Grant Ave.). Hollywood stars have been known to fly up just for one meal here. Try the Peking duck, but order 24 hours ahead. Dinner for two: $35.

**LA BOURGOGNE** (***) (320 Mason St.). Best French restaurant in town, and that's going some. Dinner for two: $45.

**L'ETOILE** (**) (1075 California St.). Opulent Louis XVI setting at the Huntington Hotel. Dinner for two: $45.

**LE TRIANON** (***) (242 O'Farrell St.). Another superb French spot. Dinner for two: $40.

**L'ODEON** (**) (565 Clay St.). A strange but workable combination of French and Greek food. Dinner for two: $40.

**L'ORANGERIE** (**) (419 O'Farrell St.). Menu superb, but small. One of the best French restaurants. Dinner for two: $45.

**THE MANDARIN** (***) (900 North Point St. at Ghirardelli Sq.). Cantonese at its best. Try the beggar's chicken. Dinner for two: $35.

**RISTORANTE ORSI** (**) (375 Bush St.). Some of the finest Italian cooking outside North Beach. Dinner for two: $35.

**SAM'S GRILL** (***) (374 Bush St.). For seafood, Sam's is in the top two. No frills. In the financial district. Great lunch spot. Lunch for two: $15.

**SCHROEDER'S** (**) (240 Front St.). For lunch. Totally masculine, beer-hall atmosphere, though ladies are now allowed any time of the day. Lunch for two: $10.

**TADICH GRILL** (***) (240 California St.). In the same class as Sam's. It's packed every noon, so get there early. Seafood. Lunch for two: $12.

**TRADER VIC'S** (\*\*) (20 Cosmo Pl.). San Francisco has one too. Dinner for two: $30.

**VANESSI'S** (\*\*) (498 Broadway). Try it when you're exploring the Broadway scene. A good Italian spot. Dinner for two: $20.

**YAMATO** (\*\*\*) (717 California St.). Best in Japanese eating. Take a client for lunch or spouse for dinner. Dinner for two: $25.

## Recommended Reading

THE DOLPHIN GUIDE TO SAN FRANCISCO AND THE BAY AREA by Curt Gentry. (Doubleday, Dolphin Books, $1.25).

INSIDER'S GUIDE TO FUN AND SERIOUS DRINKING IN SAN FRANCISCO by George Green, Edward Everett with William Gong. (VCIM/SF Publications, $1.85).

THE GOOD TIMES MANUAL by Russel Riera and C. J. Smith. (Moss Publications, $1.95).

BEAR FLAG REPUBLIC (110 Sutter St., San Francisco, Calif. 94104. Subscription only.) Monthly newsletter from San Francisco on hotels and restaurants.

AN OPINIONATED GUIDE TO SAN FRANCISCO by Franz Hansell. (Ballantine Books, $1.95).

# SEATTLE

If business brings you to Seattle, try to plan your trip on either end of a weekend so you can make your stay as long as possible. Seattle is richer in natural endowments than any other city in the U.S. Weather permitting, it is a pity not to see as much of the Puget Sound area as possible.

First off, get yourself some wheels. A car is an absolute must even for a brief stay, not only for sight-seeing but also because cabs can be scarcer than cops at crucial hours.

The city was a bargain when the settlers bought it for $16,000 from Chief Seattle in 1851 and it is still a bargain to the visitor today. You need not spend a fortune to enjoy it.

Seattle is an outdoors city as is exemplified by the awesome presence of 14,410-ft. Mt. Rainier, which is visible throughout the entire city on clear days. But there are plenty of London-like days, too, when it seems it will never stop raining. Which is all the more reason to enjoy outdoor activities when the rain finally does cease.

But those rains mean water—and Seattle has plenty of it. There's Elliott Bay just off the shore of downtown and the better residential areas; the 20-mile long Lake Washington, which edges the city to the east and makes for sporty sailing in the fall and spring; and the ship canal connecting the two, with its picturesque rotting hulks and salmon-boat terminals.

Downtown is clean, modern, and tidy—a convenient place to do business, but a hard place to generate much excitement. A city that was settled predominantly by farm stock from the northern Midwest, Seattle still is early to bed and early to rise (8:00 A.M. calls are not unusual). On weekends, any time of year, the city empties for skiing, hiking, boating, and other sports.

## Hotels

In downtown Seattle itself, there are only a few good hotels. The venerable old **Olympic Hotel,** flagship of the giant chain of Western International Hotels, is very well preserved, but service has slowed and the food has fallen off as the flagship has drifted embarrassingly into the red. Currently, the most popular hotel downtown is Western's modern cylindrical tower, the **Washington Plaza,** with its splendid views and friendly service. If a convention at Seattle Center, site of the '62 World's Fair, is what brings you to town, the **Royal Inn** and the **Century House** are handy. The **Edgewater Inn,** while a bit faded, is near the Center, and from it you can also drop a fishing line into Elliott Bay.

At the Seattle-Tacoma International Airport, the **Sea-Tac Motor Inn,** a purple Polynesian palace on twenty-four acres, offers lots of luxury and plenty of facilities. But most local businessmen prefer the older **Hyatt House** and its more settled staff. Probably the best solution is to drive up Interstate 5 a few miles to the shopping center called Southcenter and stay at the **Doubletree Inn,** a swinging place removed from the gaudy strip, close to the airport, and attracting a smarter set.

Bellevue, a city of 60,000 across Lake Washington from Seattle, might be your destination. If so, the choice is clearly the **Bellevue Holiday Inn,** an attractively designed motel with ambitious restaurants and bars. The other likely location outside of downtown would be the district surrounding the University of Washington. The **Sherwood Motor Inn,** a little far away on Interstate 5, is the modern place, but a striking old hotel now remodeled into the **University Tower** is the best bet.

## Restaurants

Once quartered, things will start looking up. The restaurant scene, for one thing, is very satisfying for a city of this size and youth.

Downtown these are standouts: **Benihana of Tokyo,** a good example of the chain and nicely tucked into a plaza across from the Olympic; **Canlis',** a steak house that does all you could ever hope for with that genre and throws in a terrific view and a fine wine cellar to boot; **Mirabeau,** an extremely good French restaurant (on good nights) atop the town's tallest building, the 50-story Seattle First National Bank Building (but remember to exercise firm control over your waiter); **El Gaucho,** another steak house, and a great place to go late in the evening, when their hunt breakfast begins; **Trader Vic's,** particularly for the European food and the meats roasted in the Chinese ovens; and **Rosellini's 410,** a sometimes-great place with a San Francisco-style menu of American and French and Italian specialties. It is a strong suit, and the quality is just as good at lunch.

There is a good deal more. Many will naturally seek a seafood restaurant, particularly one located on the water. Most of these are poor, suffering from touristitis just as the **Space Needle** does (a nice place to visit, but you wouldn't want to eat there). Best choices are **Frastani's,** on Pier 70, a reconditioned old pier now chockablock with shops and shoppers; **Ivar's Salmon House** on Lake Union, which is authentically designed to look like a Northwest Indian longhouse and cooks the salmon Indian-style, splayed over alder wood fires; and **Ray's Boat House,** a delightful, if off-center, place for lunch, looking out over Puget Sound, and the most serious about doing justice to the delectable local catch.

The town's gourmet Mecca is Pioneer Square, the heart of the old city, which is currently undergoing one of the most careful historic rehabilitations anywhere in the U.S. The area is a delightful place to spend some time, particularly around lunchtime when the downtown lawyers and government workers and architects descend upon The Square. It offers some very sophisticated art galleries (Polly Fried-lander's and the Foster/White Gallery would be the best), dozens of good shops (the most convenient collection is to be found in the Grand Central Arcade, First and South Main, an old hotel turned into a high-class Ghirardelli Square), outdoor cafés in the summer, and pleasant surprises like the tiny little **Amstelredamme Café,** 89 South Washington Street, featuring a playroom for children in the rear, cappuccino for tired mothers in the front, and a selection of locally made toys.

The restaurants in Pioneer Square are everywhere, wildly varying in quality. The **Brasserie Pittsbourg** in the basement of the grand old Pioneer Building is the one restaurant you should not leave the city without visiting: it is a brasserie more Parisian than those in Paris, THE place for lunch among the young sophisticates, and a place where the most demanding diner can find a regional specialty that does French justice to the ingredients.

Less raucous but just as perfectionist is the **Prague,** noted for Czech cooking up and down the West Coast: elegant decor, lovely presentation, and a superb handling of meat. Another good place, an

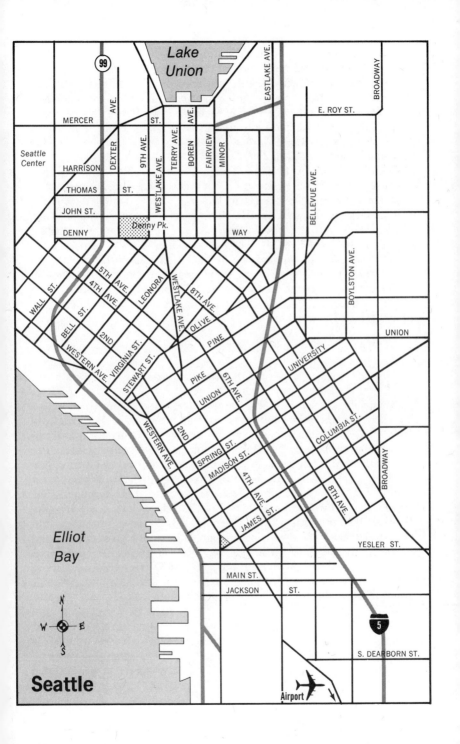

English one, is **Mr. Pickwick's Eating House.** After that, expect to get more atmosphere than good cooking for your tariff.

As a West Coast city, Seattle has a respectable little Chinatown, which is also worth a gastronomic pilgrimage, although not much else attracts. The **Four Seas** and the **Eight Immortals** are the two best places. Two good Japanese restaurants with tatami rooms are also in the area: the grand **Bush Garden** and the less grand but better **Nikko,** boasting a genuine sushi bar.

Best of all, however, is the **Yangtze Szechuan Restaurant,** incongruously located in Bellevue's Crossroads Shopping Center. The Yangtze is the best restaurant in the state, and possibly one of the best Chinese restaurants outside Peking. As the menu contains items indescribably hot, it is best to leave the ordering to the owners (Paul Yang will be most helpful). The suburbs, incidentally, contain three other good places: **Domani,** an Italian restaurant in Kirkland, **Le Provençal** a French spot in the same small town north of Bellevue, and **Henri de Navarre,** a Parisian establishment in Edmonds, just north of Seattle. Otherwise, in the suburbs, save your money for other forms of entertainment.

## Potpourri

Night life proper is thin. Name entertainment stops by at the crowded **Trojan Horse** downtown and at the grander **Jack McGovern's** on Lake Union, where you can also consume a passable meal. You might also check the **Marine Room** at the Olympic Hotel. The dominant style is more likely to be a local group of two performing at cheerful places like **The Wharf** (overlooking the wonderfully romantic fleet of Alaskan purse-seiners moored at Fisherman's Terminal), the **Chowder House** (Pier 70), the **Edgewater,** or the **Doubletree Inn.** The music is a little better down in Pioneer Square: jazz at the **Merchants Café** that is just as splendid as the restoration, and bluegrass at the funky **Inside Passage.** If things get too slow, you might repair to the **Mirabeau Bar,** 46 stories above the twinkling city. Should your quest for female companionship have failed to this point, then you had better plan to register at one of the airport motels.

One useful way to spend time is on the city's burgeoning cultural events. The **Seattle Opera Association,** mounting five productions a year, is capable of excellence, particularly if it is an Italian opera they are doing. Next would come the **Seattle Repertory Theater,** serving up accessible plays with excellent casts and solid productions. The **Seattle Symphony Orchestra** performs every two or three weeks.

Those demanding more unusual music (or drama) should check the calendar at the University of Washington, a large multiversity with strong performing arts traditions.

There are also some **sports** events worth taking in. The NBA Supersonics are still some distance from a title, but at least tickets are easy to get. The Western Hockey League Totems put a scrappy face on their losing efforts. Most popular—and hardest to get tickets for—is the football at U.W. stadium. Horse racing is at a beautiful—and fast—track: Longacres.

For your own exercise you will find lots of public tennis courts, bikes to rent (near the Arboretum is a good place to get one), and some excellent public golf courses (hilly, short Jackson to the north and scenic Jefferson to the south); of the private courses, there are venerable Seattle Gold (a bit of an old man's course), narrow Broadmoor, and one backbreaker: Sahale.

You won't want to leave the Queen City without some gifts, so the last day might be a good one for shopping. You'll have the most fun at one of the last remaining farmer's markets in the nation, the **Pike Place Market,** at the west end of Pike Street. It is a bustling, aromatic, sprawling warren of old buildings, glistening fresh vegetables, ethnic restaurants, and endless odds and ends. It also boasts one of the best coffee shops anywhere, and a good gift stop, **Starbuck's.** Other notable stores in town are: The **Fifth Avenue Record Shop** (1330 5th Ave.), one of the few record stores truly dedicated to the collector and classical-music connoisseur; **Keeg's** on Broadway, for tasteful home furnishings; **Globe Antiques** (1524 E. Olive Way), and **William L. Davis** (5th and University) for antiques, a surprisingly good buy out here, especially in undervalued colonial items; **Sur La Table** (78 Stewart) for very high-quality cookware; the **Northwest Craft Center** at Seattle Center, for ceramics from the region which many feel to be the best in the country; and the **University of Washington Bookstore,** second biggest college bookstore in America. There are also some very good department stores: **Frederick and Nelson,** beloved of old Seattle families and part of Marshall Field Group; **I. Magnin** (with the most stylish men's shop in the city); the Bergdorf-like **Nordstroms,** and the Bloomingdale-like **Bon Marché.** If you want to see what Seattle men want to look like, visit **Albert Ltd.** (5th and University) for clothes.

A good way to end your visit is to walk down to the place where

Seattle began: the central waterfront. Tourist traps abound, so buy your fish and chips at the **Sourdough** (Pier 57), and get out on the end of a pier, like Pier 56, where you can smell the fresh air. If the weather is smiling, you might have a glimpse of why it is many businessmen prefer to stay put in Seattle, even at considerable cuts in salary. The water is everywhere, the mountains jump out of the Sound in front of you, and the city itself—manageably small enough to encourage a rare urban optimism—continues its rapid growth on the flanks of a sunken volcano, striking modern office towers where once the last great forest of the Western world towered.

# HOTELS

*Good*

**BELLEVUE HOLIDAY INN** (1121 Main St., Bellevue). Easy access to the Freeway and the airport. Handsomely laid out, like a cloister, and offering uneven but ambitiously gourmet fare.

**DOUBLETREE INN** (at Southcenter, Interstates 5 & 405). A swinger's spot, with fine jazz on Sunday afternoons, good food and good rooms. Lots of salesmen on the prowl Friday nights.

**OLYMPIC HOTEL** (4th Ave. & Seneca St.). Clearly at the center of town, with four acceptable restaurants and a very nice bar. Small rooms, lots of conventions, but here's where the presidents stay.

**SEA-TAC MOTOR INN** (at the airport). Pools, lakes, outside elevators, fancy food, and a decor drawing on all the bad taste you ever dreamed of. Big, comfortable, bustling.

**WASHINGTON PLAZA** (5th Ave. at Westlake Ave.). Convention central at times, and the service can be slow, but here's how to take advantage of the best view and the best hotel restaurant.

*Acceptable*

**CAMLIN** (9th Ave. & Pine St.). A little off-center, but you get a pool, lanais, quiet, and good service. The bar upstairs is nice.

**CENTURY HOUSE** (8th Ave. & Bell St.). Near Seattle Center and has very good rates. You can sing-along in the bar if you wish.

**EDGEWATER INN** (Pier 67). Athletes and entertainers stay here. Be sure to get a waterside room or else you'll hear trains all night. Very lively.

**HILTON AIRPORT** (at Sea-Tac airport). It doesn't look like much, but there are large rooms and a putting green and some seclusion.

**HILTON DOWNTOWN** (6th Ave. & University St.). A bare-bones feel about the place, but the service is prompt and the views are high level. A struggling fancy restaurant topside.

**HOLIDAY INN OF SEA-TAC** (at the airport). Busy with small conventions. A revolving restaurant up top features singing waitresses and a view of numerous parking lots. Good service.

**HYATT HOUSE** (at the airport). The first one here: rambling, well like, jammed. Has all the facilities, sauna to putting green.

**DUNES** (1711 W. Meeker St., Kent). Boeing-bound businessmen will like this place. Good food, dancing in the evenings. Jammed with aerospace executives at lunch.

**ROOSEVELT** (7th Ave. & Pine St.). Lots of summer tour groups, but free from conventions. Quite good food. Nice location for shoppers.

**ROYAL INN** (8th Ave. & Denny Way). Close to the Center, small and ordinary except for the therapy pool and outside elevator (for a 3-story building).

**SHERWOOD MOTOR INN** (Interstate 5 at 50th St.). New and swinging, with a lively medieval cellar restaurant. Close to U.W.

**THUNDERBIRD-BELLEVUE** (Interstate 405 & N.E. 8th, Bellevue). Gaudy and awfully close to the Freeway, but well located and comfortable.

**UNIVERSITY TOWER** (Brooklyn Ave. & 45th St.). Good views, a bustling University district outside, and pretty good food downstairs.

# RESTAURANTS

**BENIHANA OF TOKYO** (**) (5th Ave. & University St.). The waiters here don't display quite the usual Benihana wizardry at the table-grill, but the bar is great and the view out to the IBM courtyard is notable. Dinner for two: approximately $25.

**BRASSERIE PITTSBOURG** (***) (1st Ave. & Cherry St.). Add an oyster vender out front and you'd be in Paris. May be moving a few blocks, but François Kissel will still be in charge. Good wines. Don't miss the mousse. Dinner for two: approximately $30.

**BUSH GARDEN** (*) (614 Maynard Ave. S). Heavy on the flowing waterfalls, a bit touristified, but they know how to cook too. Nice way to spend an evening. Dinner for two: approximately $20.

**CANLIS'** (**) (2576 Aurora Ave. N.). Restful and expert, with a dazzling view of Lake Union. Clams bordelaise, a peppercorn steak, and a rare Medoc from the special collection would be as good a meal as the town offers. Dinner for two: $45.

**DOMANI** (\*\*) (9714 Juanita Dr., Kirkland). The best Italian food around, short of Vancouver. Fritto misto is the best bet. No reservations, though. Dinner for two: $25.

**EIGHT IMMORTALS** (\*) (509 7th Ave. S.). Not as jammed as the others in Chinatown, and a little nicer inside. Ask for any special fresh fish. Dinner for two: $20.

**EL GAUCHO** (\*) (624 Olive Way). Very nice steaks, but better known for the mammoth hunt breakfasts served after midnight. Dark and atmospheric. Dinner for two: $30.

**FOUR SEAS** (\*\*) (714 S. King St.). The most accessible Chinese restaurant, with glorious steamed rock cod when they're in. Let the waiter order for you. Dinner for two: $25.

**FRASTANI'S** (\*) (Pier 70). A handsome room with a poor view and bumbling service, but if you're firm they'll do Italian seafood reasonably well. Dinner for two: $25.

**HENRI DE NAVARRE** (\*\*) (417 Main St., Edmonds). Banal decor, overcome by very good cooking. The best dish is the rack of lamb. Delicious pâté, well-selected wines. Dinner for two: $45.

**HINDQUARTER** (\*) (120 Lakeside). Probably the best of the steak-and-salad bar spots, with a friendly staff and a nice view of a sailboat marina. Dinner for two: $20.

**HORATIO'S** (1200 Westlake Ave.). Very popular, with overkill decor of an eighteenth century ship and serving "wenches." Steaks are always good. Dinner for two: $30.

**IVAR'S SALMON HOUSE** (\*) (401 N.E. Northlake Way). Alder-smoked salmon in a nice room overlooking Lake Union. Very popular with families. Dinner for two: $15.

**JAVA** (\*\*) (212 4th Ave. S.). An unlikely place, but here is excellent, cheap Indonesian fare. Order extra portions of the specialty satés. Dinner for two: $15.

**MIRABEAU** (\*\*) (Seattle First National Bank Building, 46th floor). An enormous French menu, a splendid view, and a kitchen capable of wonders. Great for lunch (stick with the day's "specialties"), and—if you get a good waiter—a nice way to spend a big evening. Scampi and the pheasant are notable. Dinner for two: $40.

**MISTER D'S** (\*) (1001 First Ave.). A zany place, with the best Greek cooking in town. Run-down, and the indispensable chef may not be there. Dinner for two: $15.

**MR. PICKWICK'S EATING HOUSE** (\*) (222 S. Main St.). Cozy and cute, with nice soups and good desserts, and a valiant try to make English food delicious. Dinner for two: $20.

**NIKKO** (\*\*) (Rainier & King). For those who want reasonably authentic Japanese food, particularly raw fish. Best salmon in town. Dinner for two: $20.

**PRAGUE** (\*\*) (1st Ave. & Main St.). Great soups, a lovely way with pork and beef, and an elegant room with the best service in town. Much lighter food than your image of Czech cooking suggests. Dinner for two: $30.

**PROVENCAL** (\*\*) (212 Central Way, Kirkland). The nicest and friendliest of the French restaurants, quiet and composed. Sensational oyster dish, and a wonderful tournedos in a pastry shell. Unusual wines. Dinner for two: $35.

**RAY'S BOAT HOUSE** (\*) (6049 Seaview Ave. N.W.). A good view of the boating, eager service, and a nice way with seafood. Clean, modern decor. Dinner for two: $25.

**ROSELLINI'S 410** (\*\*) (410 University St.). Very popular hangout for lunch, especially for Democratic politicians. Good waiters can steer you to a delicious Italian-French dinner. Excellent bar. Dinner for two: $40.

**SNOQUALMIE FALLS LODGE** (\*) (North Bend). A local tradition is to drive the family up to the lodge for a huge farm breakfast on Sundays. Nice anytime. Dinner for two: $20.

**THIRTEEN COINS** (\*) (125 Boren Ave.). Open 24 hours, and containing a large, fancy short-order menu. Great feel to the place, especially sitting at the counter. Dinner for two: $20.

**TRADER VIC'S** (\*\*) (5th & Westlake aves.). Fashionable at lunch, with a great late-hours bar, and a menu spanning East and West. Indonesian lamb roast is the best dish. Superb salads. Dinner for two: $40.

**WINDJAMMER** (\*) (7001 Seaview Ave. N.W., at Shilshole Marina). Nicely decorated rooms, with a terrific dance floor. The menu offers Maine lobster, but otherwise doesn't measure up to the view. Dinner for two: $30.

**YANGTZE SZECHUAN** (\*\*\*) (Crossroads, Bellevue). A grandmaster chef serving up the spicy cooking of Szechuan, a western Chinese province. It actually helps your health in rainy weather, and is sensationally good. Let Paul Yang order for you. Dinner for two: $25 to $40.

## *Recommended Reading*

GUIDEBOOK TO PUGET SOUND by Byron Fish. (Ward Ritchie Press, $1.95.) Rather brief about Seattle, and strong on history. Readable, if not very probing.

OUR TOWN   (Design Source, $1.) A good compendium of attractions, advertising-influenced.

SEATTLE HEDONIST    (Hedonist Publishing Co., $1.65). Stresses the unconventional, and not much use to anyone over thirty. Erratic judgments.

THE POOR MAN'S GUIDE TO SEATTLE RESTAURANTS    (Trojan Lithograph, $1.50). Out-of-the-way places, with little discrimination.

SUNSET TRAVEL GUIDE TO WASHINGTON    (Lane Magazine and Book Co., $2.95). The usual thorough job, with no ratings of private institutions. The best book for out-of-Seattle travels.

A GOURMET'S NOTEBOOK    (Argus Publishing Co., $15 a year, subscriptions only.) The most demanding restaurant guide, with monthly reports and discoveries. Likely to know the best new places.

# TORONTO

Incorporated in 1783 as the Town of York, Toronto (the word is Indian for meeting place) is today the fastest growing city in North America, and the heart of English Canada. Settled by British Empire Loyalists, Toronto is still conservative by nature. But waves of immigrants during the past two decades have forced a change upon this commercial and industrial center on the shores of Lake Ontario.

Toronto is a city that's fighting—so far successfully—to preserve its neighborhoods from encroaching high-risers, and to continue its growth without falling prey to the crime and decay of cities like New York and Detroit.

English reserve overrides all emotions, but the prevailing mood of Toronto is smug—not surprising considering the broadcast networks and most newsweeklies have done rave features on the city within the past two years. Vance Packard has called Toronto "the most civilized city in North America," but while it is indeed a city that works, it is not yet a mature cosmopolitan metropolis.

Once known as "Hogtown" and "Toronto the Good," Toronto is trying to shake its bumpkin image and become urbane and sophisticated overnight. Nudie shows and massage parlors have sprouted along Yonge Street (the main drag, pronounced Young), the Mynah Bird on Yorkville Avenue (since closed) briefly featured a nude chef, and the porno shops proliferate. But along with the tastelessness are coming, slowly but unrelentingly, restaurants catering to more discerning tastes, sophisticated boutiques, gourmet food shops, high fashion for the well-dressed woman lacking Jackie Onassis' budget.

Speaking of money, the Canadian dollar floats against the greenback and usually runs at a premium. Yankee dollars will be accepted at most places, but usually at a discount. Hotels will change money, but the best rate is to be had at the chartered banks. There's a branch on every corner, open from 10:00 A.M. to 3:00 P.M., many later on Fridays.

## *Hotels*

More excellent hotels than one would expect, a good number of good hostelries, and a raft in the fair-to-middling range. So finding a suitable room should be no problem. Best of the lot are the **Castle Harbour,** the **Hyatt Regency,** the **Inn on the Park,** the **Prince,** the **Sutton Place Hotel,** the **Toronto,** and the **Winslow Arms.**

The **Hyatt Regency** is the city's most Continental hotel, reflecting the touches of manager Frans Schutsman, who came to the hotel via Raffles in Singapore and the Cavalieri in Rome.

The **Inn on the Park** is another gem, worth the 15-minute taxi ride from downtown. Set on a 20-acre park, it's a resort unto itself, and even Toronto couples (married, that is) come here to unwind on a weekend.

The **Sutton Place Hotel** is centrally located and a bit hectic, but the staff still tries to add some personal touches for guests.

**Castle Harbour** is a twin-towered behemoth on a redeveloped waterfront area, and overlooks the city and Lake Ontario.

The **Prince** is indeed regal, and is more like a resort than a hotel, with 15 acres to squander on an ice-skating rink, playground, putting green, and bicycle path.

The **Toronto** is a Western International showcase that prides itself on soundproofing and luxury touches geared for the discriminating business traveler.

The **Windsor Arms** is tiny (85 rooms), but worth trying. Many rooms have Canadian pine antiques. The staff gets to know you—and serve you—in a hurry.

Failing these, the **Bristol Place Hotel,** the **Park Place,** the **Royal York,** or the **Westbury** should do nicely.

## *Restaurants*

Toronto is coming into its own as a good city for food. For years a populace that equated fine food with the bill got what it deserved —expensive, mediocre restaurants. That has largely changed, but vestiges remain. Wine lists are sadly limited—by the Ontario Liquor Control Board. Only a few restaurants go through the bother of acquiring the special license needed.

Few restaurants have bars or cocktail lounges, so if you have to

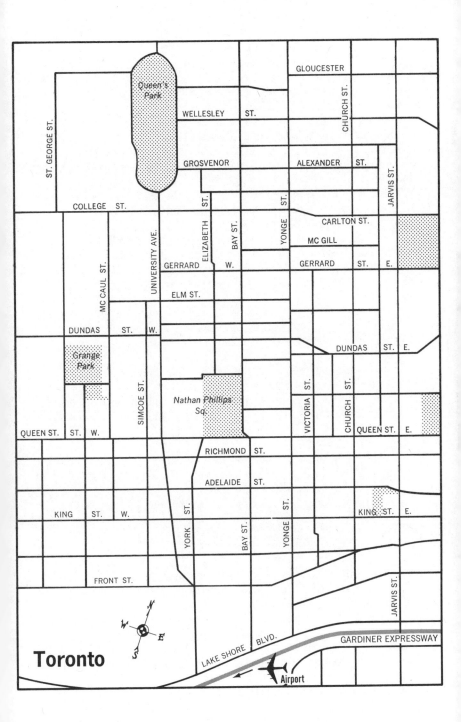

wait for seating, it will usually be at the door. Many restaurants are closed Sundays, some for lunch as well. Many close at 10:00 or 11:00 P.M., and waiters can be very frosty to strangers.

The range of restaurants in town is quite broad, but English, French, and French-Canadian styles are most common, naturally.

Probably the most famous restaurant in the city is actually three restaurants in one, **Three Small Rooms,** which is definitely worth at least one visit. Its monastery-like ambiance and crisp service, plus its limited but meticulously prepared menu, almost equal the reputation and bill.

The **Café de l'Auberge,** in the Inn on the Park, is another place to bring someone special—business contact or otherwise. Cuisine, wine, service, and prices are of high standard.

The **Westbury Hotel Dining Room** is likewise well known, and deservedly. The scampi is an award-winner the equal of royalty. In the same league—in price and quality—is **Winston's.** It's especially fashionable with local society and usually packed, so don't miss your reservation.

**Napoleon** is another showcase where the French cuisine and wine list match the surroundings. **L'Aiglon** is likewise famous for its haute cuisine, as is **Chez Gaston. Auberge Gavroche** also deserves distinctive mention.

If you want to try Arctic Char, or a broad range of other seafood dishes, try **Moorings** or **La Residence.**

No big city is without its pasta palace, and in Toronto it's **La Scala,** which is very strong on Italian veal dishes. **Don Vincenzo's** is just a notch below, and justly prides itself on seafood dishes, Italian-style.

If you are as much a gourmand as a gourmet, head for **Troy's.** It's small, with two sittings at 6:30 and 8:30. The limited menu changes every fortnight, but quality—and quantity—do not.

For a good steak in a nice setting, **Barberians** is your best bet.


## *Potpourri*


There's hardly a "swinging" place in town you wouldn't want to take your sister to, or meet her there. But don't let that fool you. There's plenty of fun to be had.

The liveliest watering hole in town after five is the **SRO Bar** in the Hyatt Regency, a favorite of singles and would-be singles. **"22"** at the Windsor Arms is only slightly less sociable, and far less frenetic. The **Scotch Room** at the Inn on the Park is also a favorite singles meeting place.

For a quieter drink there's the **Liberty Bar** at the Royal York,

**Stop 33** atop Sutton Place, the **Polo Lounge** at the Westbury, or **Malloney's** on Grenville Street. TV and radio personalities hang out at the **Bombay Bicycle Club,** which proprietor Julie also promotes for cocktail-hour singles gazing.

There's dancing at the **Imperial Room** at the Royal York, the **Odyssey Lounge** atop the Hyatt Regency, **Pompeii's** in the Waldorf Astoria basement, **Café de l'Auberge** at the Inn on the Park, **Franz Josef Supper Club,** and a few other spots. The Imperial Room gets the name performers, with some in concert at Massey Hall on Victoria Street.

The real action, though, has moved from downtown out to the airport strip. Along Dixon and Airport Roads nineteen different rooms in nine hotels offer entertainment six nights a week—all the way from tasteful trios to hard rock.

**Attila's Cave** at the Airport Hilton, the closest thing on the strip to a singles bar (stewardesses the main attraction) has been the most successful in recent years. Decor is from the Flintstones, music hard rock. **Bachelor's Lounge** upstairs, with an omniscient pianist, is a bit more intimate.

Back downtown, avoid the once popular **Maxwell's Plum** on Yorkville Avenue. **Pip's** on lower Jarvis Street is lively, and **The Studio,** in the basement of the Four Seasons Motor Hotel on Jarvis, continues to draw a chic crowd across the age spectrum.

Toronto sees itself as a major jazz center, too. Most reliable is the **Colonial Tavern,** 201 Yonge Street, where eclectic bookings have included Muddy Waters, Gary Burton, and Dizzy Gillespie. For local jazz try **George's Spaghetti House,** 290 Dunda East. Go to **Bourbon Street,** 180 Queen Street West, for Dixieland.

Upstairs from George's Spaghetti House is **Castle George,** the only good cheek-to-cheek place out of the hotels—and a favorite cheaters' hangout.

The best spot for folk music is the **Riverboat,** 134 Yorkville Avenue, where folks like James Taylor and Gordon Lightfoot used to play before they become famous.

The Yonge Street Mall, from King to Gerrard, is pleasant in summer with greenery, outdoor cafés, and local craftsmen. But it can get jammed with strollers, and late at night is best left to the potheads.

The performing arts have become very much a part of the Toronto scene in recent years. The symphony, in residence at **Massey Hall** during the winter months, is passably good. The opera is not. The National Ballet, as well as other ballet companies, comes frequently to cavernous **O'Keefe Centre** (sit in the orchestra). If it's in town, the Royal Winnipeg Ballet is an unexpected delight.

Pre-Broadway tours now often hit Toronto, as do many road companies, performing at both O'Keefe and the **Royal Alexandra Theatre.**

Toronto has inherited the British mania for **sports.** Hockey is kingpin, of course, but good luck on getting a ticket for the Maple Leafs. Business contacts are your best bet.

The World Hockey entry, the Toronto Toros, draws good crowds at Varsity Stadium—where tickets are cheaper and easier to come by.

The Canadian Football League Toronto Argonauts are worth a look—you'll hear a lot of familiar names if you follow college football in the States.

There's racing almost year-round at Greenwood—standardbreds and thoroughbreds—and thoroughbred racing in season at Woodbine.

If you have some spare hours to just look around town, Toronto has quite a range of interesting diversions.

There is an ample supply of parks, snowed over in winter but beautifully maintained in summer. In Toronto the parks are for people; the signs say: "Please Walk on the Grass."

**Allan Gardens** hosts a 33,000-square-foot greenhouse with botanical displays. **Edwards Gardens** is 35 acres of rolling lawns, shady arbors, little bridges, and beautifully fashioned rock and formal gardens. **High Park** is the largest, has a small zoo, teahouse, baseball fields, stunning gardens, and gurgling rill. The **Riverdale Zoo,** at Sumach and Winchester, is an oldie but goodie.

If you want to do some shopping, head for the Yorkville area. It was once a hippie haven, but the opening of the Hyatt Regency spurred a revival. The streets are full of rebuilt shops featuring everything from llama skins and needlepoint to books and furniture.

For Canadiana, visit the **Canadian Guild of Crafts** for a good selection of Eskimo work at reasonable prices, and a superb collection of earthy Canadian pottery.

## *Nitty Gritty*

## HOTELS

*Superior*

**CASTLE HARBOUR** (1 Harbour Sq.). A twin-towered behemoth on a developed waterfront area that overlooks the city and Lake Ontario.

**HYATT REGENCY TORONTO** (21 Avenue Rd.). A bit away from downtown, but service and Continental touches worth it. Excellent public rooms.

**INN ON THE PARK** (1100 Eglinton Ave. E.). About a 15-minute cab ride from downtown, but a world in itself. Pools, tennis courts, putting green, gym with sauna. Never the air of a convention hotel.

**THE PRINCE** (900 York Mills Rd.). Indeed regal, and is more like a resort than a hotel with 15 acres to squander on an ice-skating rink, playground, putting green, and bicycle path.

**SUTTON PLACE** (955 Bay St.). Well located, always busy, but the staff will remember you. The Royal Hunt Room lays the most expansive Sunday brunch table in town.

The **TORONTO** (145 Richmond St.). A Western International showcase that prides itself on soundproofing and luxury touches geared for the discriminating business traveler.

**WINDSOR ARMS** (22 St. Thomas St.). Small, ivy-covered hostelry, a gem from another era. Still one of the cheapest hotels downtown. Katy Hepburn's Toronto hideaway.

*Good*

**BRISTOL PLACE** (950 Dixon Rd.). On the airport strip. Popular among travelers with business in Toronto's fast-expanding northern quarters and northwest suburbs.

**PARK PLAZA** (4 Avenue Rd.). Quiet and comfy, more decorous than the Hyatt across the street. Recently refurbished. South wing has far more charm.

**ROYAL YORK** (100 Front St. W.). Opened in 1929, the Grande Dame of Canadian Pacific's string of hotels and by far the best-known hotel in town. Caters to heavy convention business.

**WESTBURY** (475 Yonge St.). Quiet, unpretentious, well located. Fine dining room and cocktail lounges.

*Acceptable*

**CONSTELLATION** (900 Dixon Rd.). On the airport strip, next to the smaller Bristol Place. Handy, lively in the evenings.

**FOUR SEASONS SHERATON** (123 Queen St. W.). Lays claim to title of largest convention hotel (1,466 rooms) in North America. It packs them in week after week. Recommended only for good downtown location and the Cambridge Club, a first-class health club/fitness institute in the bowels of the hotel. Cambridge Club facilities, otherwise limited to select private membership, may be used by hotel guests for a few dollars per session.

**HOLIDAY INN, DON VALLEY** (1250 Eglinton Ave. E.). Holiday Inn, but in pleasant wooded setting and closer to northeast end of town.

**HOLIDAY INN, DOWNTOWN** (89 Chestnut St.). Largest Holiday Inn in Canada, with 750 rooms. Efficient, bustling, right downtown—at back steps of City Hall. Pleasant revolving bar as crown.

**LORD SIMCOE** (150 King St. W.). Aging not too gracefully, but still good service and location. Moderate rates.

**TORONTO AIRPORT HILTON** (5875 Airport Rd.). Nothing spectacular—not the best of the hotels near the airport.

# RESTAURANTS

**ACADIAN ROOM** (*) (Royal York Hotel). Maritime flavor. Try the creamy king crab with chanterelles on rice. Gets crowded and noisy, but service is attentive. Dinner for two: $30.

**ACROPOLE** (*) (18 Dundas St. W.). Upstairs Greek restaurant where you head for the kitchen to select your food. Lamb dishes first class. Good Greek wines but no ouzo. No credit cards. Dinner for two: $15.

**AUBERGE GAVROCHE** (***) (90 Avenue Rd.). Intimate hideaway with vintage records by the likes of Edith Piaf. Salads a delight, especially the endive. Recommended: duck, served with unexpected white wine and muscat sauce, and rabbit chasseur. Insist on crème caramel for dessert. Dinner for two: $45.

**BARBERIANS** (**) (7 Elm St.). Comfortable downtown steak house. Nureyev brought the Canadian National Ballet Company here more than once. Wise to call for reservations. Dinner for two: $35.

**BURGUNDY ROOM** (**) (Constellation Hotel). Weekdays rushed, service better on weekends. Avoid the scampi. Try the veal or rack of lamb. Dinner for two: $35.

**CAFE DE L'AUBERGE** (***) (Inn on the Park). The place for the special client. Try the chicken Kiev or Dover sole, which is the real McCoy flown to Canada daily. Impressive but expensive wine list. Dinner for two: $50.

**CARMAN'S CLUB** (**) (26 Alexander St.). Steak house replete with antiques, objets d'art—and bad oil paintings. Steaks, chef's salad, and Viennese pastries are superb. Avoid early dinners on hockey nights. It's near Maple Leaf Gardens, and jammed. Dinner for two: $25.

**CHEZ GASTON** (***) (595 Markham St.). Scene right out of St. Germain des Prés—white stucco walls adorned with nudes, old prints, and vintage posters. Good bouillabaisse, tournedos, and rack of lamb. Moules a specialty. Dinner for two: $30.

**CORNUCOPIA** (*) (101 Richmond St. W.). Ersatz greenhouse with hanging plants. Imaginative salads and good roast beef. Best for lunch. Unlicensed. Brown sugar for the tea. Lunch for two: $10.

**COSSACKS** (\*\*) (269 Queen St. W.). Russianesque. Red damask walls, waiters in silk smocks. Ladies get unpriced menus. Try the Georgian skewered lamb and mushrooms in Cossack sauce. Expensive Beluga caviar not in keeping with generally moderate prices. Dinner for two: $25.

**DON VINCENZO'S** (\*\*) (679 Mt. Pleasant Ave.). Off the beaten track. Intimate grotto decor. Put yourself in the owner's hands and he'll cook you up a fine meal. Excellent fish entrées. Reasonably good wine list. Dinner for two: $25.

**DOWNSTAIRS ATTIC** (\*) (225 Yonge St.). Downstairs from the bar, The Silver Rail, with its sepia photos and other memorabilia. Seafood the specialty, steak house the style. Dinner for two: $25.

**ED'S WAREHOUSE** (\*) (270 King St. W.). First-class beef—only roast beef and steak served—amid antiques and Tiffany lamps. Antique games and red hangings give distinct bawdy house flavor. Reservations for dinner; be early for lunch. Dinner for two: $20.

**FERNANDO'S** (\*\*) (36A Prince Arthur Ave.). Opened in 1974 and shows great promise. Chef is Westbury Dining Room grad. Bias is Spanish. Order the Solomillo Manchego, an excellent tender filet smothered in subtle herb sauce. Dinner for two: $30.

**FRANZ JOSEF SUPPER CLUB** (\*\*) (121 Front St. W.). Underrated. Packed weekends. Plush decor and restrained dance orchestra. Richly sauced veal and fish dishes. The hot Viennese apple strudel is a must dessert. Gourmet menu every other Tuesday. Good Rhine Wine list. Dinner for two: $45.

**L'AIGLON** (\*\*\*) (121 Yorkville Ave.). Classic French elegance. Skip the house pâté. Service superb. Good selection of veal dishes. One of the city's better wine lists. Has withstood the changing tides of Yorkville. Dinner for two: $40.

**LA RESIDENCE** (\*\*) (Cara Inn). Simple low-key spot with superb fish dishes. Start with the crab claw, and then try the trout stuffed with shrimp and mussels, sautéed and finished with cucumber and lemon. One of the few spots around to push fiddleheads, a leafy vegetable that grows wild in Canada's maritime provinces. Dinner for two: $35.

**LA SCALA** (\*\*\*) (1121 Bay St.). Limited high-quality menu. Minestrone Milanese more than just another Italian soup. Veal dishes superb, especially the scaloppine Marsala. Wine list strong on both French and Italian. One of the few restaurants in town with a cocktail lounge. Close to provincial parliament, frequented by lawyers, politicians, and sports figures. Dinner for two: $30.

**LE PROVENCAL** (\*) (23 St. Thomas St.). Gaily decorated rooms. Stick to fish or game birds, such as roast quail en cocotte or Coquille St. Jacques. Waiters' team approach varies from smooth-as-silk to miss-by-a-mile. Tuesday is gourmet night. Dinner for two: $35.

**MICHI** (*) (328 Queen St. W.). Unpretentious, just good basic Japanese fare. Sushis and tempuras commendable. Reservations recommended in the evening. Dinner for two: $10.

**MISTER TONY'S** (*) (100 Cumberland St.). Brought fine dining to Toronto, but no longer what it was. The Cordon Bleu is disappointing. Try the shrimps mignonette, in delicate butter sauce. The gateau St. Honoré is sinfully rich. Dinner for two: $40.

**MONSIEUR DRAY** (**) (142 Cumberland St.). Small but uncrowded. Three days' marinating makes pheasant forestière a tender game dish. Garlic shrimps and tournedos the chef's specialities. Dinner for two: $20.

**MOORINGS** (***) (404 Yonge St.). Tables cramped, but the waiters care. Try the distinctly Canadian Arctic char, with Béarnaise or anchovy sauce, or the escargots Marsellaise with lemon and sauce. Dinner for two: $30.

**NAPOLEON** (***) (79 Grenville St.). Ivory and gold dining room is impressive but not intimidating; ditto for the menu. Start with escargots à la crème, follow with a fine artichoke salad, duckling in fig and brandy sauce. Impressive wine list. Dinner for two: $35.

**NOODLES** (**) (60 Bloor St. W., entrance on Bay). Very avant-garde for Toronto, all done up in neon, glass, and orange tile. Original menu. Fine Tuscan manicotti. Outstanding watercress and avocado salad. Wine list has length and strength, including many private imports. Dinner for two: $25.

**POMPEII'S COURT** (*) (80 Charles St. E.). Slightly sinister basement hideaway with good Continental cuisine and dance music. Maître d' George is an original. Dinner for two: $30.

**SAI WOO** (*) (123A Dundas St. W.). Best Chinese food in Toronto. No frills, not even tablecloths. But service prompt and confident. Unlicensed, no credit cards. Dinner for two: $12.

**THREE SMALL ROOMS** (**) (22 St. Thomas St.). One of the three rooms is the restaurant. Very good, but still overrated. Once described as "the world's most luxurious monastery cell," it has a cold atmosphere, unwarmed by Baroque music. Wine list the longest in Canada, some bottles priced as high as $250. Menu limited, changes regularly. Particular care to game in season. Caesar's salad excellent. Elegant and expensive. Dinner for two: $60. The second room is the **Wine Cellar** (**) where you must order wine. Seats only 25. Food selection centers around cheese fondues. Inspired list of wines and brandies. Excellent service. Dinner for two: $25. **The Grill** (*) is the least inviting of the three rooms. Try to get one of the two tables in the brick alcove. Menu on a blackboard. Try the trout Lapland. Dinner for two: $20.

**TROY'S** (\*\*\*) (31 Marlborough Ave). Not for the faint of stomach. Two sittings, 6:30 and 8:30. Limited menu changes every few weeks. Good wine list, some exclusive burgundies. A recent menu included cream of pumpkin soup, a rich pâté with tomato and pine nut sauce, a mousseline of guinea fowl, and a buoyant hazelnut torte. Dinner for two: $30.

**TRUFFLES** (\*) (Hyatt Regency Hotel). Very posh, but fails to shake being in a hotel. Quality Continental cuisine, quantity greater. Very good, but expensive. Dinner for two: $50.

**WESTBURY HOTEL DINING ROOM** (\*\*\*). Off-putting hotel decor as setting for a true gourmet table. Chef Tony Roldan's renowned scampi dish deserves the grand prix Gastronomique rating— and serving them is quite a show. The wine list is excellent, but too dear. Baked whole Pacific salmon another gourmet delight. Dinner for two: $60.

**WINSTON'S** (\*\*) (104 Adelaide St. W.). Clientele financial at lunch, uppercrust in the evening. Be on time for reservations; the place is packed. Especially good wine cellar. Especially recommended: the duck Montmorency, in a lightly sweetened cherry wine sauce. The cheese cake is the best in Canada. Dinner for two: $50.

## *Recommended Reading*

TORONTO CALENDAR MAGAZINE   On a few select newsstands for 50¢.

TORONTO LIFE   A 75¢ magazine available everywhere.

KEY TO TORONTO   A magazine distributed free at most hotels, good on what's going on but undiscerning in its restaurant reviews.

DINING OUT IN TORONTO by Jerry Brown and Sid Adilman. (Greywood Publishing, $1.75.) Also has short sections on museums, parks, etc.

EXPLORING TORONTO, PAST & PRESENT by Donald Boyce Kirkup. $4.95.) Paperbound collection of aerial photos.

TORONTO by Jacob Spelt. (Collier-Macmillan Canada Ltd., $4.95.) The most informative book on the city.

# WASHINGTON

Everyone knows people in Washington: a college classmate who joined the Foreign Service, a partner in your law firm serving a stint as an Assistant Secretary, a guy from your industry trade association. Look them up. Washington, although the number of theaters and fine restaurants is burgeoning, is essentially a home-oriented town, where the favorite diversion is talk, talk, talk. Chances are that none of the night spots will give you as gay a time—or as good an insight into what makes the capital tick—as an evening spent with an old friend. He'll be a lot more likely than the officials you have business with to invite you to tag along to one of the numerous cocktail parties where the government's real powers often let their hair at least halfway down.

If he asks you to dinner at his house in Cleveland Park or Potomac, chances are that the next-door neighbor who drops by can help with your particular problem as much as the appointments on your official schedules. Politics—in its broadest sense—is what makes Washington go, and it is never bad form to ask a direct question or raise a most specific request for aid. If the answer is "no," you'll be told so in equally specific terms and no hard feelings.

## *Hotels*

Most Washington regulars have a favorite they keep coming back to but, short of that, location may well be your No. 1 consideration. Many trips to Washington involve a good bit of scooting around from one appointment to another and, unless you are going to sign on a limousine for the day, you'll want to at least end up near your room. For cabs in Washington are so cheap that it doesn't pay the cabbies to fight rush-hour traffic and they just disappear from the streets around 4:00 P.M.

Location is one reason the new challengers haven't really managed to catch the **Hay-Adams** in the rivalry for top hotel. **The Madison,** the **Watergate** (despite the jokes the name of the complex now sets off), and the **Embassy Row** all provide a level of personalized service that is in the luxury class, but that across-from-the-White-House site remains in the sole possession of the **Hay-Adams.** Just one notch down in quality, the **Mayflower, Statler Hilton,** and new **Loew's L'Enfant** are making especially keen pitches to prove themselves to traveling businessmen, so should be willing to walk the extra mile for you. **Loew's,** right near the headquarters of the Transportation and Housing and Urban Development departments, offers special rates to executives in those industries. But it may make good sense to choose a decidedly inferior hostelry that's handy to the offices of the particular agencies you deal with: the **Roger Smith,** for instance, is conveniently close to the World Bank installation and just a block from all the Executive Office agencies. And suburban locations are best if your itinerary is primarily military.

## *Restaurants*

Eating out in Washington is still something locals do to complement their conversation, rather than as an end in itself. But considering that when Kennedy was inaugurated no place in town was offering notable cooking, the proliferation of fine restaurants is remarkable. The best vie among themselves in the rather narrow confines of class French haute cuisine, and really top-notch beef or seafood houses are still scarce.

**Jean-Pierre** gets first place in the rankings for food, edging out the others by little personal gastronomic inventions, such as a squab mousse appetizer. But you go there for the food, period. The service is attentive, but the chef-owner has held decor and even table settings to an almost Spartan simplicity—his personal revolt against the frou-frou of French restaurants that get by on kitsch and charm rather than their kitchen.

**Toque d'Argent,** just above Georgetown, comes closest to having it all: superlative cooking and service, plus a grandly elegant setting. The other French restaurants in the same reliably tops category—**Grenouille** and **Bagatelle**—are in less showy settings. The two longer-established tabernacles of haute cuisine—**Rive Gauche** and **Jockey Club**—can zoom to the top of the list with a particular meal, but can't be counted on day-in day-out anymore, and are particularly prone to give haughty and inattentive service to patrons who are not regulars.

The large foreign community in Washington supports a wide variety of restaurants featuring national dishes. None are of the three-star class, but they are quite equal to pleasant neighborhood restaurants in Madrid or Peking. If your hometown doesn't have a good Middle East restaurant or one featuring Hungarian or Oriental food, seek out one of Washington's.

For steak, the **Palm,** started by young Washington businessmen who felt the lack of a good local beef house, easily takes top honors, and the swift service and tables spaced far enough apart to insure privacy make it a good choice for a meal during which there will be a high quotient of business discussion. It is also likely to produce the largest bill of any restaurant in Washington. **Paul Young's,** with a Roumanian-flavored American menu, is another place that can be counted on to provide an unobtrusive backdrop for business talk. Seafood in Washington isn't as good as it should be, considering the proximity of Chesapeake Bay, but **Chesapeake Inn, Adam's Ark,** and **O'Donnell's** can still provide a feast for Midwesterners who find fresh fish and crustaceans hard to come by.

Every government building has some sort of eating facility, and at the very least they can provide you with quick sustenance at lunch. At the best, they offer waitress service, pleasant surroundings, and food as good as most company executive dining rooms. Among the best are those in the new Executive Office Building and the Federal Judicial Center. Their locations aren't advertised, but the public is welcome. No drinks, however. The one institutional dining facility in town that's extraordinary is at the International Monetary Fund; if you have contacts there, be shameless in goading them into inviting you to lunch—it's like the private dining room of a top Continental bank.

Every hotel, of course, has its own dining room plus coffee shop, and in general they reflect the tone and quality of the hotel: clubby Old-World at the **Hay-Adams,** cabin-class Atlantic crossing (circa 1939) at the **Sheraton Park** and **Shoreham,** mod and swingy at **Loew's L'Enfant.** But only the **Montpelier** at the Madison has a noteworthy life of its own.

## Potpourri

There's not too much in the line of swinging night life in town. The **Blue Room** at the Shoreham Americana showcases name enter-

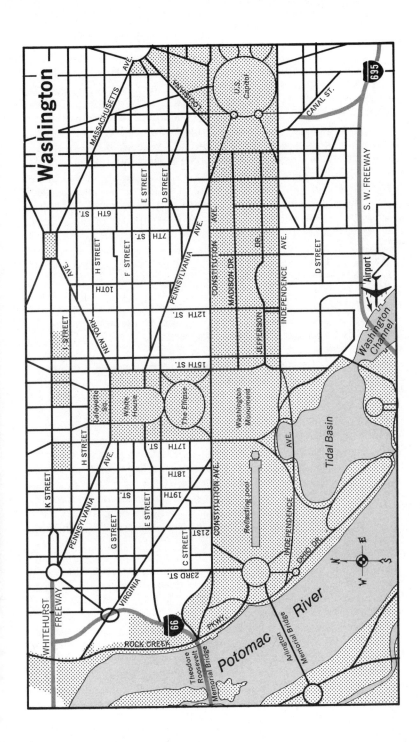

tainers. There are three good jazz spots in Georgetown—**Blues Alley** for Dixieland, **Etcetera** for mainstream, and **Cellar Door** for folk and soft rock. **Clyde's,** in Georgetown, is the most popular saloon in town, and you can get an omelet there as late at 2:00 A.M.

But there's a rich choice of comfortable cocktail lounges where you can sit long into the evening in congenial conversation. Among them: the **Quorum** at Loew's L'Enfant, **Peacock Lounge** in Les Champs in the Watergate, **Grande Scène Lounge** atop Kennedy Center, **Marquee Lounge** in the Shoreham Americana (where satirist Mark Russell throws barbs at politicians in the news), and the flock of private clubs which are so prevalent in Washington that even middle-level brass belong to, say, the International or the Capitol Hill or the National Press. You'll have no trouble arranging a visitor's card at one.

Mating habits change in Washington as elsewhere, and singles bars are perfectly respectable spots for the unattached to meet those similarly inclined. The blocks of Pennsylvania Avenue just above the Capitol and just below Washington Circle are the centers.

Mating of a more primitive sort is offered by the women who prowl 14th Street from U downtown to about K; just below their turf are raw skin bars that are tawdry, but safe. Note: Washington's crime situation is made much of, but the normal caution you should use in any big city will stand you in good stead. If you don't venture well off the beaten track, you're unlikely to run into any trouble.

Washington now offers an array of theatergoing opportunities that will be hard to believe if you haven't been in town for a few years. No fewer than seven professional stages are kept going most of the time, plus a steady stream of performances by local and visiting orchestras, ballet companies, and soloists. If you bring the kids, they may want to check if a rock concert is on at **Constitution Hall.** The world's top chamber music groups give performances almost every Friday at the **Library of Congress;** your Congressman can arrange tickets for you.

The **dinner theater** phenomenon has caught on stronger in suburban Washington than any place else in the country, but like most compromises, it doesn't provide very good dinner or very good theater; you might suggest one, though, if you have to spend an evening with a sister-in-law you don't much go for.

**Kennedy Center** has made the major difference in the performing arts in D.C. A visit there is a must, even if only to promenade through its Grand Foyer and stand on the balcony looking out over the Potomac or on the roof terrace overseeing the Monuments. A fine theater, playhouse, concert hall, and opera house are all contained in the massive center, as well as three restaurants, and a lot of space is still unused. It's elegant enough so that if you wear a tux you won't be alone, and it is of-the-people enough so that faded jeans won't stand out either.

**Football** is the one topic that can get Washingtonians off politics— at least as long as the Redskins are winning. But obtaining game tickets is out of the question unless you have a contact with season tickets. If he offers you one, it shows how much he values either your business or your friendship. The Capitol Bullets are a new favorite for business entertaining, but the **basketball** team plays in a new arena a good 45 minutes from downtown, so if you go, wangle a ride with a local. Washington hopes for a baseball team remain just hopes.

The number one pastime for most visitors is unabashed sight-seeing. And why not? The city is a collection of national shrines and sights unequaled elsewhere. So if possible, bring the family along. For chic and for shopping, your spouse may have half a dozen preferences to Washington, but there's no other business city so great for the kids. Apart from the number and variety of things to see, it's eminently copeable: the open space and low buildings make it easy to keep a sense of where you are, and the very fact that the town *does* attract so many tourists means it has aids for them—ranging from easily available maps to troops of volunteers who man booths on the Mall just to hand out directions and advice.

Many businessmen bring a child along to Washington. You can park him in one of the **Smithsonian** museums, say, for two hours with certitude that there will be plenty to absorb him. Watching a session of one of the houses of **Congress,** or hearing a case argued at the **Supreme Court,** or even (if your child's brash enough it can be done) slipping into a press conference by a cabinet member, can do as much as a year of civics in detailing just how decisions are made in this particular democracy.

But businessmen in Washington have a way of forgetting that they can be tourists too. At the simplest level, walking from appointment to appointment rather than cabbing it can disclose grand vistas and charming buildings. But in Washington, as really no place else in the U.S., the museums and monuments are interspersed with the office buildings, so it's feasible to recharge your batteries between calls with a quiet moment with a Rubens or Renoir. The **National Gallery,** with perhaps the best collection of pictures in the country, is just across the street from the Federal Trade Commission; the ornate Victorian charm of the **Renwick Gallery** is sandwiched between the two Executive Buildings; the **National Collection** (strongest on American art) and the **National Portrait Gallery** are together in a building just across the street from the Tariff Commission.

If you enjoy shopping for take-home gifts, walk the crowded streets of Georgetown, where boutiques, antique shops, and bookstores are squeezed together in yeasty confusion and evening hours are the norm. But if you don't, just put yourself in the hands of a personal shopper at **Garfinckel's.** The toniest shopping area has shifted from downtown to the city's Maryland border at Wisconsin and Western, in the four blocks stretching from **Saks Fifth Avenue** to **Lord & Taylor.**

## *Nitty Gritty*

## HOTELS

### *Superior*

**EMBASSY ROW** (2015 Massachusetts Ave. N.W.). Unusual location among the embassies makes it a bit out of the way for most businessmen, but the level of service and elegant ambiance make it first class.

**HAY-ADAMS** (800 16th St., N.W.). Local ownership has kept the high quality at what was the flagship of the Manger chain. Deluxe touches like terry-cloth bathrobes hanging in closet. Family retainer-type service. Unparalleled location. Free parking.

**MADISON** (15th & M sts., N.W.). Some visiting executives complain about the prices, but this is one hotel you can count on always to get everything right. Especially if you are going to need special services while in town, this should be your pick.

**WATERGATE** (2650 Virginia Ave., N.W.). Besides being a sight for the tour buses now, this has all the accoutrements of a deluxe hotel. Particularly advisable if traveling with spouse, since many luxury shops are in the complex. Kennedy Center right next door.

### *Good*

**CHANNEL INN** Motel (650 Water St., S.W.). Is acquiring an enviable reputation. A beautiful waterfront location that will help turn a business trip into a vacation. Not, however, handy to most government offices.

**GEORGETOWN INN** (1310 Wisconsin Ave. N.W.). The best choice if you want to be among the hopping street life of Georgetown. Small rooms, but pleasant decor and service.

**GRAMERCY INN** (1616 Rhode Island Ave. N.W.). Typical luxury in-town motel, with the usual pluses of such places: pool, free parking.

**HOLIDAY INN** (1501 Rhode Island Ave. N.W.). As usual, this chain offers a totally acceptable room. Two other Holiday Inns in the midtown area are equally acceptable and two in nearby Virginia are convenient to the Pentagon, CIA, Patent Office, and National Airport.

**JEFFERSON HOTEL** (16th & M sts. N.W.). A real find. The charm and attention of an old-fashioned European hotel. A genuine bargain for those who don't demand a lot of extras.

**LOEW'S L'ENFANT PLAZA HOTEL** (480 L'Enfant Plaza East, S.W.). Eerily isolated at night but management tries to make up for the odd location with extra luxury touches in room furnishings. Handy if your business is at DOT or HUD.

**MARRIOTT KEY BRIDGE** (1401 Lee Highway, Arlington). Washington is the headquarters for this now-international chain, so individual inn managers are kept on their toes. This and two nearby Marriott motor hotels are especially handy for business at the Pentagon, CIA, and Patent Office. The Marriott at Dulles should be considered if you come in there on a late flight or have an early morning flight out.

**MAYFLOWER HOTEL** (1127 Connecticut Ave. N.W.). A conscientious attempt is being made to bring this hostelry back to its old eminence. That means your requests for special attention will trigger quick service. Many rooms quite small.

**QUALITY INN CAPITOL HILL** (415 New Jersey Ave., N.W.). The neighborhood's a bit spooky at night, but the amenities are luxury-motel standard, and if you want to be within walking distance of Congress it's clearly your best choice. Another Quality Inn in Arlington is closest hotel to the Pentagon. New one going up on Thomas Circle.

**RAMADA INN DOWNTOWN** (Thomas Circle). Glass-domed, year-round swimming pool is most distinctive feature. Otherwise a typical in-town luxury motel. Rosslyn, Virginia, Ramada handy to Pentagon, CIA, Patent Office, and National Airport.

**SHERATON-CARLTON** (16th & K sts., N.W.). Doesn't do the Old-World charm trick as well as the Hay-Adams, just a block away, but it's an acceptable alternative.

**SHOREHAM AMERICANA** (2500 Calvert St. N.W.). Like the *Queen Mary* on one of its less distinguished crossings. Although it's hard for a hotel this huge and convention-prone to be truly fine, they try hard.

**STATLER HILTON** (16th and K sts., N.W.). Boxy rooms in

Washington's first post-World War II hotel. Has had massive renovation job, and management is determinedly seeking business travelers. Midway between government offices and the "new downtown" of law firms and trade associations.

**WASHINGTON HILTON** (1919 Connecticut Ave. N.W.). Hilton does do the big-city-hotel-as-machine gambit well, and this is no exception. Location is convenient to almost nothing. Just out of first cab zone; taxis from here are more expensive and therefore easier to get.

**WELLINGTON** (2505 Wisconsin Ave. N.W.). Primarily an apartment hotel. Check it out if you need to be in town longer than a week. Residential neighborhood.

*Acceptable*

**BARBIZON TERRACE HOTEL** (2118 Wyoming Ave. N.W.). If economy must get high priority, this is your best buy. Rooms small. New. A bit off the beaten track.

**GEORGETOWN DUTCH INN** (1075 Thomas Jefferson St., N.W.). Suites only. Side-street charm in Georgetown. Free parking. A good buy, especially if you're with your family.

**HOWARD JOHNSON'S MOTOR LODGE** (2601 Virginia Ave., N.W.). Where the lookout man for the Watergate burglary muffed it. No other distinction.

**ROGER SMITH** (1775 Pennsylvania Ave., N.W.). Respectable second-rate hotel with an absolutely first-rate location. Nearest World Bank complex, Executive Office Buildings, USIA.

**WASHINGTON** (515 15th St., N.W.). Another respectable second-rate hotel with an absolutely first-rate location. Nearest Treasury, Commerce, D.C. Government Offices, stores.

# RESTAURANTS

**ADAM'S ARK** (**) (2001 Wisconsin Ave., N.W.). Best trout in D.C. served in pleasant surroundings. Other seafood, too, of course. Same management runs **ADAM'S RIB,** with a less distinguished but more general menu, at 2100 Pennsylvania. Dinner for two: $20 to $25.

**ANNA MARIA'S** (*) (1737 Connecticut Ave., N.W.). Food—conventional Italian—is only adequate, but a big plus is the 4:00 A.M. closing, unique in Washington. That draws a more chic crowd than you'd expect. Dinner for two: under $20.

**BAGATELLE** (***) (2000 K St., N.W.). Garden-like ambiance as amiable as the cooking, which is near the top of the town's classic French restaurants. Among D.C.'s newest high-rise office towers;

many top law firms and trade associations nearby. Dinner for two: $40.

**BIXBY'S WAREHOUSE** (*) (1211 Connecticut Ave., N.W.). A favorite of the aggressively in young crowd. Frenchified menu can be quite OK if you're looking for that trendy setting. Dinner for two: under $20.

**BLACKIE'S HOUSE OF BEEF** (*) (22nd and M sts., N.W.). Maze of rooms in New Orleans-style building is fun and tourists like its reasonably priced, reasonably good steak. Half-dozen other Blackie places around town are all reliable though not memorable. Dinner for two: $30.

**EL BODEGON** (**) (1637 R St., N.W.). Conscientiously prepared, wide-ranging Spanish menu. Friendly owners circulate with *porron,* pouring wine down customers' throats à la *The Sun Also Rises.* Questionable neighborhood; cab there and back. Dinner for two: $25.

**CANTINA D'ITALIA** (***) (1214A 18th St., N.W.). Excellent Northern Italian food with emphasis on veal. Many Washingtonians who care about food rather than chi-chi rate this the town's best. Dinner for two: $30 to $40.

**CHEZ BROWN** (*) (519 13th St., N.W.). Very few selections, each prepared with care. Handy midtown location. One of the few spots where you'll see Washington's black professionals and businessmen. Dinner for two: $20.

**CHEZ CAMILLE** (**) (1737 De Sales St., N.W.). A highly personalized French restaurant that emphasizes plain good cooking rather than haute cuisine. Very loyal following. Dinner for two: $30.

**CHEZ FRANCOIS** (*) (818 Connecticut Ave., N.W.). Great bargain. Provincial French cooking, costumed waitresses, lots of pottery —all done pretty well. Dinner for two: $25.

**CLASS REUNION** (*) (1726 H. St., N.W.). Pictures of Ed Murrow and Dave Garroway on the walls; "Moon River" and "Stardust" on the Muzak. Aimed at those who view the 1950s as the Good Old Days. Generous drinks, edible food. All dishes: $3.

**COSTIN'S** (*) (14th & F sts., N.W.). Best restaurant in the midtown, Treasury-Commerce area. Prime ribs, crab imperial. Don't expect quick service. Dinner for two: $35.

**CSIKOS** (*) (3601 Connecticut Ave., N.W.). Hungarian specialties in spacious dining room reminiscent of faded Mittel Europe splendor. Enjoyable. Dinner for two: $25.

**EMPRESS** (*) (1018 Vermont Ave., N.W.). Popular with Chiang Kai-shek loyalists and rated high by many Washington food critics. Also two suburban locations. Dinner for two: under $20.

**EXCHANGE** (**) (1730 Pennsylvania Ave., N.W.). The best of a batch of new-type saloons with hip young waiters, good drinks, and rare roast beef. M Street location—same name and management—not nearly as good. Dinner for two: $15.

**GANGPLANK** (*) (650 Maine Ave., S.W.). Food's OK but the real attraction here is the setting, on a boat floating in Washington Channel; gorgeous view at sunset. Dinner for two: $30.

**GAYLORD** (**) (1731 Connecticut Ave., N.W.). A curry restaurant in a converted townhouse. Try the lamb dishes; Indian breads are great. Occidentals get mild seasoning unless more exotic is ordered. Dinner for two: $20.

**GOLDEN PALACE** (***) (726 7th St., N.W.). Unquestionably the best in Washington's Chinatown. Reservations are essential. Try birds' nest soup, shrimp with black bean sauce. Prix fixe dinners at $3.50, and à la carte up from there.

**GOLDEN TABLE** (*) (528 23rd St., N.W.). Again location is the chief feature; really the only restaurant near the State Department. Menu offers unremarkable variety of American and Continental dishes, decently prepared, and the ambiance is most pleasant. Dinner for two: $25.

**GRANDE SCENE** (**) (Kennedy Center). Most elegant setting in town. When everything is working right food and service can match, but all too often the coffee is cold and the quenelles too spicy. Ambitious classic French menu. Dinner for two: $45.

**GRENOUILLE** (***) (1075 Thomas Jefferson St.). Newest Georgetown gem. Top-notch French cooking with attention to detail. Small, cozy room. Dinner for two: $40 to $50.

**HAMBURGER HAMLET** (**) (5225 Wisconsin Ave., N.W.). Best hamburger place in town. Eastern outpost of California chain. Very appetizing sandwiches and fountain drinks; beer, too. Cocktails served in book-lined library. Sumptuous snack: $3 a person.

**HARVEY'S** (*) (1001 18th St., N.W.). New site for a restaurant that your grandfather loved. Coasting on its reputation now, but the location's at the heart of Washington's "new downtown," just steps from K Street. Dinner for two: $30.

**IRON GATE INN** (*) (1734 N St., N.W., rear). Good Middle Eastern cooking. Long a favorite with young Washingtonians. Outdoor dining in season. Dinner for two: under $15.

**JACQUELINE'S** (*) (1921 Pennsylvania Ave., N.W.). French bistro cooking, intimate checkered tablecloth atmosphere. Loyal following. Outdoor dining in season. Dinner for two: $30.

**JEAN-PIERRE** (***) (1835 K St., N.W.). The best cooking in town, period. Tables so close you hear two other conversations along with your own, and decor aggressively simple. But Jean-Pierre's personal variations on classic French cuisine ensure memorable meals. Dinner for two: $50.

**JOCKEY CLUB** (\*\*) (2100 Mass. Ave., N.W.). Can rise to the occasion and serve French food as good as any in town, but not reliable, and those who aren't regular patrons can get short shrift. Associated Sea Catch room specializes in guess what. Dinner for two: $45.

**BILLY MARTIN'S CARRIAGE HOUSE.** (\*) (1238 Wisconsin Ave., N.W.). Congenial Georgetown spot. Conventional menu. Dinner for two: $25.

**MONOCLE** (\*) (107 D St., N.E.). Best of an unimpressive assortment on Capitol Hill. Crowded at lunch, not at dinner. Known for its duck, but also offers wide variety of other meat and fish dishes. Dinner for two: $25.

**MONTPELIER RESTAURANT** (\*\*) (15th & M sts., N.W.). Decor and service held to highest standards. Gracious. Varied menu has French flair. If you're in town on Sunday, have brunch here. Dinner for two: $50.

**NICOISE** (\*\*) (1721 Wisconsin Ave., N.W.). Works hard at being a "fun" place. Roller-skating waiters and naughty songs sung by the staff. Many celebrities. Provincial French cooking that isn't bad. Dinner for two: $35.

**O'DONNELL'S SEA GRILL** (\*) (1221 E St., N.W.). Often a lunch stop on package bus tours, but despite that a favorite with downtown businessmen looking for good seafood simply prepared. Norfolks and gumbos among best bets. Dinner for two: $25.

**PALM** (\*\*\*) (1225 19th St.). Copy of famous New York restaurant. Best in Washington for steaks; also features lobsters. Good for business conversations. Dinner for two: $50.

**PROVENCAL** (\*\*) (1234 20th St., N.W.). Country French cooking of a high order. Crowded and chummy. Service with goodwill rather than elegance. Dinner for two: $30.

**RIVE GAUCHE** (\*\*) (3200 M St., N.W.). The granddaddy of all French cuisine in Washington, but now highly variable. Those who aren't regulars often get haughty, disparaging treatment. Recent ownership change adds more question marks. But there's no limit to their ability when everything clicks. Dinner for two: $45.

**SANS SOUCI** (\*\*) (726 17th St., N.W.). The patrons are the big attraction. If you can get in at lunch—and your best chance is a lobbyist who has a permanent reservation—you're sure to see someone to impress the folks back home: Henry Kissinger, Sally Quinn, or Art Buchwald. After dark, it's no longer chic. Food is good enough to stand on its own, though few notice. Dinner for two: $30.

**1789** (*) (1226 36th St., N.W.). On Georgetown University campus. Particularly popular with alumni and neighbors. A good bet for visitors with family in tow. Dinner for two: $25.

**TIO PEPE** (**) (2809 M St., N.W.). Spanish specialties blandized for American tastes. Many give it top rank. Dinner for two: $30.

**TRADER VIC'S** (**) (16th and L sts., N.W.). This chain is so well known it's easy to forget how really good its Polynesian cooking is. Attentive staff always makes dining out fun. Dinner for two: $30.

**YENCHING PALACE** (**) (3524 Connecticut Ave., N.W.). Mainland Chinese diplomats have made this out-of-the-way restaurant their favorite. High-quality Chinese cooking almost totally unrelated to the usual Chinatown glop. Dinner for two: $20.

**PAUL YOUNG'S** (**) (1120 Connecticut Ave., N.W.). A businessmen's favorite. Widely spaced tables make it ideal place for serious talk over meals. Roumanian-flavored American menu. Dinner for two: $25.

**DUKE ZEIBERT'S** (*) (1722 L St., N.W.). Lindy-esque: bustling waiters, hearty good fellowship, stewed chicken. Popular with sports figures. Dinner for two: $25.

*Not Recommended*

**HOGATE'S** (9th and Maine, S.W.). This old Washington institution provided a fun waterfront visit even when the food was greasy. But since the Marriott organization took it over in a new homogenous setting, there's no reason at all to go there.

**HOT SHOPPES.** Nineteen locations in the area. You expect fast service and palatable food, and will be disappointed on both counts.

**II CAESARS** (527 13th St., N.W.). Handy midtown location may tempt you to overlook the MGM papier-mâché decor, but the food is worse than the setting.

### Recommended Reading

NEW YORK TIMES GUIDE TO THE NATION'S CAPITAL, edited by Alvin Shuster. (Bantam, $1.25). Best on detailed workings of the government.

WASHINGTON, D.C. (Hastings House, $9.95). Originally put together in the 1930s under the aegis of the WPA. Gives a detailed history of the development of the city.

WASHINGTON GUIDEBOOK by John and Katharine Walker. (Metro, $1).

RAND MC NALLY GUIDE TO WASHINGTON, D.C. by Andrew Hepburn.

(Rand McNally, $1.95). Good on outside-of-Washington day trips to such attractions as Bull Run or the Shenandoah Valley apple country.

WASHINGTON, D.C. GUIDE by Jane Dutton. (Determined Productions, $2.50). A small-format compilation of useful addresses and phone numbers. Has graphics and makes a nice souvenir.

CAPITAL FEASTS by Janet Staihar and Richard Barnes. (Rock Creek, $3.50). Reproductions of the menus of the town's better restaurants.

# HOW TO STRETCH
# YOUR EXPENSE ACCOUNT

George Washington was the first American on record to wrestle with a sizable expense account. And he didn't do badly. In fact, if he were around today, many an executive would be happy to "let George do it" when an expense report has to be filed. Old George turned in an expense account of $449,261.51 for the eight years he was fighting the British. A sample entry: $411 for reconnoitering the East River, and Long Island Sound as far as Mamaroneck.*

Today's sharp-eyed comptrollers and accountants in the business world would doubtless disapprove of such expenditures. But Washington was, after all, a General dealing with the government. And even then Uncle Sam had a funny way of accounting for money when it came to the military.

Let's face it—very few people make money on their expense accounts. If you have an expense account, there's a good reason for it. And despite all the barroom braggadocio you've heard about how guys keep mistresses on the "old E.A.," or how they squirreled away enough to put a pool table in the den, it's the rare chap who profits from an expense account.

Indeed, if he did, he wouldn't have his job—or his expense account —for long.

There is the story of the wire service reporter, for example, who, while hot on the trail of a kidnap story, had to charter a plane to get to a small town where the kidnapper was shooting it out with police. He reached the town, all right, and got his story—but then came the moment of truth. How to account for the $1,400 he had spent on the

* *George Washington's Expense Account,* by Marvin Kitman (Simon & Schuster, $5.95).

plane. Obviously, he had a legitimate reason for spending the money, and his editor had approved the outlay. But editors don't audit expense reports. The imaginative reporter therefore explained that he had accidentally run into a cow while racing in his car to the small town, and had to pay a farmer $1,400 compensation for the animal. Accountants got hold of the reporter's report, and determined that no cow is worth that much. They notified the reporter and advised him that the animal must have been a bull, and would he please adjust his expense accordingly.

There are times when all of us who wrestle with expense reports have to come up with a little bull of our own. It's hoped the following pages will be of use.

## *Domestic Air Travel*

Businessmen who fly waste more money on air fare than on any other business expense, with the possible exception of entertainment. Reasons: they fly first-class too often, fly when it is often most expensive, and seldom, if ever, take advantage of package deals which tourists routinely enjoy. Flying first-class is absurd, unless there is no room in coach on a "must" flight.

Many companies permit only certain key executives to travel in the front of the plane. Others insist a flight be of a certain duration—and, therefore, discomfort level—before first-class is allowed. The reasoning is faulty in both cases.

First, what's good for the goose is good for the gander. If a company's top executives must fly very often, the company should have its own plane or planes. If not, the same flying rules should apply to top execs as apply to juniors. To differentiate among executives is poor for morale. It also encourages the less privileged to rationalize hours spent goofing off, and even overcharging on their expense accounts.

Second, the comfort of the passenger may or may not be affected by the length of the flight. If anything, the shorter flights are more often the most crowded, and first-class might make sense here—especially if the traveling businessman has an important meeting shortly after landing. Few businessmen schedule important meetings right after long flights, however.

On average, the first-class fare is close to double the tourist fare on domestic flights. If you can trim that much right off the top on some of your trips, you are way ahead of the game in stretching your expenses.

The second area where it is easy to save is scheduling. When you fly can mean a difference of up to 25% of the cost. Say you are in New York and have to make a trip to Los Angeles. Let's assume you are going economy class. The basic air fare, as of this writing, is $194 one way, or $388 round trip. But you can save $78 in round-trip fare by flying at night. Westbound, for example, Eastern Airlines presently has one flight from Kennedy and one from LaGuardia which leave shortly after 9:00 P.M., making one stop in Atlanta. The flights arrive in Los Angeles about 2:00 A.M. local time. Eastbound, there is a direct, one-stop flight without aircraft change leaving L.A. at 10:00 P.M. and arriving at LaGuardia at 7:34 A.M. While your appointment schedule might not permit you to fly both directions at night, you can save $39 by flying at least one way in the evening.

Not only is the time that you fly important, so is the day. United Airlines, for example, currently will give you a 25% discount on round-trip coach fares if you are flying 1,500 miles or more—provided you buy your ticket a week in advance and leave and return on Tuesday, Wednesday, or Thursday, after a week to nine-day stay. Obviously, you can't take advantage of such discounts on that many trips. But the savings are substantial enough to possibly stretch a trip, or tack a mini-vacation on to it. To wit: New York to Los Angeles, you can save $96 round trip. To San Francisco, $96; to Denver, $67; to Las Vegas, $89.

Another way you can save money when traveling is by taking advantage of package deals which might be available. These include substantial savings on hotels, ground transportation, and car rentals. There are myriad packages available, many of which businessmen could—but don't—use. It certainly doesn't hurt to ask about them when making reservations.

Just one example—Fly/Drive tours. They can result in substantial savings so long as you agree to stay in the same hotel or hotel chain for a minimum period, and fly the same airline round trip. The car rental is practically a free bonus. Rates on these deals are constantly changing, but they are well worth looking into. Most airlines have them—as most airlines are in some way linked with hotel and motel chains.

Note: Many times it is possible to stop—for free—between destinations. It's possible on some airlines, for example, to get a free stopover in Miami if you are flying New York to Los Angeles, or the reverse. This is good to keep in mind if you plan on a mini-vacation enroute to or returning from a business trip.

Of course it is impossible to take advantage of these and other options if you don't know about them. And here is where a good travel agent comes in. Pardon us, but this does NOT mean an efficient company transportation expert, if your employer has one. Your company agent will book your flights according to the schedule you or your secretary provides. He will book hotels according to the location you prefer. He can be very efficient—but not cost conscious, at least not of *your* expenses. Remember, company transportation people are NOT compensated by the airlines in any way. They are, in effect, free help for them.

Travel agents, on the other hand, make their living from the carriers. (They seldom charge you for their services, except where special communications or other charges are incurred.) There are more than 9,000 travel agents now operating in the U.S., and over the past five years airlines have paid a cool $300 million in commissions to them. No wonder. They sold over $4 billion worth of airlines tickets.

Picking a good travel agent is something like finding a good lawyer —unfortunately, trial and error and word-of-mouth are the most effective methods. But a good travel agent—who costs you nothing— can save you a bundle on your business and vacation trips by taking advantage of options you probably never heard of.

Okay, you say, you sit in the back of the plane, fly at night, at midweek, hook up a deal for a car rental and hotel room. All you wind up with is receipts for less money spent than if you had flown first-class on a Friday morning and had booked a car and hotel room à la carte.

There are several ways you can benefit directly. First, of course, is the fact that your total expense budget is less depleted because of what you saved. If you are on an annual budget, that means there is more left in your budget for other types of expenses—which may or may not be so difficult to account for.

Second, there are ways you can translate those savings into cash, if you must, to make up for other legitimate expenses which are not so easy to justify. One way is through your air travel or other credit card. You purchase the more expensive, but justified, ticket with the card. Then you exchange the ticket for a cheaper one, plus the difference in cash. For your expense report, you use your credit card bill as a receipt.

If you need an actual copy of your flight ticket, see your travel agent. He should be able to help you out.

## *International Air Travel*

Whenever your company sends you overseas, it knows the tab will be high. But it need not be nearly as high as the company anticipates.

And you can benefit—one way or another—by not spending so much on air travel, hotels, and incidentals.

As with domestic air travel, many companies permit first-class air travel because of the time spent in the air. The theory, of course, is that you will be more comfortable in first-class. That's certainly so. But traveling tourist—unless the plane is jammed—is not all *that* unpleasant. In fact, if you are on an evening jumbo jet and the plane is not very crowded, you can often stretch across several seats in coach and sleep like a baby, which you may not be able to do in first-class. And by flying in the back of the plane you can cut almost 50% off your round-trip fare.

But where you can really save is on package deals, some of which are tailored for the business traveler.

The key, once again, is in timing. Off season (November to April) there are countless deals available on trans-Atlantic flights. Example: Let's say you are bound to London or Paris for a week, Saturday through Saturday, with Monday through Friday set aside for business. If you fly first-class, your off-season fare to either city is, as of this writing, $1,206 from New York. The round-trip tourist fare to either city is $612 (of course rates will vary somewhat over time).

In addition you have ground costs, especially your hotel. Let's say you stay at the Ritz in Paris, or the Savoy in London. The current costs at those hotels for seven nights are currently $623 and $387 respectively. You also have to transport yourself to and from the airport, and perhaps hire a car to get about. Figure at least $100 ground costs. Thus, your total tab to Paris is $1,929 first-class, $1,235 tourist. To London, it's $1,593 first cabin, and $999 in the back of the plane.

Air France now has one package deal—called L'Aristocrate—which can save you hundreds to either destination. The one-week trips include round-trip air fare (tourist), de luxe accommodations, and some extras. In Paris, you can stay at the same Ritz—or the Crillon, Plaza-Athénée or George V, which are all in the same league. In London, you can stay at the same Savoy. Yet the package cost—Saturday to Saturday—is only $699 to Paris (*vs*. $1,235 on your own) and $599 to London (*vs*. $999). And the extras thrown in include three or four dinners, show or theater tickets, and sight-seeing by private car.

Similarly, TWA has an off-season package to Paris for from $412 to $489 which includes round-trip air fare (tourist) and accommodations.

Virtually every trans-Atlantic carrier has some sort of package available (though by the time you read this they may be somewhat different from those described above). This is true even if you aren't sure when you will return from your destination. Pan Am, for example, offers its business passengers to Brussels and other destinations Eurotelpasses good at 163 hotels in 142 cities throughout Europe. The indefinite pass assures you a single room with private bath and Continental breakfast each day for only $16.50 per night—with no reservations needed.

Moral: Be sure and ask the airline or your travel agent about special packages before you book your plane and hotel.

## To and From the Airport

Most companies put you on the honor system when it comes to tabs under $25—such as transportation around town and to and from airports. And here is where you can stockpile quite a bit of cash to use for unaccountable, but legitimate expenses.

When traveling, resist the impulse to queue up for a taxi when your plane lands. Cabs are expensive. And if you don't know the city well, you run the risk of a time-and-money-consuming joyride. Every major airport is serviced by buses which often make stops at major hotels.

As long as you don't arrive at an ungodly hour, these buses are usually frequent enough so that you lose little time against taking a taxi. And the cost differences are normally well worth the wait. At present prices, figuring in the tip, in New York it's about $14 cheaper to take the bus into the city from JFK, $5 cheaper from LaGuardia, $10 or so from Newark. In Philadelphia, the bus saves you at least $5. And on and on.

Some cities—such as Cleveland and Toronto—have rapid transit service to and from the airport. It's not very chi-chi, but much cheaper and even faster than taking a cab. And you don't get any lip.

Similarly, you can often forego hopping into a cab when you are getting around in a city. Take a few minutes to familiarize yourself with whatever public transportation is available, and how well it operates. It is always cheaper and sometimes (as in New York) much faster than grabbing a cab. And there are no receipts to worry about.

If you must rent a car—as might be the case in a city like Los Angeles—see the tips in the next section.

## When You Do the Driving

We all know the gleeful George in the office who drives his Volkswagen on company business every chance he gets—and dutifully collects the 15¢ per mile the company allows. There's no doubt about it, he's way ahead of the game in the short run. He might spend only $6 for gas and oil for every hundred miles he travels, but the company gives him $15—plus tolls, parking, etc. But out of the $9 per 100-mile "profit" comes a lot of wear and tear on the family wheels, not to mention on poor George who is 6 ft. 3 in. and gets mighty cramped behind the wheel of the VW.

You might clear a few dollars by driving your economy car on business, but they are really hard-earned dollars. And it's hardly impressing if you have to put any customers or clients in your car. A blown sales commission—or lost job—is a high price to pay for the few cents you squeeze from the company.

If you do a fair amount of driving on business, you have two other options: rent cars as you go, or lease a car.

Obviously, renting a car on a day-to-day basis can be costly. Don't forget to ask about the company discount. Many companies are entitled to a 20% discount from major car rental companies, but they neglect to tell their employees about it. Be sure to ask. Note: many companies prefer to insure their employees against accidents when driving rented cars on company business. So don't automatically take the car rental company's daily insurance. It could be wiped off your expense report when you submit a bill.

Leasing a car on an annual basis might not appeal to your company, since you don't need the car all that much.

In such a situation, you might suggest paying part of the leasing cost—instead of paying for your own car—and have the right to use the car on your own time. Such an arrangement can save the company money, and can save you quite a bit, as well.

Example: Suppose you are in the market for a new car. Let's say it's a new Ford Torino you want. Suggested list price is $4,200. If you buy it at a nice 12% discount, after shopping around a bit and doing your best haggling, your net cost is $3,700. When you include insurance, license, gas, oil, tires, maintenance, etc., your annual cost of operating that car for three years is about $2,780 a year, assuming you drive 16,700 miles annually.

The lease cost for the same car—with the same expenses, and for the same annual mileage—is about $2,850 annually, or only $210 more, total. If you put a substantial number of company miles on your own or rented cars, you should be able to get your company to contribute substantially toward the auto lease. If you get, say, $1,000 from your company toward the lease, you are much farther ahead of the game than gleeful George—and much more comfortable too. And, your company is saving money besides.

# PARKING

If you have to use your own or a rented car on business, there are some cities where the parking fees can do outrageous things to your expense budget. In New York City, for example, it can cost $12 or more to park for the day in midtown.

If you are out of town and need to use a car, find out in advance if the hotel or motel you are staying at has free parking. That benefit can be well worth the extra couple of dollars the hotel or motel might charge.

Some car rental companies will offer you discounts on parking at their lots.

Finally, it can pay to walk a bit, too. In New York City, for example, it's only about $4 per day to park west of Broadway—but more than double that a few blocks east.

## *When It Comes to Lunch*

The expense-account lunch is so accepted in American business today that it is hard to conceive of any major business deals taking place without martinis and foie gras. Damned few fine restaurants could survive these days without expense-account customers. Long live lunches on the old E.A.

The truth is, though, that there is more fooling with lunchtime accounting than in any other expense area. If all the people who are reported on expense reports actually ate in all the restaurants named, there wouldn't be a morsel of food left in America. Just because it's easy, more finagling goes on in accounting for lunch than anywhere else on an expense report.

But it can be very foolish to monkey with lunch reports. For one thing, it is easy for your boss to check up on you, if he is an s.o.b., or if he is looking for a reason to nail you. I once received a phone call from a friend's boss who wanted to know when and where my friend and I had an expense-account lunch, and what we talked about. I tried to cover for him, but was so dumbfounded, I couldn't. My friend was nailed.

"I never run out of restaurants to list," another friend of mine told me some time ago, "I just run out of names." My friend liked to take his then-girlfriend out to lunch a lot. His now-girlfriend currently buys him an occasional sandwich at noon—between his job interviews.

Another reason why it's not wise to bury other expenses under "lunch" is this: How much can you actually bury? The equivalent of one or two lunches a week? How often can you have business lunches, every day? Your boss will be wise to you after a while, and even if he does the same thing himself, it puts you in a very bad light.

If you do have to invent luncheon partners occasionally, be a little creative. Don't use the same names all the time. Check your previous reports to see that you don't form a pattern. And use names of people you actually know, preferably those you do entertain often. Otherwise, a chance meeting between your boss and your bogus luncheon partner could be disastrous.

Make sure that your numbers look right for the restaurant you name. Don't put down $24.90 for a lunch at a restaurant like Lutèce, for example. It is impossible for one person—let alone two—to eat there for that amount. And don't always use round numbers.

Try not to use restaurants with which your boss is familiar. He will know right away if your figures are out of line. Or, as happened to one salesman I know, your boss may have lunched in that restaurant that day—and can recall not seeing you there.

The point is, don't make the phony lunch look obvious in any way. This can be a fine art. There is the story, for example, about the young executive who put his country club dues on his E.A., only to be told by his boss that the company wouldn't cover such an expense, even though he entertained customers there. He resubmitted his expense report and his boss asked, "Did you eliminate the club dues from your expense report?" "No," replied the young exec, "but now you can't find them."

Another danger in listing phony lunches is that you will get too used to it—and not be able to use lunch for legitimate business purposes. This will hurt your effectiveness, your reputation, and your value to the company. Oh, yes, your integrity, too. There was a well-known public relations executive in New York, for example, who, judging by his expense report, was on a first-name basis with every newspaper and magazine reporter in the country. In fact, he really didn't entertain any—but simply took their names from a writer's association directory. For years he fooled his employer and pocketed a little bonus every month. Eventually, in no small measure because he was on such poor terms with the working press, he was let go by his employer. He then had to turn to the same press people for leads on public relation jobs, and for references. But the few who really knew him were wise to his game and resented having their names used on his expense reports. Naturally, they didn't do anything to help him find a new job.

## *At the Mahogany*

It doesn't take any talent at all to spend a small fortune at the bar entertaining someone. If you have important clients or business contacts who like to imbibe—and who doesn't—it pays to know your way around the mahogany. For one thing, it's often money spent on booze that you have to bury in your expense report under other areas, and the less spent the better. For another, spending money at the bar wisely can earn you that beautiful image you want of being a nice guy, quick with a buck, always the first to reach for a tab, etc.

Be very selective about where you drink, but once you have chosen a suitable watering hole or two, make sure you become known there. Find out the bartenders' names and have them know yours. And this most of all: Tip, tip, tip. A friendly bartender can be extremely valuable to you. He'll buy you drinks. He'll let you leave a tab for a day or so. He'll be faster to reach for the other guy's tab when drinks are ordered. He'll cash your personal checks upon occasion. And, he'll even furnish you with blank receipts if you need them. There are more than a few bartenders in New York, for example, who supply their steady customers with blank credit card receipts, with their customer's card number and name imprinted on them.

Tip your bartenders early and often. Even if you have only one drink—including just a soft drink—leave a minimum of $1. If you have a sizable tab, leave at least 15%. And whenever possible, tip the bartender in cash, rather than putting it on your credit card. The bartender gets his tip right away, no matter how you do it. But, if you tip on your credit card, the boss knows how much the bartender is being tipped too.

As Pat Campbell, the impish bartender at Charley O's in New York explains, "It's much more personal to get your tip in cash—and I always remember people who tip that way."

The bartender is king in a bar. He pours and sells the booze; he is the only one who cannot lose. The owner, the customer, the manager—all can lose money in a bar. But not the bartender. All bars are run on percentages—so much return is expected on so much volume. Any restaurant manager worth his salt calculates what his return should be, then perhaps tries to boost volume if he wants to increase profits. He doesn't monkey with how that percentage is reached, because he knows he is liable to find out some rather unpleasant things about his staff.

Any place where cash money changes hands there is some stealing. A clever bartender can steal an owner or a customer blind and he will never see a thing. He controls the amount of booze that goes into a glass (in all but those horrid "measured shot" places which deserve to be banned). He determines who gets a free drink now and then. And, of course, he controls the percentage of profit the owner gets. If he steals a bit, but the percentage stays where it should be, no savvy owner is going to do a thing to him.

Moral: Know your bartender. He's one man whose friendship can easily be bought.

## Credit Cards

Most businessmen have a pocket full of credit cards—but few really know how to use them. For business expenses as well as personal ones, your cards can actually earn you money. You can get, in effect, two months worth of interest-free loans by juggling your cards right.

Here's how it works: Suppose you habitually use four credit cards, both travel and entertainment and bank-charge cards. By using these cards just before the billing dates—which are imprinted on the cards —you maximize the time it takes for the bill to be computed and sent to you. It usually takes 30 days or longer. Once billed, you have close to another month before interest is computed.

If you are a highly organized type, you can even make money by putting cash in the bank when you make a charge, and pocket the interest which accrues while you await the bill.

Don't forget, too, that if you make a sizable purchase and offer to pay cash instead of charging it on a credit card, many retailers will offer you a discount. They, of course, lose up to 9% of the retail cost of anything charged on credit cards (except their own credit cards, of course).

Note: If you have several credit cards, be sure to get credit card insurance. Even though you can only be held liable for $50 per card in case of loss and unauthorized use, that can add up. If you have 20 cards, for example, you can lose $1,000.

Even if you do have insurance, you should notify the card companies immediately if you lose your cards. One easy way of keeping a record of all your cards and their numbers is simply to lay them out flat on the surface of a copying machine. On one sheet of paper you'll have copies of all your cards.

Note to American Express card holders: Ever wonder what Am-

exco thinks of you? If you have a personal—rather than a corporate
—account look at the last three digits of your card. They can range
from 100 to 800. The lower the number, the better the customer you
are in terms of use of the card and promptness in payment.

## Tickets

If you take clients or customers to a ball game or the theater once
in a while, you can wind up spending a lot of money on tickets. And
this can be money wasted.

For all sports events, first of all inquire in your own backyard for
tickets. These days many companies have season tickets for major
football, basketball, hockey, and baseball teams. Rare is the company
that uses every ticket to every game, however. If your timing is right,
you might be able to pick up tickets when you need them, at no cost
at all to you.

Your company public relations man is the one to speak to. But
remember that he is probably badgered quite often for tickets. So
explain why you want them and don't make a pest of yourself.

Theater tickets can be tricky. But resist to the death the temptation
to simply call a ticket agent. Call the theater first and ask when tickets
will be available. Often, expensive tickets can be had to hit shows
even on the day of the performance. These "house seats," which are
reserved for possible VIPs, are usually among the best in the theater.

On Broadway, it's now possible to buy tickets for half-price to all
shows not sold out that night. While this limits your selection of plays,
the savings are substantial.

If you buy tickets at the theater itself, use your American Express
card. From time to time, Amex works out special promotions with
restaurants. Nowadays, for example, if you buy theater tickets on
your Amex card, you get a receipt good for $5 at all Restaurant
Associate eateries, provided your bill is over $15.

## Keeping Records

A few years ago there was a movie about a young hippie and his
pregnant wife who wanted to have their child naturally, without a
doctor, in their cold-water flat. The girl's father stopped by on a
visit, found out and objected. In the course of the film, he was constantly jotting down numbers, which turned out to be reminders and

entries for his expense account. The baby turned out fine—and presumably so did the expense account.

Hollywood didn't intend it, but the story illustrates how important it is to keep accurate, up-to-date records of your expenses. And how important it is to make a practice of doing so, regardless of the circumstances.

A pocket calendar, into which you can also stuff receipts, is probably the most convenient place to record expenses. But don't be too cryptic. Describe the expense, as well as recording the date and amount of the expense. The IRS will accept such a diary if you have to support your deductions.

But no matter how meticulous you might be, you can easily overlook some out-of-pocket expenses. Taxi rides, tolls, phone calls, tips are frequently forgotten.

One way to keep a check on yourself is to keep your company and your personal money separate. On trips, for example, one ITT executive I know puts his own money in an envelope and seals it until he is flying home. That way he knows exactly how much he has spent on company business. When flying abroad, he takes his advance in traveler's checks, which he exchanges into local currency when he arrives in the countries he must visit. He keeps all "leftover" foreign currency until he is back home, and then converts all of it into U.S. dollars. He then simply adds that amount to any traveler's checks he still has, subtracts that from his advance, and knows precisely how much he has to account for. If he spends any money on gifts, or other personal items, he simply charges them on his credit card.

He swears that once he figures out exactly how much he has to account for with the company, he has very little trouble justifying it—even if he does use some of the ways suggested in this book from time to time.